T0159116

FRONDS
AND
ANEMONES

Essays on Gardening and Nature

DR. WILLIAM ALLAN PLUMMER

FRONDS AND ANEMONES
ESSAYS ON GARDENING AND NATURE

Copyright © 2017 Dr. William Allan Plummer.

All rights reserved. No part of this book may be used or reproduced by any means, graphic, electronic, or mechanical, including photocopying, recording, taping or by any information storage retrieval system without the written permission of the author except in the case of brief quotations embodied in critical articles and reviews.

iUniverse books may be ordered through booksellers or by contacting:

iUniverse
1663 Liberty Drive
Bloomington, IN 47403
www.iuniverse.com
1-800-Authors (1-800-288-4677)

Because of the dynamic nature of the Internet, any web addresses or links contained in this book may have changed since publication and may no longer be valid. The views expressed in this work are solely those of the author and do not necessarily reflect the views of the publisher, and the publisher hereby disclaims any responsibility for them.

Any people depicted in stock imagery provided by Thinkstock are models, and such images are being used for illustrative purposes only. Certain stock imagery © Thinkstock.

ISBN: 978-1-5320-1449-9 (sc)
ISBN: 978-1-5320-1450-5 (e)

Print information available on the last page.

iUniverse rev. date: 02/08/2017

In memory of my dad,

who gave to me a love of both nature and gardening

If you have a Garden and a Library,
you have everything you need.
—Marcus Tullius Cicero

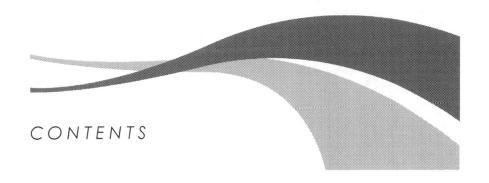

CONTENTS

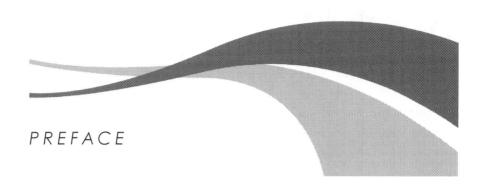

PREFACE

The majority of these articles have appeared in *Screeches* (the quarterly newsletter of Spencer Crest Nature Center, Corning, New York). Others have appeared in *The Corning Leader*, *Green Dragon Tales* (the newsletter of the Adirondack Chapter of the North American Rock Garden Society), the *Hardy Fern Foundation Quarterly*, *The Fiddlehead Forum* of the American Fern Society, and the *Rock Garden Quarterly* of the North American Rock Garden Society.

My interest in nature was stimulated one winter by the sight of snowbirds, slate-colored juncos, in our backyard in Wilkes-Barre, Pennsylvania. That same spring, I saw the yellow-bellied sapsucker during its migration, and I was hooked. The article, "Early Bird Watching," is the account of my discovery. Although we lived in the city, the hill was about a quarter mile from the Susquehanna River and extended more than a quarter mile, making it an ideal resting spot for migrant birds. My interest in birds then extended to wildflowers, and in 1943 and 1944, I was nature director at the Wyoming Valley Boy Scout Council's Camp Acahela at the confluence of the Tobyhanna and Lehigh Rivers. Following military service, I entered college, and in 1947 and 1948, I served on the staff of Philmont Scout Ranch in Cimarron, New Mexico, as a trail guide. During graduate school and my early years in Corning, my interest in nature lay dormant, only to be rekindled when we built a home on a heavily wooded lot in Gang Mills in the town of Erwin. The site had mature white and red oaks, white pine, red and sugar maples, shagbark hickory, black cherry, and Pennsylvania ash with an understory of witch hazel, hawthorn, viburnum, wildflowers, and ferns and called out for adding to the existing flora; a call that I answered and that I am still responding to. An account of this is given in "Evolution of a Garden."

As the reader will soon discover, I am an incorrigible punster, for which I make no apology. I hope you will enjoy reading these articles as I certainly have enjoyed writing them.

The title of this collection of writings was inspired by a story that appeared in the *Fiddlehead Forum*, the publication of the American Fern Society. A husband and wife were both avid gardeners and vied in outdoing each other. One fall day, the wife filled a vase with a beautiful bouquet of windflowers. The husband, not to be outdone, removed the windflowers from the vase and replaced them with ferns that he had just picked, exclaiming, "With fronds like these, who needs anemones?"

COMMON NAMES /
LATIN NAMES

In ornithology, very few birders use the Latin name for a bird species. In fact, the only Latin bird name I know is *Turdus migratorious* for our American robin. Instead, the common names of birds, at least in the United States, have been standardized. It is not "Canadian goose"; it is "Canada goose." The same goes for mammals and insects. We recognize *Homo sapiens*, but not *Odocoileus virginianus*—every gardener's adversary—as the white-tailed deer. Nor do we know *Danaus plexippes* as the amazing migratory monarch butterfly.

Contrariwise, dedicated gardeners use Latin names almost exclusively. I think this is so for a number of reasons. Many plants not native to the States have no common names or have made-up common names. *Kiringeshoma palmata* is a Japanese plant that goes by the common name yellow wax bells. I've always known it by its botanical moniker, and I had to look up the common name recently. Many plants have more than one common name, and often the same common name can apply to two different plants. When we buy a plant, we want to know exactly what plant we are buying. A third reason is that Linnaeus's binomial system tells us something about the plant. It may be descriptive, as in *diphylla* for twinleaf; tell where it was found, as in *virginianum*; or honor the discoverer of the plant, as in *Lewisia*. Many Latin names are literal translations of the common name. For example, New England aster is *Aster novae-angliae*. Which came first, the chicken or the egg? The most difficulty many of us have with Latin names is pronunciation, but here we do not have to worry about that. To make the text somewhat easier to read, I use mostly common names, but where there may be confusion, I add the Latin names for clarity.

CHAPTER 1

EARLY BIRD WATCHING

As noted in the preface, I became interested in birds one winter when I sighted a flock of slate-colored juncos. That spring, the hermit thrush and the yellow-bellied sapsucker came through on their migration. Although we lived in Wilkes-Barre, we were only several hundred yards from the Susquehanna River and our house backed up to a hill that extended south for a quarter mile. Most of the backyards on North Main Street were undeveloped because of the steepness of the hill. The west side of the hill had few homes and contained a couple cemeteries. In short, it was a great place to catch the spring and fall migrations, as it provided a stopover for them. Early mornings were an ideal time to spend an hour or two spotting and identifying the migratory birds. I was able to do this while attending Coughlin High School and later Wilkes College. Toward the end, I was able to identify most of the birds by sound as well as by sight. One Christmas, I was given an album of bird songs. This was the first recording (78 rpm in red vinyl) produced by Sapsucker Woods. One of those years, I built a flicker house and erected it on a chestnut oak on the hill in our backyard.

In our scout troop, there were a half dozen of us, including our scoutmaster, my dad, who would go out on a Saturday or Sunday morning to some favorite birding spots. During the week, I might take walks along the Susquehanna after classes, looking for birds. We participated in the Audubon Christmas Bird Count one or two

Decembers. One fall, we journeyed to Hawk Mountain to see the hawk migration.

Because of my interest in nature, principally birds and wildflowers, and because the college students were off to war, I was appointed nature counselor while in high school and held that position for two summers. The scout camp, Camp Acahela, was located at the edge of the Poconos where the Lehigh and Tobyhanna Rivers join. We would take groups of Scouts up and down the Lehigh River, finding and identifying birds. In the evenings, you could hear the hermit thrushes calling, and there was many a covey of ruffed grouse that we would put to flight on our hikes.

During my college years, I was fortunate to serve for two summers as a trail guide at the Philmont Scout Ranch in Cimarron, New Mexico. Thus I was able to add a number of western species to my life list. I still treasure Roger Tory Peterson's *A Field Guide to Western Birds*,[1] presented to me by the Philmont Exploration Unit #26 from the Kansas City Area Council. In the east, we have only the blue jay and the ruby-throated hummingbird. In the west, there are nine jays and thirteen hummingbirds. The red-shafted flicker was indistinguishable from our yellow-shafted species except for the color change. The "Beep, beep!" roadrunner is familiar to all. Another intriguing bird from the west is the water ouzel—the bird that walks underwater.

A couple of incidents come to mind when I think back over those early bird-watching years. At that time, the pileated woodpecker had not made its dramatic comeback and was quite rare. We did see some evidence of their presence but were never able to spot them. Now they are a fairly common sight. In fact, they are residents in our area. In a recent Christmas card, my cocounselor from Camp Acahela mentioned seeing them. Forty and fifty years ago, the tufted titmice had just begun to extend their range northward. We were out camping on Labor Day weekend, and one of our troop members was intrigued by the name. Whenever he spotted a bird, he would call out, "Tufted titmouse." To his complete surprise and ours, believe it or not, there they were. They are now common residents.

I located a list "Birds Identified in 1944" among some papers I

---

[1]   Peterson, *A Field Guide to Western Birds*.

had saved. It lists seventy-one birds seen between January 1 and May 14. Among the winter residents were juncos, evening grosbeaks, tree sparrows, chickadees, tufted titmice, song sparrows, downy woodpeckers, and horned larks. By the second week of March, the migrants began to move through. A meadowlark and bluebird were sighted on March 12 and a robin on March 20. On March 19, a dozen hermit thrushes were seen, and four weeks later, their song was heard. In the first week of April, flocks of white-throated and chipping sparrows and alder flycatchers passed through, along with a few golden-crowned kinglets and brown creepers. The next week, I saw ruby-crowned kinglets, yellow-bellied sapsuckers, white-breasted nuthatches, and a couple of flickers. In mid-April, I added a spotted sandpiper and the vesper sparrow to the list. At the end of April, towhees came through en masse. In the first week of May, fourteen birds were added, including six warblers, a brown-headed nuthatch, a Baltimore oriole, three catbirds, and the nighthawk. The second week garnered six more warblers, a couple of flycatchers, the scarlet tanager, the rose-breasted grosbeak, and a wood thrush. The scarlet tanager was recorded as singing on May 12. I have no surviving record, but I suspect between then and the end of school, the summer at the scout camp, our fall camping, and the fall migration, I must have added another dozen to that list.

For the Birds

Birds need food, water, shelter, and nesting sites. An excellent book is Verne Davison's *Attracting Birds from the Prairies to the Atlantic*.[2] One section lists each bird and its food preferences. Another section lists plants and which birds utilize them, whether for food, shelter, or nest building.

Food may be berries, nuts, seeds, flower heads, nectar, or insects. A pond or a birdbath can provide water. Many birds like running water. Nests can be on the ground, in vines, in shrubs or trees, in tree cavities, or in bird boxes. Dense evergreens provide excellent shelter, as does any dense vegetation. If you have a bird feeder, provide

---

[2]   Davison, *Attracting Birds from the Prairies to the Atlantic*.

some nearby shelter from predators. Don't be too neat. The mess, such as a brush pile or seedpods on flowers, will provide shelter and food respectively. Provide some nesting materials for our feathered friends.

Most birds, including hummingbirds, eat insects, spiders, and other animal food (e.g., ants are a favorite food of the flicker). Avoid the use of pesticides. Select shrubs and trees that provide berries. Forsythia is beautiful, but use it sparingly. Avoid plants that can be invasive. Honeysuckle and autumn olive have been touted as food sources but are overrunning the upper meadow at Spencer Crest Nature Center. Norway maple, burning bush, barberry, and multiflora rose are others that can get out of hand and crowd out our native shrubs and trees. Instead, make use of our native trees and shrubs, including the viburnums, dogwoods, and winterberry. The serviceberry, also known as shadblow and Juneberry, flowers in late April; the berries, ripening in June, provide an early source of fruit and one of its common names. Grapes and blueberries are so relished that commercial growers have to protect their crop. The pileated woodpecker will eat berries, and I have seen it eating the berries of my flowering dogwood and those of American holly. Berries will provide food for migrating birds, such as cedar waxwings. They will gorge themselves on mountain ash berries and get drunk on the fermented berries. Would they be in danger of being grounded for FWI (flying while intoxicated)? Some berries don't become palatable until after a frost and can provide food for winter residents and spring migrators. Native trees that provide food for birds include black gum, sweet gum, chokecherry, pin cherry, crab apple, dogwoods, sassafras, shadblow, hawthorn, southern magnolia, mountain ash, and red cedar. Some of the native shrubs to include are sumac, chokeberry, coralberry, elderberry, inkberry, huckleberry, blueberry, grapes, hackberry, spicebush, viburnums, and winterberry. Birds will also eat the fruit of Virginia creeper and poison ivy. In fact, that is how poison ivy spreads. On several occasions, I have found a single seedling of *Rhus radicans* growing in my garden.

Seeds are favorite food of finches, nuthatches, chickadees, titmice, blue jays, and cardinals. All of the conifers, such as white pine, eastern hemlock, red cedar, Colorado spruce, balsam fir, and larch provide seeds relished by both birds and squirrels. Squirrels can really strip a pinecone down to the core. Alders, ashes, and birches all have catkin-like pods, containing small seeds, while the seeds of maple and witch hazel are substantial in size. One year, we had a ruffed grouse feeding on the hop hornbeam. Sunflowers, asters, thistles, zinnia, chicory, and dandelion are a few herbaceous plants providing seeds for many birds. The larger birds with their larger beaks are able to eat the nutmeats provided by beech, the shagbark hickory and its clan, and the large variety of oaks.

Hummingbirds drink nectar and can be attracted by providing a source of sugar water, colored red, as they are attracted by this color, like waving red in front of a bull. Red-flowering plants include azaleas, bee balm, fuchsia, cardinal flower, penstemon, hibiscus, and gladiola. Other flowers that attract hummingbirds are coralberry, weigela, bugleweed, Turk's cap lily, milkweeds, thistle, tulip tree, and zinnia.

Birds build nests on the ground, in bushes, in trees, on ledges, and in cavities. Putting up a ledge for a robin or a bird box for woodpeckers or chickadees and the like does not guarantee that they will use it. For example, I built a bird box with an opening for a chickadee, but a nuthatch decided it was prime real estate and proceeded to enlarge the opening. Our son and his wife gave us a birch-bark-nesting box as a Christmas present one year. That spring, a wren decided to build its nest in the feeder. A week later, a chickadee, having completed its courtship, made the same decision. One morning, we looked out from the family room window. There was the chickadee attempting to remove the wren's nesting material. It had hold of a twig in its beak and was attempting to dislodge it. It was flapping its wings like crazy, but the twig would not budge. It gave up, but when the wren fledglings had flown the coop, it claimed possession and has maintained its lease in the ensuing years. Phoebes will build on a ledge or projection, and one year, a phoebe built a nest on top of our electric meter that was located on the laundry porch. Another year, it attempted, without success, to plaster its nest on the molding above the laundry door. I never did discover where it did build its nest that year.

Juncos

It all started when I was fourteen and noticed a small gray bird with white on its tail when it flew. A few months later, a hermit thrush stopped on its migration up the Susquehanna watershed, and then there was a yellow-bellied sapsucker. That was my introduction to birds and nature. From that day on, juncos have had a special place in my heart and mind. It was a common winter bird in Pennsylvania but migrated north to breed, so it disappeared in late spring only to be seen again the next fall. The same thing was true in our area when I moved to Corning in the mid-50s. In the Adirondacks and the higher Catskills, they are among the most numerous nesting birds. In the southern tier, they could be found in evergreen woods at higher elevations.

The first time I remember seeing a junco in the summer was in the late '60s in western New York around Olean, the icebox of New York. But one summer, a number of years ago, I was pleasantly surprised to see my friend and later to see fledglings in my yard. Since then, nary a summer has gone by that I have not noticed breeding pairs. They generally raise two broods a year in our state. In contrast to the tufted titmouse, cardinals, and mockingbirds, which have extended their range northward, the junco appears to have extended its breeding range southward. Twenty years ago, they did not breed close to Lake Erie or Ontario. Perhaps today they do.

Although juncos are predominantly a ground-nesting bird, nests in evergreens are not uncommon. They have been known to nest as high as eighteen feet above ground on top of an abandoned barn swallow nest. One year, I discovered a nest about thirty inches high in a dwarf Alberta spruce on my patio. We have two hanging planters with fuchsias on either side of our sliding doors. I discovered after the fact that a junco had built its nest in one of them. This was six feet above the patio, whereas the nest in the Alberta spruce was less than three feet from the ground.

Cowbirds lay their eggs in other bird's nests, foisting their parental duties onto the surrogate parents. Their eggs have a shorter incubation period, so they hatch before those of the host. One year, we looked out our family room window at breakfast to see this enormous fledging squawking like crazy with its mouth agape, demanding to be fed. The mama junco appeared, one-fourth the size of her *baby*, and proceeded to feed it. The baby, if you haven't guessed it, was a cowbird. The surrogate parents were feeding the cowbird fledgling as their own.

Some years, the juncos seemed more numerous than ever. Every time I would go out in the yard or around the neighborhood, I would hear a lot of twittering. My friends seemed to like conversing with me and I with them.

Come fall, the snowbirds will head south to the Carolinas, Georgia, or Alabama. In March, they will head north again, traveling in flocks that may number a thousand. The birds we see in the winter at our feeding stations are most likely their cousins who have summered in Canada.

Tree-Os

Three birds that can be found climbing up, down, and around trees are the nuthatch, downy woodpecker, and brown creeper.

The white-breasted nuthatch is the most common of the nuthatches or nuthacks, for there is a smaller, rustier version in the red-breasted, which is a winter visitor in these parts. The white-breasted nuthatch is generally a yearlong resident, although some of those seen in the winter may breed farther north. The red-breasted, although migratory, has been recorded as nesting in the Finger Lakes region. It prefers coniferous forests, whereas the white-breasted nuthatch prefers deciduous forests. A hundred years ago, there was a rare sighting of a southern species, the brown-headed nuthatch, near Elmira.

The nuthatch has been given the appellation of the upside-down bird and the topsy-turvy bird, since it is most commonly spotted circling a tree head down in its search for insects. It is also called the tree mouse. Frequenting bird feeders for sunflower seeds, it will invariably fly away with the seed and stash it in the bark of a tree. It reminds me of a penguin with its gray-and-white- waistcoat. Its "Yank! Yank!" call is quite distinctive.

I have, over the years, erected birdhouses for chickadees and nuthatches, with the recommended entrance-hole sizes. However, the nuthatch, with a mind of its own, decided that it preferred the chickadee or titmouse box and proceeded to enlarge the hole to its liking. Their courtship was enchanting. The male would find a twig for the nest and would proceed to sweep his head back and forth while uttering a low murmuring sound.

The downy is the smallest of the woodpeckers and is essentially a small version of the hairy. Young boys get down on their chins before they sprout hair, so is this where the appellation arises? The species name reflects this. It is "pubescens" for the downy as opposed to "villosus," shaggy or hairy, for the hairy. The downy frequents open woodlands, whereas the hairy prefers the deeper woods. As with the other woodpeckers, the distinguishing feature of the males is a patch of red. It is the most common woodpecker, and unlike the flicker is a year-round resident. For a few years after we first moved to our present home, we had a downy that was almost white. The normal black barring was a very light gray. Our neighbors and we called our visitor Casper, the Friendly Ghost.

The third member of this *tree-o* is the brown creeper. It is a small, inconspicuous brown bird that starts at the bottom of a tree and circles the trunk upward in its search for food; then, it flies to the bottom of a neighboring tree and repeats its foraging. It has a needle-like sharp, curved bill that it uses to probe for insects. Some birds will be year-round residents, and others will winter in the southern states. It is a common breeder at higher elevations as far south as North Carolina and breeds occasionally at lower elevations. Unlike the nuthatch and the downy, it does not nest in a cavity but instead builds a nest behind a loose shingle of bark on a dead or dying tree.

Eastern Phoebes

When we came home from vacation one April, we noticed bird droppings, moss, and soil on our laundry porch. It was cleaned up and reappeared the next day. A phoebe was trying to build a nest on the molding on the inside of the porch. There was more of the nesting material on the floor than on the trim. To discourage it, we put up some plastic bags. They finally got the message and chose the top of the electric meter that sits inside the porch along the one wall. Another pair had nested there some fifteen to twenty years earlier. After finishing the nest, which took a couple of weeks, she started to lay her eggs. Unfortunately, someone else did also. That someone else was a cowbird. Since cowbirds are so numerous in spite of the scarcity of cows in the neighborhood, I decided to help the phoebe along. The last time this happened, I disposed of the cowbird's egg, only to have her lay another one. The problem is that the alien egg hatches before the host's eggs. The cowbird nestling bonds to the hosts and demands and gets its ration of food and then some. Perhaps my small act will do something to redress the balance.

Some seventy-six species[3] are known to be hosts to the cowbird's eggs. The phoebe, at 3 percent, is one of the ten most-favored victims, the list being headed by the yellow warbler (12 percent) followed by the red-eyed vireo (9 percent) and the song sparrow (7.5 percent). The junco is favored only once out of two hundred nests. The cowbird will even occasionally parasitize hole nesters, such as the bluebird and the nuthatch. It will rarely penetrate deep into a woodland, but a greater number of birds are being victimized because of the increase in woodland fringes due to housing developments.

My Friend Flicker

The golden-shafted flicker is one of the more common woodpeckers and is quite distinctive. Most woodpeckers are basically black and white, but the flicker is brown. Most woodpeckers don't have yellow feathers, but the underside of the flicker's wings and tail is a golden yellow. It is a very distinctive bird, having a white rump that is prominent when it flies, and it has that distinctive undulating flight of all the woodpeckers. At Philmont Scout Ranch in New Mexico, I became familiar with the red-shafted flicker on which the yellow feathers are replaced by red feathers. This may or may not be a separate species. In the areas where they overlap, there is considerable inbreeding with all sorts of gradations between the two. Most woodpeckers search for insects on trees, but the flicker prefers to hunt for ants on the ground.

---

3   Bull, *Birds of New York State.*

One of my bird projects in Scouting was to build a birdhouse, and I chose to build a flicker house. I erected it on a large chestnut oak on the hill in our backyard. The flickers approved and took up residence. It was fun and instructive to watch the male and female birds sharing the incubation and feeding. What a racket the young'uns would make when the parent returned with food and proceeded to regurgitate it for the fledglings. Then the day came when it was time to leave the nest. One other thing I remember from those early years was that a church at the end of the block had a metal roof. Oh, how a flicker loved to use that as a sounding board and how the neighbors somehow failed to appreciate the amorous calling of the male flicker to his potential mate

Pileated Woodpecker

One Friday in December some years ago, during a snowstorm, I heard a chucking call that I identified as the pileated woodpecker. I looked out the window to locate it. It flew down and lit on a snow-laden branch of a flowering dogwood, bending it down still more. Fascinated, I watched as it proceeded to eat the berries. I went into the other room to get my camera, but on returning, I found it had flown to a neighboring oak where it slowly ascended, knocking off pieces of bark in its search for insects. A day or two later, as I pulled into the driveway, I saw the pileated fly from the dogwood by the front door to one of the oaks. I thought this most unusual, but I pulled out my copy of *Attracting Birds: From the Prairies to the Atlantic*[4] from my bookshelf. Looking up "woodpecker, pileated," I found that animal food constitutes only 45 percent of its diet in the winter. Some choice plant foods are beech, black cherry, chokecherry, corn, Virginia creeper, dogwoods (both alternate-leaf and flowering dogwood), elderberry, sassafras, and acorns. In addition, it has been known to come to bird feeders occasionally for nutmeats and suet.

The next week, I was in my den, working on the computer and listening to WSKG, our local PBS station, when I again heard the pileated. He was only five feet away, eating berries on the dogwoods

---

[4]   Davison, *Attracting Birds from the Prairies to the Atlantic*.

by the front door. Both male and female had come this time. I found my camera, but by the time I got it loaded, they had flown away.

My neighbor across the street has an American holly, and one year, it was loaded with its red berries. Several pileated woodpeckers would visit, hang from a branch, and eat the berries until they were all gone. I wonder if we will have some holly trees in the surrounding woods. Visiting my neighbor the other day, I noticed a number of holly seedlings. One afternoon, walking back up the hill to the lab after lunch, I saw a female pileated and several fledgings.

Yellow-Bellied Sapsuckers

Every birder is familiar with Sapsucker Woods, even if he or she has never seen the avian species for which it was named. It is a migratory woodpecker that, like the flicker, has an un-woodpecker-like trait. It drills for sap! It is just as mixed up as the flicker, which has an affinity for anthills. My first experience was one spring when growing up. I was out on one of my early morning forays and saw this woodpecker-like bird, circling a tree. When it flew, it had the typical undulating flight of woodpeckers and white on the wing. On going up to the tree, I saw there was this neat little circle of holes all around the trunk. One might not always spot the migrating birds, but the distinctive series of holes is a dead giveaway that Kilroy was here. Often, people will ask me about concentric holes on their trees. The answer is easy; you have had a visit from the yellow-bellied sapsucker. I have not actually seen it in our neighborhood, but my neighbor has a tree with those holes in its trunk.

Red-Winged Blackbirds

As part of an assignment in Tom McGrath's contemporary biology course at our local community college, which I audited one fall, we were asked to choose a bird that we saw on our field trip to Montezuma National Wildlife Refuge. We were to report on when it leaves in the fall, where it goes, and when it returns in the spring. I chose *Aegelaius phoeniceus*, the red-winged blackbird. It has a wide breeding range, extending from southern Canada to the Bahamas, Cuba, and Costa Rica. In the fall, it swarms by the tens of thousands in roosts and during migrations. On October 12, 1960, at the Clay Swamp roost in Onondaga County, numerous observers estimated three hundred thousand birds. In Montezuma marshes, one hundred thousand birds were reported on November 9, 1955. C. F. Stone and V. Burtch[5] banded numerous nestlings at Branchport. The following winter, twenty-eight were recovered in North Carolina, another fifteen in South Carolina, and one each in Georgia and Texas. During the spring migration, one hundred thousand were recorded at Montezuma on March 22, 1958. In the early 1900s, Arthur Allen[6] kept a three-year record of redwings migrating through Ithaca. From their plumage, he was able to distinguish males from females and adult birds from those hatched the previous year. The record he reports is for 1911, and as he remarks, the actual dates will vary from year to year, but the order in which the males and females and migrants and residents arrive will remain. (I wonder if there has been any significant shift in the ninety years since Dr. Allen made his study.) Here is what he found: males arrive on the scene, followed two weeks later by the resident females. The migrants that appear are presumably on their way to Canada, while the immature birds that will take up residence may have been searching for green pastures.

Vagrants	February 25–March 4
Migrant Adult Males	March 3–April 21
Resident Adult Males	March 25–April 10
Migrant Females and Immature Males	March 29–April 24
Resident Adult Females	April 10–May 1
Resident Immature Males	May 6–June 1
Resident Immature Females	May 10–June 11

Although a few wandering redwings can appear in late February, it is not until a month later that the resident males arrive.

---

5   Bull, *Birds of New York State*, 526–528.
6   Arthur A. Allen, *The Book of Bird Life* (Princeton, NJ: D. Van Nostrand, Inc., 1961).

CHAPTER 2

EVOLUTION OF A GARDEN

We had bought a house in South Corning, New York, and in 1962, a new subdivision in Gang Mills, Town of Erwin, across the Cohocton River from Painted Post, was announced. We knew that Corning Glass Works had plans to build their new research facilities on land in the Town of Erwin adjoining this subdivision. The area had been logged in the 1800s; the hamlet took its name from the gang saws used to cut the lumber. Huge rafts would be built from the lumber, and in the spring floods, they would be floated down the Chemung to the Susquehanna to the Chesapeake. When we bought our lot, they had only started to cut down the trees for the road that was to be Fox Lane (named after an early settler). We walked up the partially cleared road with the real estate agent to a small creek that flowed diagonally across the road. He said, "I think your lot begins about here." Our response was "We'll buy it." It turned out, in my opinion, to be the best lot in the entire development. It had a diversity of trees and shrubs and had enough of a slope to provide interest but not so steep as to cause difficulties siting our house. An added bonus was that it was on a dead-end street. The Cape Cod Royal Barry Wills house that we had built fit beautifully on the lot. The creek was diverted to the opposite side of the road and after several floods, starting in the year we built, was put underground.

The trees on the lot were mainly white pine, white and red

oak, shagbark hickory, red and sugar maple, hop hornbeam, black cherry, Pennsylvania ash, and pagoda dogwood. Shrubs included witch hazel, hawthorn, and maple-leaf viburnum. Among the ferns and wildflowers on the lot, as I remember, were partridgeberry, gaywings, winterberry, rue anemone, round-leaf hepatica, Bishop's cap, foamflower, wild sarsparilla, mayapple, shinleaf, starflower, Solomon's seal, false Solomon's seal, Virginia creeper, low-bush blueberry, woodland aster, blue-stemmed goldenrod, Christmas fern, and marginal wood fern.

In 1964, we had our house built, saving as many trees as we could and protecting the others from damage from bulldozers. We planted lawn only in the open areas around the house, leaving the front and backwoods as woods. That winter, for $100, we had a landscape plan prepared, and in summer, I took a vacation from sailing and proceeded to plant shrubs and trees as per our plan. To prepare the soil, a friend who had a stable provided truckloads of horse manure that I roto-tilled into the front woods and driveway planting area.

The front of the driveway was flanked with Sargent's junipers. A row of hemlock was planted along the south border, and others randomly sited on the lot. Four Colorado spruce were originally planted—three by the driveway and one near the northwest corner. Along the north border we planted a number of mountain laurel. A shrub border at the front of the lot contained snowberry, Japanese honeysuckle, Carolina allspice (*Calycanthus floridus*), spicebush (*Lindera benzoin*), shrub dogwoods, and viburnums. For the front foundation planting, we used a number of Japanese holly (*Ilex crenata convexa*) and Japanese andromeda (*Pieris japonica*). In a small bed by the front door, we planted a pyracantha that we planned to espalier. We planted Pfitzer junipers in front of the bedroom wing. My dad brought up some rosebay rhododendrons (*Rhododendron maximum*) from the Poconos. One of these, we planted at the corner of the house, and some, we planted in the woods. A white birch clump was sited at the intersection of the two walks. Rockspray cotoneasters (*Cotoneaster horizontalis*) were planted as a groundcover next to the walk leading to the laundry door.

The front stoop and the laundry porch were laid using random flagstones edged with bricks. To continue that theme, the two three-foot-wide sidewalks also used random flagstone laid in a sand base. Years later, the stones were lifted and relaid in concrete. The other major project that first year was putting in a flagstone patio off the living room. Here we used rectangular flagstones. My wife calculated sizes, the quantity, and the pattern for the flagstones. A sand base was used for the patio.

Since both my wife and I were in Scouting and familiar with our native wildflowers, we embarked on a project to introduce additional wildflowers and ferns to those already on our lot. For the first several years, we concentrated on planting the front woods. The first thing we did was design and lay our paths. To provide additional interest, we constructed a small pond. Unfortunately, we did not have the foresight to make it larger or deeper or to include running water. When full, it is only three inches deep. We found a large flat stone and positioned it at the head of the pond. An offshoot of the main path circles above the pond. The path continues north and swings east past a white pine. The path continues eastward and emerges at the bedroom wing of our home.

We also discovered a large boulder in the neighborhood, and we prevailed upon our plumber to use his backhoe to have it brought and partially buried between an oak and a hickory next to the path. (Rocks should not just sit on the surface. Ideally, they should be buried to about one-third of their height.) Consequently, I dug a hole six to nine inches deep in preparation. I was at work when the plumber came with the backhoe and the rock. As my wife related the story, our two boys and several other children from the neighborhood followed the backhoe, like the rats following the Pied Piper of Hamlin. With her fear for the safety of all, it was dumped in sideways, and I had to use a crowbar to flip it 90 degrees. This became our "sitting stone." After that first year, I was hooked on gardening and took a vacation from sailing for a number of years.

We repopulated the front woods, which had been denuded during the construction, with plants from untouched areas of the lot. Some plants we rescued from construction sites in the development, but most were bought from mail order and local nurseries. Trilliums came from a nearby creek area, and we found a massive sod of trailing arbutus (*Epigea repens*) pushed aside to the side of a new road being put in. A couple of pink lady's slippers (*Cypripedium acaule*) were among the rescued plants. The arbutus slowly declined over several years. The lady slippers persisted for some twenty years and then failed to flower and finally died, never forming clumps. The trillium, however, proceeded to self-sow. I discovered that in the first year, they send up one leaf, the next year two leaves, and then three, and a few years later, they flower. They now number several hundred plants. The seedlings were transplanted and now cover a large expanse in the front woods. In later years, they have been transplanted to other areas so that when you walk the paths, you will likely spot two or three trillium here and another three there. One large clump with a dozen blooms appeared on the edge of the patio. Contrariwise, I have not had much success with red trillium, also known as stinking Benjamin (*Trillium erectum*). But yellow trillium (*Trillium luteum*) has done well for me and now grows in several locations. The prairie trillium (*Trillium recurvatum*) that I brought back from Indiana is thriving. In addition to these, I have more than a half dozen other species. I have added many more wildflowers over the years. Those that have done particularly well are bloodroot, twinleaf, blue cohosh, Virginia bluebells, wild ginger, Allegheny spurge, and bugbane. Trout lily covers large expanses in the spring before it disappears. It is only now after these many years that I have begun to get significant bloom from the trout lilies.

In those first years, we discovered the minor bulbs and planted snowdrops, winter aconite, crocus, chiondoxa, and scilla. The crocuses have not done well, with only a few strays remaining, probably because of voles or chipmunks. The snowdrops have self-seeded and have begun to spread. We divided and transplanted the expanding clumps. The chiondoxa and scilla have seeded around with abandon. In the spring, they carpet almost the entire front woods, dying back a month or so later. Lately the scilla and chiondoxa have begun to spread into the back woods. They have also spread into the lawn with a vengeance. In the spring, I rue the day we planted the scilla and chiondoxa. They detract from the native spring flowers, like trillium and bloodroot. The winter aconite is being used principally at the driveway entrance, providing sheets of yellow in early spring. This too is spreading into the back woods. I have not had much success with species tulips or with dwarf iris. Ah, but the daffodils! The early, midseason, and late daffodils fill the shrub/perennial bed with white and yellow blooms for weeks and weeks, the dwarf varieties being especially delightful.

Early on, we lost two large white oaks off the patio because of grade changes. We had plenty of firewood, so I had the happy thought of having it sawed into eight- or nine-inch sections and sinking them to use for the path on the north side of the house. When they rotted years later, I cast concrete stepping-stones as replacements. This walk has been extended down into the back woods. One of the early wildflowers I bought was goldenstar (*Chrysogonum virginianum*), and I planted it in the front woods. It survived but was not thriving. I then transplanted it as a groundcover between the stepping-stones to the north of the house. It has thrived in its new location and makes a spectacular display when in flower, handsome throughout the year with scattered bloom in late summer and fall.

To provide more light and air in the front woods, I have had the trees limbed up forty feet or so. It improves air circulation, enhances the appearance of the trees, and as a bonus, provides room for the second tier of trees to thrive as well as the third tier of shrubs, which are underplanted with ferns and wildflowers.

As my interest grew, I discovered the local gardening club and national organizations, such as the American Rock Garden Society. Although I wasn't into rock gardening at the time, their interests extended to woodland plants as well. As I learned later, they were an eclectic group of top-notch gardeners. Their quarterly journal carried articles of interest as well as ads for nurseries offering a wide range of plants. As my gardening interests grew, I joined the American Fern Society, the American Rhododendron Society, and the American Holly Society. Again, the articles and ads broadened my horizons. I devoured gardening books, especially those by Donald Wyman. I searched out nearby nurseries and a host of mail-order nurseries that offered plants of interest, both native and nonnative. I found sources for ferns, wildflowers, native shrubs and trees, rhododendrons, and unusual plants that were not available locally.

There was one flowering dogwood in the back woods. It is such a great native tree that we planted several more—one across the path from our sitting rock and two more by the front entrance (one with white and the other with red flowers). We planted another by the patio in back and still another at the back corner of the house. In the following years, we planted a dozen seedlings in random sites in our woods. Another eastern native we planted was eastern redbud, but we chose *Cercis canadensis alba*, a white-flowering selection.

Through my reading of garden books, I learned of the cornelian cherry (*Cornus mas*) and the Chinese dogwood (*Cornus kousa chinensis*). The cornelian cherry, a native of Eastern Europe, flowers early along with forsythia. It has yellow blooms followed by cherry-like drupes. Two of these were planted, one in the woods south of the driveway and the other bordering the front lot line. They bring welcome bloom along with forsythia in the spring. The Kousa dogwood was planted just off the patio in back. At the time it was planted, I was unaware of the added bonus provided by its brown, flaking bark. This has raspberry-like fruit.

Another plant highly recommended by Donald Wyman was Dr. Merrill magnolia. This was planted in the back next to the house to the north of the patio. It grew into a magnificent specimen, albeit casting dense shade on the bed to the north. It bloomed early and prolifically and was much appreciated by our neighbors, who got the full benefit of sight and smell. Ah, but it flowered for all too short a time. Indeed, one year, we went home for Easter. It was coming into bloom when we left on Friday. It was a hot weekend, and when we arrived home Sunday afternoon, all the petals had fallen.

Still another plant getting high marks was red-veined Enkianthus (*Enkianthus campanulata*). This is in the Ericaceous family, which includes blueberries, laurel, and rhododendrons. The bell-like flowers bloom in the spring. It forms a nicely shaped bush with gray trunks, providing interest when not in bloom. But it is in the fall when it comes into its second season of glory, the leaves turning an intense orange. This was planted just before our big white pine near the northwest corner of our woods.

In our journeys, we saw an interesting and different spruce and on inquiring learned it was a Serbian spruce (*Picea omorika*). We found a nursery close by that had this spruce, bought it, and planted it at the driveway entrance, replacing a Colorado spruce. The Colorado spruces are so overused that this narrow, weeping spruce is a most welcome addition, adding interest to the driveway entrance.

The rhododendrons available locally were the old ironclads that had the native Rosebay rhododendron in their heritage, such as *Roseum elegans*, Nova Zembla, and Cunningham's White. Membership in the Rhododendron Society gave me access to information on the new hybrids being introduced, and attendance at chapter meetings allowed me to meet some of the great hybridizers and growers in the field. We met David Leach, author of *Rhododendrons of the World*[7] and visited him in Brookville, Pennsylvania. One of his introductions was Janet Blair, named for Miss Blair, a '40s, '50s, and '60s movie star, who hailed from Brookville. This has large pink trusses and was sited in the front foundation planting. Two somewhat tender hybrids, Scintillation and David Gable, were planted on the north side of the house, giving them protection from the wind. A number of years the flower buds got blasted, and they failed to bloom. But they have performed well overall. Another of the hybridizers active at that time was Tony Shamarello, and we purchased several of his selections, planting them as a backdrop for our sitting rock. Sited across from the rock is *Rhododendron smirnowii*, a species native to the Caucasus Mountains. This is a hardy pink-flowering plant with dark, glossy leaves, having indumentum on the underside. Through the Rhododendron Society, we met Orlando "Lanny" Pride, who had a nursery in Butler, Pennsylvania, specializing in Rhododendrons, Azaleas, and American holly. Lanny had developed a hardy strain of holly and contended that once the taproot got below the frost line, they could withstand anything. Our neighbor and we purchased several of his hollies, male and female.

I don't remember where I saw it, but when I did, I knew that I had to have it in my garden. This was the Japanese paperbark maple, *Acer griseum*. The reddish-brown bark exfoliates, providing year-round interest. Its small trifoliate leaves lend a delicacy to it. In the fall, the tree waits until all the other trees have turned color and dropped their leaves. Then and only then do the leaves turn gorgeous reddish orange before being shed.

Guy Nearing was another of the hybridizers at the time, but he concentrated on using the native *Rhododendron minus* as a parent. This is one of the small-leaved rhododendrons, and Nearing was one of the first to use this as a parent. Since then, many others have, notably P. J. Mezitt of Weston Nurseries, who introduced the

---

[7] David G. Leach, *Rhododendrons of the World* (New York: Charles Scribner's Sons, 1961).

PJM series of rhododendrons. My favorite of Nearing's introductions is the hybrid rhododendron "Windbeam." One on the side of the driveway has been allowed to grow as it will. It has an irregular growth habit and is about seven to eight feet tall. Another beside the path to the laundry door has been pruned yearly to keep it in a rounded shape at five feet in height. The small flowers open white in May and turn to a lovely pink.

The epimedium from my dad, *Epimedium rubrum*, was used to line the paths into the front woods. This is a great plant for dry shade. It flowers in the spring along with the new growth. The attractive foliage persists into late fall. The clumps kept enlarging, and as they continued to increase, they were divided and used to line the entire length of the driveway. They continued to increase and were used to border the walk around the garage. At that time, not many varieties were available, but I added a yellow-flowering form and a dwarf white epimedium. The dwarf white variety lined the path past the pond, and the yellow lined a portion of the path in the front woods. Years later, the yellow epimedium was transplanted as a border for the path off the patio. I still get plants growing from roots left behind. The dwarf white was transplanted to use as an edging for a portion of the patio. Several years ago, after Darrell Probst's explorations in China and his hybridizing efforts, the number of species, hybrids, and cultivars of epimedium available has mushroomed almost out of sight. I have added a few more of the new introductions, some lining a path along the astilbe bed and others at the edge of the patio. I would add more but am limited by available space.

The naïve pinxterbloom azalea (*Rhododendron periclymenoides*) was growing in the woods in the development. One specimen was in our back woods but lacked enough light to bloom. I am attempting to add this and other native azaleas. One that I planted years ago is the pinkshell azalea (*Rhododendron vaseyi*). This is found only in four counties of North Carolina and is named for its discoverer, George Vasey. It has never failed to bloom in all the years I have had it. It has lovely pink flowers, hence its common name. It is seven to eight feet tall and makes an impressive sight in the spring. A few years ago, I bought a small plant of *R. vaseyi White Find*, but it has yet to bloom. Another perfectly hardy southern azalea is the plumleaf azalea (*Rhododendron prunifolium*). This is unusual in that it blooms in August with orange trusses. In a severe winter, this has suffered some dieback but still managed to flower. Other native azaleas are added as sources are found.

We had an aunt and uncle who bought a farm in northern Indiana on which to build their home. Walking through the woods on their farm, we discovered several wildflowers of interest, such as the prairie trillium (*Trillium recurvatum*). They also had a paw paw patch. We brought several of each home with us. Both have made themselves at home. The prairie trillium has adapted nicely and is spreading throughout. The paw paws bloom regularly but have failed to set fruit. Both paw paw and sassafras send out root suckers that over time will create groves. I suspect that the paw paws I brought home are clones and need to be cross-pollinated. Accordingly, I have bought some young trees, and perhaps now I will get fruit. A friend gave me a persimmon tree. They need to be cross-pollinated, and so now I have two small persimmon trees. I may or may not live to taste their fruit. Closer to home, my neighbor had a massive basswood tree that he had to have cut down. Years and years later, I discovered about a dozen saplings of basswood springing up all over my woods. Welcome, neighbor!

Five years after our initial planting, plus the additions we had made, the garden had begun to take shape, and we decided to host friends and neighbors to a garden party each spring when the garden was at its peak. We would have wine and cheese on the patio. Guests would often haul me off, asking about particular plants. On those few occasions when it rained, we would move inside, looking out at the garden from the family room or the living room. If there were a break in the rain, a few hardy souls would venture outside to see more. One year, the Seventh District of the Federated Garden Clubs of New York had their annual meeting in Corning and presented me with two awards, honoring my garden.

Our local rock garden chapter has held a number of their meetings in our garden. The garden is listed as open to visitors, and on a number of occasions, rock garden members have stopped on their way to and from meetings. In many years, instead of garden parties, we have held an "open garden," sending out invitations. In 2015, we had a two-day celebration of "Fifty Years in the Garden" with 150 to 200 visitors.

My wife kept suggesting that I ought to build a stone wall to separate the front lawn from the woods. Finally acting on her suggestion, I undertook that daunting task. Our lot and the creek across the road provided a ready source of stones. I started at the north end where the path emerged from the woods with two layers of stone. As I worked west and then south, the ground rose to a height of some two feet before again falling. I followed Linc Foster's[8] guidance to build a firm foundation and backfill it to provide good drainage. One recommendation I could not follow was to plant as I went. After a whole summer of backbreaking work, the wall was finished. Almost forty years later, it still stands as sturdy as the day it was built. The wall really makes the garden. It is handsome when plants are blooming and especially attractive in the winter, covered in snow, and it is fascinating to see the wall emerge from its snowy blanket. It mostly faces east and only gets the morning sun, but many rock garden plants do well with the light they receive.

Our contractor built an east-facing wall in the back of the house to provide a level site for the flagstone patio. The wall is in deep shade from trees in our back woods. I am not sure I ever planted anything in this wall, but it abounds with ferns and flowers, many rooted deeply in the crevices. The contractor also built a low south-facing wall off the driveway to accommodate the change in level from the house to the garage. Although it is a south-facing wall, both sun-lovers like sedum and shade-lovers like maidenhair spleenwort thrive. It has abundant light in early spring and then filtered light the remainder of the year, which apparently satisfies both plants. On the opposite side of the driveway, I needed to extend the area to provide a winter parking place for my sailboat, resulting in still another wall. The steps leading off the patio are lined with walls. When we enclosed the back porch, the rock wall coming down from the patio was extended to the south side of the porch and planted with dwarf rhododendrons. One of my problem areas was a triangular section abutting the back porch and the garage. It was too shady for grass and too small for much else. After I extended the wall, I decided to build a triangular raised bed, surrounded by a flagstone walk. In this raised bed, I am growing several dwarf conifers. On the shady

---

8   Foster, *Rock Gardening*.

north side of the raised bed, I planted a ramonda, a hardy relative of African violets. Ramondas prefer a shady site, and it is happy on the north face of this raised bed. At the base of this wall, two maidenhair spleenworts have arrived on their own, an unplanned but welcome addition.

The first fifteen to twenty years in our garden, the deer population was small and generally traversed north of us. As the herd expanded, they started using my garden on their travels. I lost a number of plants, many well established. I had a nice selection of dwarf hemlocks. These are on the top of their menu, and I lost them all. In the summer, any member of the lily family is deer fodder, especially Solomon's seal and trillium. They would eat the leaves on the Solomon's seal, leaving a bare yellow stalk. Although laurel and rhododendron are poisonous to deer, they will eat enough to kill the plant but apparently not enough to cause them much discomfort. Unprotected rhododendrons in the neighborhood have nothing below the foraging height of deer. With all my plants scattered throughout our lot, the only viable solution was to erect a deer fence. To make it less obtrusive, I built it behind the front shrub border and angled it back at the driveway so that the gate was forty feet back from the end of the drive. This left plants outside the fence vulnerable to deer foraging. Most of the plants in the shrub border are deer resistant, and only minor foraging has occurred. On either side of the driveway, I have planted rhododendrons. Each fall, I erect a five-foot fence to protect these plants, removing it in the spring. Deer do not like small enclosures, and they have not jumped the fence to eat my rhododendrons.

What remains of some of the original plants? The Pfitzer junipers were the first plants to be removed. Early on, we decided that they were not a good choice. They would need extensive pruning to keep them in scale, and there were more interesting plants. They were given to a neighbor and are now massive, as they have not been pruned. The Sargent's junipers at the driveway entrance are gone, having become two leggy and not responsive to pruning. The driveway entrance planting has been completely redesigned. The clump white birch is also gone; it got birch-leaf minor, and its roots were causing problems. I replaced it with a Japanese snowbell tree (*Styrax japonica*). The cotoneasters were not performing as expected and were dug up. A variety of low-growing shrubs replaced them—heaths, azaleas, and a Japanese spirea. The magnolia by the patio was plagued with scale, and the resulting black smut made a mess of the house. It was a beautifully shaped tree and provided lovely fragrant white blooms in early spring. Trying to control the scale was too daunting a task. This bed was dug up and planted with perennials. Three of the Colorado spruces are gone, leaving one to the south of the driveway. This has been trimmed up to twenty feet. The hedge of Canadian hemlocks lacked sun to make a dense hedge. All were cut down save one on either end. Various rhododendrons were planted in their stead.

When we planted the front border, we relied on the suggestions offered to us, some native and some nonnative plants. As we gained experience, we realized that the nonnative shrubs, such as the Japanese honeysuckles, were poor choices. These and the other nonnative shrubs in the front border were removed. They have been replaced with native shrubs.

Much of the original lawn area is gone. The lawn south of the driveway has been eliminated; there was just too much shade from my neighbor's trees and mine. There was grass in the bed between the walks and the house. With the addition of rhododendrons to this bed, the grass has been replaced with myrtle. There was a small triangular plot behind the garage. That is now gone. There was a grass swath leading north from the patio that has been removed and replaced with rectangular stepping stones interplanted with wild strawberry, barren strawberry, foamflower, and whatever else decides to seed in. The construction of the stone wall eliminated more of the front lawn. The front bed has been enlarged on a number of occasions, further reducing the amount of greensward to about one thousand square feet. This bed has evolved over the years. The junipers at the rear of the bed were replaced by a number of the small-leaved rhododendrons. In front of the rhododendrons are a dozen or so hellebores with flowers ranging from white to dark purple. These bloom in early spring, and their attractive foliage provides year-round interest. They seed prolifically, the seedlings needing to be removed constantly. In the spring, this bed is abloom with daffodils, hyacinths, grape hyacinths, chiondoxa, leucojums, and other spring bulbs in profusion as well as some dwarf rhododendrons.

A Franklinia tree (*Franklinia alatamaha*) and a Japanese stewartia (*Stewartia psuedocamellia*) provide vertical interest to this bed. False anemone (*Anemonopsis japonica*) provides summer bloom. In the fall, many of our native plants, like asters and goldenrod, do well with the light they receive.

The garden is not finished and never will be. That is the beauty of a garden. I am still adding plants even after fifty years. Many of the shrubs and trees are still small, and the garden will change as these plants grow and mature. Some plants may have to be removed. Others will need to be pruned to maintain their form or to keep them in scale. The woods garden will evolve as some plants spread and fill in while others disappear. Volunteers will continue to appear and may be treated as weeds or transplanted to other beds. The stone wall separating the woods from the lawn has stood more than forty years and seems as sturdy as when it was built. It provides a perfect foil for the front lawn. Plants will continue to seed into the wall, and the rock garden on top will improve with each coming year.

In the early years, the garden was 90 percent work and 10 percent enjoyment. Now, in these later years, this has been reversed. What a delight it is in the early spring to stroll the paths and spot leaf and flower buds expanding and later to see flowers blooming, to see fiddleheads emerging, or to be overwhelmed at the height of spring with the sheer magnificence of so much in bloom. In summer, we enjoy the cool comfort of the shade and the variety of foliage from the large leaves of mayapples to the tiny foliage of the wild lily of the valley. In the fall, we delight in the asters and goldenrods, the ripening berries, and later the trees and shrubs as they change color. And finally in the winter, we have snow covering the wall, snow outlining every branch of bush and tree after a snowfall, and snow on the fallen leaves with the moss-covered paths meandering throughout the woods.

CHAPTER 3
AMONG FRONDS

Ferns in the Garden

(Adapted from the November–December 1988 issue of the *Fiddlehead Forum* of the American Fern Society.)

I have three-quarter acres of land, composed largely of maple, oak, pine, and hickory. Except for a small lawn in front, the rest of the front lot has been left in woods, underplanted with dogwood, wildflowers, and ferns. In this front section, there is a small pool surrounded by an island formed by paths. One portion of the path is surrounded on both sides by the northern maidenhair (*Adiatum pedatum*). Maidenhair is also used to border a path leading to my neighbor as well as for accent elsewhere in the garden. The effect of the border is dramatic in the spring and throughout most of the summer. By September, the afternoon sun takes its toll along the front paths, and the maidenhair tends to get a little ratty. My only real complaint is that I wish it would unroll its fronds in early May rather than in early June. I was fortunate that I had access to an area under development that had abundant maidenhair ferns, so I was able to use them with abandon. At one stage, they formed semicircular plantings around three crab apples. I estimate that I have had about one hundred linear feet of maidenhair lining my paths.

The other dramatic use of ferns is on the patio on the east side of the house. The patio is constructed of rectangular flagstones, and the border contains irregularly shaped planting pockets. A perennial garden lies to the north of the patio, separated from the patio by dwarf evergreens and a variety of ferns planted in the above-mentioned pockets. These include Christmas fern, lady-in-red fern, Japanese painted fern, holly fern, and hart's tongue fern. The autumn fern (*Dryopteris erythrosa*) provides additional color in the spring. This combination makes an interesting contrast of color, form, texture, and height. The bulblet ferns particularly make handsome clumps. Another border of the patio contains a large and spreading clump of the Himalayan maidenhair (*Adiatum venustum*).

The interrupted fern (*Osmunda claytonia*) was also rescued from a development site and is used to line an entire bank, serving as a backdrop for a planting of wildflowers. I like to use Christmas fern and marginal wood fern, both of which are abundant in the area, as accents. These are particularly effective when used at a turn in the path or at the base of a tree or a rock. The stone walls are home to a variety of ferns, some planned and some unplanned. Among those ferns that were planted in the walls are maidenhair spleenwort, polypody fern, fragile fern, marginal wood fern, Goldie's fern, spinulose wood fern, lady fern, Christmas fern, and the bulblet fern. An attempt is made to restrict the spreaders to the banks as much as possible. These include ostrich fern, hay-scented fern, lady fern, and southern beech fern.

Flagstone steps lead off the patio to the south. Stone walls that create raised beds border the steps. The bulblet fern grows very assertively in the crevices and in the planting areas but is easily controlled. Japanese painted ferns lend color and interest as accent plants at the base of the steps and elsewhere. In the early years, this was being constantly divided for gifts, thereby keeping the clumps small. Lately, the clumps have been allowed to increase in size, thus providing a very effective accent in the more formal parts of the garden. This fern has also volunteered in some of the walls.

Hooked on Ferns

Unlike my early interest from my youth in songbirds and wildflowers of northeastern Pennsylvania, my interest in ferns was kindled and my interest in wildflowers reignited when we bought a wooded lot in a new development. There were marginal wood ferns and Christmas ferns on the property and maidenhair, interrupted, and cinnamon ferns abounded in the surrounding woods. To learn more about ferns, I bought Gordon Foster's newly published book *The Gardener's Fern Book*.[9] It was published in 1964, the same year we built our home. Some years later, I had the pleasure of meeting and hearing Gordon Foster in Rochester, New York.

I rescued ferns from lots that were being developed, including a host of maidenhair ferns whose habitat was to be destroyed. I joined the American Fern Society, grew a few ferns from spores, notably Braun's holly fern. I use ferns throughout the wooded property as well as incorporating them into the landscaping of our flagstone patio. But although I had a deep interest in ferns, I think I became hooked through Sue Olsen and Judith Jones when I started adding nonnative ferns to the garden to the extent that I cut a new path through the woods, which I dubbed "Pteridophyte Ptrail."

Fascinating Fronds

Ferns are fascinating for a number of reasons, not the least of are the shape and arrangement of the sori (*sorus* is the technical term for the cases that hold the spores; the plural is *sori*). It is often the shape, location, and arrangement of the sori that aids in the identification of ferns. The spores are the invisible seeds whereof Gadshill says in Henry IV, "We have the receipt of fern-seed, we walk invisible." Of course, they are not actually seeds since they do not produce a new fern. Instead, the spores, given the right conditions, begin dividing and give rise to prothallia. The prothallia, as they mature, produce male and female sex organs on the underside. Sperm cells from the antheridia find their way to the archegonia and fertilize the egg cells. These egg cells then divide, giving rise to sporophytes and eventually new ferns. If prothallia from different species are both present, hybrids can occur. The wood ferns, genus *Dryopteris*, are very prone to hybridization. But back to the story of the sori.

---

[9] Foster, *The Gardener's Fern Book.*

The northern maidenhair is one of the more widely distributed ferns, ranging from east to west, from northern Quebec to Alaska, and as far south as Georgia and Central California. The sori are found on the edge of the frond and are oblong in shape. In other maidenhairs, they will also be on a frond but may be round or short. Other ferns with sori near the margin are bracken, cliff brakes, and rock brakes.

In the spleenworts (*Asplenium*), the sori are elongate on either side of the vein. The two most common spleenworts are the ebony spleenwort and the maidenhair spleenwort. This is another genus that readily hybridizes. Not only can the aspleniums hybridize among themselves; they can also hybridize with the walking fern (*Camptosorus rhizophyllus*). The walking fern is so-called because new fronds form at the tip of a frond. One such hybrid is Scott's spleenwort, the hybrid with ebony spleenwort. Such hybrids are placed in the hybrid genus *Asplenosaurus*. Some of these are fertile and can hybridize with other species of *Asplenium* to create other fertile and sterile hybrids. Are you sori you asked?

There are three osmunda ferns, and each had its own way of displaying its sori. In all of the osmundas, some of the sterile fronds have been transformed into fertile fronds. The interrupted fern is the most common and gets its common name because its sterile fronds are interrupted on the stipe by a series of fertile fronds. They start out dark green and change to a rusty brown as they mature. The fertile fronds of the cinnamon fern are on separate stalks that are surrounded by sterile fronds. As they mature, they run from a dark gray-black to a rich cinnamon-brown and make striking displays while they last. The royal fern is different yet and is un-fernlike in appearance. Common names are locust fern and flowering fern— *locust fern* because the fronds are compound like the leaves of the locust tree and *flowering fern* because the fertile fronds at the tip of the stipe give the appearance of a flower head. It can reach six feet in height.

Two other ferns that, like the cinnamon fern, have separate stalks of fertile fronds are the ostrich fern and the sensitive fern. These two have other things in common. They both will grow in wet areas, and they both spread by underground stems. They both can grow in sunny sites, as well. Sensitive fern is abundant at Spencer Crest, and

I remember seeing vast drifts of ostrich fern along the banks of Pine Creek as we rafted down Pennsylvania's Grand Canyon a number of years ago. Sensitive fern is unfernlike in appearance, having broad, wavy fronds. The ostrich fern is a large, majestic-looking fern with it arching habit and height of five feet. Ostrich fern is commonly called the fiddlehead fern and is the fern on restaurant menus in the spring. They are reputed to be somewhat carcinogenic. These are two to be avoided in a small garden because they can take over large swaths. The fertile fronds of the ostrich fern are what give it its common name. These fertile fronds of the sensitive fern and the ostrich fern persist over winter and are often used in flower arranging.

Rattlesnake fern is the most common of the grape ferns. Why grape ferns? The sori are globular in clusters like bunches of grapes and hence the common name for the species. The sori are on a separate stalk, rising from the juncture of the leaf and main stalk. Whence the rattlesnake? Is it because it and the rattler were often found in the same area or because the long stalk with the fertile fronds on the end resembles a rattler's tail? The grape ferns are primitive ferns and have another curious and unique characteristic. They do not form fiddleheads, but they emerge doubled over.

The wood ferns (*Dryopteris*) are a confusing lot to identify. Then, to make it worse, they will hybridize readily. The most common and the easiest to identify is the marginal fern—and only if you have found one with sori. The name gives a clue to its identifications. The sori are displayed on the margins of the leaflet. It is also one of the evergreen ferns, others of which are the fragrant and spinulose wood ferns. The sori of the wood ferns are round and kidney-shaped.

The Christmas fern is another evergreen fern with yet a different way of displaying the sori. On mature plants, the fronds that carry the sori will be at the top of a stalk and will be diminished to about half the size of the sterile fronds. The contrast between the sterile and fertile fronds is striking and makes for an attractive display. The sori are round and in rows near the midrib, and they are so numerous that they will cover the back of the leaflet. This is another very common fern and will form large clumps. The new growth in spring is spectacular as the fiddleheads emerge all contorted and covered with white hairs.

The sterile and fertile fronds of most ferns are indistinguishable in size and stature. Others, like the narrow-leaved spleenwort, display dimorphism, meaning two forms. The sterile fronds are narrower, more erect, and with longer stalks. Besides those already discussed, the other ferns exhibiting dimorphism are lady ferns, crested fern, New York fern, ebony spleenwort, and netted chain fern.

The bulblet bladder fern has still another way of reproducing. In addition to producing spores, it develops small bulbs on the underside of the fronds. These drop off and can produce new ferns without going through the prothalium and gametophyte phases.

As Paul Harvey would say, "Now you know the rest of the s(t)ori." Sori about that.

Winter Fronds

Most of my fronds have gone south for the winter, but a few persist to furnish a touch of green throughout the winter. One of the most common is one of my favorites, the Christmas fern. Unlike the maidenhair, another favorite, it is evergreen—that is to say the fronds persist over winter. It is common throughout our area, occurring in scattered locations as well as in small colonies, generally in rocky, shady areas. A clump former, it slowly forms larger and larger clumps, sometimes as much as two feet in diameter. Whence its name? Well, it is evergreen and can be used in Christmas decorations. Or is it because the small leaflets are shaped like Christmas stockings? Since its growth is past, it does little harm to pick the fronds for Christmas. The old fronds do photosynthesize, so its growth may be somewhat reduced in the following year. Not only is it attractive throughout the winter, but also the emerging fronds are covered with white, wooly hairs. The uncurling of the fronds is a joy and a delight to behold.

What is the derivation of the Latin name, *Polystichum acrostichoides*? Looking up the word, *stich* in the dictionary, I learned that it has the same derivation as *stitch*. *Acro* denotes elevation as in acrobat. The name of the genus can be interpreted as "many rows," and the species as "elevated rows," presumably referring to the height of the fertile fronds. The Christmas fern is one of the easiest to recognize and identify with its dark-green fronds and each pinna or leaflet shaped like a Christmas stocking. The pinnae can vary in size, shape, and outline, but I have only been able to observe slight differences among my plants. A gardening friend has collected numerous distinctive variations, but all mine are typical of the species. Another distinctive feature is the dimorphism of the fronds. All this means is that the fronds display two forms, the fertile fronds and sterile fronds being different. The fertile fronds are much reduced in size, giving a distinctive air to the fern. Not all Christmas ferns necessarily will have fertile fronds.

The marginal or evergreen shield fern is another common and easily identified fern. From one of its names, one would be safe to surmise that it is evergreen. The fronds on the marginal wood fern are smooth, and the spores are on the margin of each leaflet, making it one of the easiest of the wood ferns to identify, hence the other common name. Simple, isn't it? Its scientific name is *Dryopteris marginalis*. The genus name is all Greek to me—*dryo*, meaning oak, and *pteris*, meaning fern, probably signifying its presence in oak woods. All the wood ferns form clumps, and next year's fronds can be found in the center covered with brown furry coats. The green of the Christmas fern is dark and lustrous, whereas the green of the wood ferns is lighter.

Another evergreen fern is the rock polypody fern. Its common name is quite descriptive, as it grows on rocks, forming large colonies by means of its many feet (poly means *many*, and *pody* means feet). It is a smaller fern, growing only six to twelve inches high, and quite distinctive in its form. Two more evergreen ferns are the ebony and maidenhair spleenwort. The ebony spleenwort could, at a cursory glance, be mistaken for a small nine- to twelve-inch Christmas fern. It can be found growing in a variety of habitats, whereas the maidenhair spleenwort prefers damp, shady rock cliffs. To the best of my knowledge, neither is found at Spencer Crest. Although the maidenhair spleenwort is usually found in nature on those damp, shady cliffs, I have several growing in a south-facing wall by my driveway. It apparently gets enough moisture and is protected from too much direct sunlight by the tall trees to the south. I have a north-facing raised bed. At the foot of this bed, two maidenhair spleenworts have self-soried and have found a more favorable habitat.

Although not evergreen, two other ferns provide interest throughout the long, cold winter. They are the sensitive and ostrich ferns. Both are unusual in that the fronds are dimorphic. The dried fertile fronds of both are frequently used in flower arrangements, and again, no harm is done to the plant. Both are aggressive plants and not suited for the small garden. The sensitive fern is extremely abundant, spreads aggressively to the point of being weedy, and will grow in full sun in damp areas.

Ladies and Gents

Ferns are asexual. There are no male and female ferns. They have no flowers and hence no seeds. Well, what about the asparagus fern? It flowers and has seeds. Just because it's called a fern doesn't mean that it is a fern. It is a nonedible relative of asparagus and a member of the lily family. It gets its fern appellation from its fernlike appearance with its feathery leaves.

So whence the "Ladies and Gents"? Well, there is a fern, *Athyrium filix-femina*, whose common name is lady fern, and there is *Dryopteris filix-mas*, with the common name of male fern. They are in different genera and do not hybridize. Instead of seeds, ferns produce spores—small, dust-like particles. In times past, people were puzzled by how ferns reproduced. So tiny are the spores that the Bard wrote, "We have the receipt of fern-seed; we walk invisible."

Well then, where do baby ferns come from? The spores, if they fall on a suitable moist surface, a heart-shaped gametophyte or prothallus develops. On the underside of the prothallus, sperm-producing antheridia grow. When the sperm is released, they swim toward the archegonia and fertilization occurs. The sperm and egg are referred to as gametes so the sexual phase is the gametophyte and the asexual phase is the sporophyte phase. So once fertilization has taken place, a new fern, a sporeling, begins to grow.

Ah, you say, but what about hybrids? If spores from two different species are sowed on the same surface, then the antheridia from one species can fertilize the archegonium from the other species. There are naturally occurring hybrids, and some genera, such as *Dryopteris*, are more propitious in producing hybrids than others. There are even hybrids of species from different genera, e.g., Scott's spleenwort is a naturally occurring hybrid between the walking fern and ebony spleenwort.

Longtime Fronds

Top on my list of ferns is our northern maidenhair, also known as five-finger fern. It is unlike any other of our native ferns. The fronds are displayed horizontally and spread out like a hand. I was fortunate in that I was able to rescue many from an area that was due for development. Consequently, I was able to use some to line paths. Others, I planted in the woods and left undisturbed. They formed a nice colony, reaching a height of eighteen inches. In a truly ideal site, they reputedly will grow to thirty inches. Not only are they handsome throughout the summer and into fall, but the emerging reddish stems and fronds are contorted and a joy to behold. There is another maidenhair fern from the northwest *Adiantum aleuticum*. The major difference is the more erect fronds on *A. aleuticum*. A few years ago, I noticed that the emerging fronds were green and not red. I checked with a fern friend, and she confirmed that this indeed is diagnostic for this fern. Of course, once the fern matures, this is not helpful. There is a dwarf form, *subpumilum*, that grows only three or four inches tall with overlapping segments. I have not had success growing this. There is also a southern maidenhair that is too tender for me, although a hardy variety has been reported. The Himalayan maidenhair (*Adiatum venustum*) is a dainty and stunning rival to our native northern maidenhair. It only grows a few inches high, spreads slowly, and can form large mats. I have lost my original clump but am trying it anew, as it is such a delightful fern. In the Northwest, it grows lustily.

Braun's holly fern is one of the ferns that I have grown from spores. It is the other native *Polystichum* in the northeast, and its range is more northerly than that of the Christmas fern. It too is a handsome fern, growing two feet tall, but shaggier and a lighter green than Christmas fern. It too increases in size by spreading outward.

The lady fern (*Athyrium filix-mas*) is a handsome fern, especially in the red form *rubellum*. A particularly intense red form is available under the name lady in red. From what I understand, it takes several years for this form to attain its distinctive red coloration of the stipes. I find it easier to identify this fern in the spring when it emerges. The stipes are covered with black hairs. This fern is a "runner," spreading by stolons, and can be a bit invasive.

Goldie's fern is the most distinctive of the wood or shield ferns. It is tall, four to five feet, with wide fronds. It has become one of my favorites, and I am forever dividing it and planting it in a new location.

Japanese painted fern is one of everyone's favorite ferns with its shades of burgundy, gray, and green. Plant it in a lightly shaded spot, as too much sun can wash out the color. It, like the lady fern, spreads, making propagation simple. In fact, it will send up new fronds all summer and into fall. When I bought this many a year ago, I would divide it and contribute it to the Corning Area Garden Club plant auction. This went on for a number of years, and I think everyone in the club had a plant. Then I visited one of my gardening friends, Paul and Grace Graham, and their plant was spectacular—a good eighteen inches in diameter. I then vowed that other garden club members could donate plants of this for the auction. In 2004, it was named Perennial Plant of the Year. There are many variations that fall under "pictum," ranging both in size and coloration. With its status as Plant of the Year, a host of named varieties were introduced, each claiming distinction. One truly different is Applecourt, with its crested fronds. Two reputed hybrids with the lady fern are Branford Rambler and Ghost.

I have come to appreciate the glade fern, also known as narrow-leaved spleenwort. It can be found under *Diplazium pycnocarpon* or *Athyrium pycnocarpum*. The sterile fronds are tall and narrow and the fertile fronds taller still. It spreads nicely by short rhizomes and is easily divided. I now have it in several spots in my woods. Northern beech fern is a delightful, distinctive fern with triangular-shaped fronds and spreads by rhizomes. It, too, is easily divided. The oak fern has somewhat the appearance of a miniature bracken fern and like bracken spreads widely. It can be easily overlooked, but when massed, it can be stunning.

Bulblet bladder fern (*Cystopteris bulbifera*) is a curious fern in that it has two methods of reproducing—by spores and by forming bulbs on the fronds, which then drop off, root, and grow into new ferns. It grows so profusely at times that I have had to rip out dozens of them. It is very attractive with its long, tapering fronds, which can reach three feet in length. Another of the bladder ferns is fragile fern (*Cystopteris fragilis*). This is more compact than the bulblet fern and makes a small, handsome fern in my rock walls. It has the distinction of being the first of my ferns to unfold its fronds in the spring.

A popular indoor fern is holly fern (*Cyrtonium falcatum*). There is one species that is hardy in the northeast, *Cyrtonium fortunei*. The holly ferns have beautiful, leathery holly-like fronds. I use this fern on either side of the steps leading off from the living room.

A few years ago, I had the pleasure and joy of visiting Clark's Reservation south of Syracuse. This is one of the few places home to the rare hart's tongue fern (*Asplenium scolopendrium*). To see an entire hillside with these long, tongue-shaped fronds blows one's mind. A friend gave me two plants, one of which he thought was a hybrid with the English form. These I planted at the edge of my patio, using oyster shells since they are lime lovers. I have added no additional source of lime in the intervening years, and they continue as healthy-looking as initially.

For years, I was successfully growing the rattlesnake fern (*Botrychium virginianum*). This is one of the grape ferns. The sterile fronds are triangular with three pinnae. The fertile frond is erect, rising several inches above the sterile fronds. It is curious in that it doesn't form a fiddlehead but simply unbends.

Fronds I've Yet to Meet

There are a half dozen of our native ferns that I would like to add to my collection. Heading the list is *Camptosaurus rhizophyllus*, the walking fern. The long, slender fronds are evergreen and will form new ferns at the tip; hence the appellation of walking fern. Next on my want list is the climbing fern. This is unique for its twining habit. One problem is that it is one of the more difficult ferns to grow. Ah, but one can dream. There are two woodsias that are not difficult to grow and would make nice additions to my rock garden in a shady site. They are rusty woodsia and blunt-lobed woodsia. For the sunny rock garden, I would like to try the hairy lip fern.

There are two cliff brakes, and either one would be nice to have for the rock garden. They are purple cliff brake and the smooth cliff brake. The netted chain fern has distinctive sterile and fertile fronds that would add interest in the garden. This is found in acidic bogs and swamps but is reputed to grow well in the average garden. The Virginia chain fern would make a nice addition but likes more moisture in its site than I could provide.

There are two of our fronds from the northwest that I have tried without success. They are the western sword fern and the deer fern. The sword fern is a magnificent fern with narrow fronds that in the northwest can grow to six feet. If it were to survive in my garden, it would not attain the stature it has in its native habitat. I should, however, be able to grow the deer fern, and it would make a delightful addition. It is evergreen with prostrate sterile fronds and erect fertile fronds.

One fern that is way too tender by two zones that would be nice to have is Plummer's woodsia (*Woodsia plummerae*) for obvious reasons. It is native to the southwest and into Mexico.

Pteridophyte Ptrail

When I started growing nonnative ferns, I conceived the idea of cutting a new trail through the back woods and lining it with my newly acquired ferns. Actually, I cut two trails to accommodate the large number of wood ferns that are hardy to zone 5. Since ferns are pteridophytes, why not call it by the alliterative Pteridophyte Ptrail? The trail starts at an existing trail that runs close to the southern border of the lot. It runs several feet from a bank, forming an island bed home to many snakeroot plants. It then crosses a path, turns north just short of my eastern lot line, and joins another woodland path.

On the left or northern side of the path are planted all the dryopteris clan, the wood ferns. For the most part, I have planted the type and not the crested forms. If a fern was zone 5 or lower and was available, I would buy it. Unfortunately, a nursery in the New York City area that had great selections closed. I am a member of the Hardy Fern Foundation, and they offer ferns that they have grown from spores. The other two sources of a good selection are two Washington state nurseries. Most of the ones I bought have prospered. I have some two dozen species, distributed along forty feet of the path.

The first section on the right side is devoted to the Polystichums, the holly ferns. These are finickier than the wood ferns, and my batting record here is around 0.500. I am growing the soft shield fern as the type not the fancy forms. This European fern is very variable, producing a variety of crested forms, finely divided forms, and dwarf forms. One could build an entire garden with the myriad forms of this fern. One of the less hardy ferns that I have tried and may try again is the Korean rock fern (*Polystichum tsus-simense*). This small, dainty fern is worth growing.

The lady ferns fill out the rest of this section. I have the unpainted as well as the painted forms of the Japanese fern, *Athyrium nipponicum*, as well as some of its hybrids with other lady ferns. My specimen of *minutissima* was doing so well I divided it and used it in the foundation planting next to the patio. This is a delightful miniature lady fern, growing three to six inches tall. The first time I saw "frizelliae," the tatting fern, I could not believe it was a fern. The fronds are twelve to eighteen inches tall, but the pinnae are reduced to beadlike balls. A most curious fern. I also moved lady in red to the foundation planting.

CHAPTER 4

FLOWERS THAT BLOOM IN THE SPRING TRA-LA

Harbingers of Spring

> Harbinger; har'bin jr. Anything that
> foreshadows a future event, an omen.

The first harbinger of spring occurs two weeks before the winter solstice. The second week into December, the sun begins to set a little later each day. A month later, both sunrise and sunset are being pushed back, and the days begin to grow appreciably longer. In January and certainly by February, the alders and birches with their catkins and the red maple are our native harbingers. Driving back from Florida, one can follow the advance of spring by the red maples. These are wind pollinated, and it is not until late April that the shad, with its small, delicate white blows, announces that spring is truly here.

Down on the forest floor, signs of spring proliferate. Trailing arbutus will be among the first to bloom, and pushing aside the leaf litter, one can see color in the buds. Mayflower is one of the loveliest of our wildflowers; it is more widely known as *trailing arbutus* and is believed by some to be the New England mayflower of the Pilgrims. It is a low-growing plant sometimes spreading into huge mats a yard square. The flowers are fragrant and may vary in color from white to pink. Many people in times past would go into the woods in April and gather arbutus by the armload. A friend of my father's was one of these, and at that time, I was not troubled by his action. But it is a slow-growing plant, perhaps spreading an inch a year in a favorable site. It is fairly abundant in our woods in the southern tier and occurs in a number of locations at Spencer Crest Nature Center. One unlikely site where it was growing at the nature center was on a slight hillock by a path that got good sun and was almost bone-dry in the summer. It can be grown from cuttings and where abundant, no landowner should object to a few cuttings. They can be taken from spring to early summer after the plants have finished blooming. Marjorie Dietz[10] in her excellent little book *The Concise Encyclopedia of Favorite Wild Flowers*, gives a photographic how-to procedure for rooting cuttings of arbutus. Grown from cuttings, they will develop a good root system. The needs of arbutus are easy to satisfy. Like many of our wildflowers, it prefers an acidic soil. If you have oaks and pines, you are all set. If not, you can increase the acidity by working in oak leaf mold or pine needles. Despite that plant growing at the nature center, arbutus should not be planted in full sun; shade or semishade is preferred as under trees or on the north side.

In the race to see which will be among the first to bloom is the dainty but rugged rue anemone. It is a small anemone-like plant with leaves like the meadow rues. It is a delicate-looking plant but tough in reality. This was one of the endemic plants on our lot. For years, it grew well and I would dig and divide the small bulbs to plant around. Then years ago, I noticed that I was losing it. A friend suggested voles as the cause. Many list it as ephemeral, but the flowers persist for a week to ten days, so that in my book it is not ephemeral. The best known of the cultivars is Schoaff's Double, which many people rave over, but it leaves me cold. It is the color, because the double green, Betty Blake is more appealing to me. There are white and pink semidoubles and single pinks. Until I get the vole problem solved, I will not be investing in these named forms, attractive as they may be.

Another of the endemic wildflowers is the round-leaved hepatica.

---

[10] Dietz, *The Concise Encyclopedia of Favorite Wild Flowers*.

Both its Latin name (hepatica) and common name (liverwort) are related to the belief that it was a cure for liver problems. Other common names are noble liverwort, liverleaf, liverweed, trefoil, herb trinity, kidneywort, and edellebere. Many of these names may be traced back to Europe and their native species of hepatica. The old leaves persist over winter, and the new furry leaves unfold in early spring. Easy to spot are the old leaves and the fattening buds of the flowers. The flowers can range in color from white to pink to dark blue. In the woods around here, it is often found at the base of an oak or rock—a likely place for a seed to lodge and to germinate. Our other native hepatica is the acute-leaved liverwort. This occurs in the hills around us, and my plants with clear pink blossoms came as a gift from a friend and neighbor. When these wildflowers bloom and the first fiddleheads of fragile fern appear, spring is surely here.

Spring Ephemerals

> Ephemeral: Lasting for a markedly brief time: Living or lasting only for a day, as certain plants or insects do such as the mayfly. From Greek: ephmeros: *epi-* + hmer, *day*.

There are those wildflowers whose flowers last for only too brief a time, and there are those plants that die back after being pollinated and setting seed. Both types are ephemeral but in different senses. There is a third type, which will die back in a dry spell but which, if given enough water, will persist until frost.

In the first category is twinleaf. The flowers of twinleaf may persist for two days if the weather is cool and they have not been pollinated. But even though the flowers are so short-lived, the form and the shape of its leaves and its intriguing seedpods warrant it a place in the garden. Added to that is that it is named for our third president, Thomas Jefferson. Both its Latin and common names are apt descriptions—"di" meaning two and "phyla" meaning leaf. The leaf is cut deeply, almost in two. The seedpod is most interesting. It is funnel-shaped and capped with a lid. When the seeds have matured, the cap opens and the seeds spill out, resulting in many seedlings the next spring. This plant develops a massive root system, and large plants are difficult to dig. Consequently, I try to dig up the yearlings to pot up or to transplant.

Bloodroot is not as ephemeral in flower as twinleaf; the flowers persist for several days until they are pollinated. The bloodroot is one of the earliest of the wildflowers to bloom, pushing up out of the ground in early to mid-April with its leaves wrapped snugly around the flower stalk. On overcast days, the flowers do not open, presumably because the plant knows that the bees will be spending the day at home in the hive. Thus the flowers may persist for a week. Given a little sun, the bud opens, revealing a charming white daisy-like flower. Massed in a colony, they present a dramatic sight. In a week, the flower has been pollinated, petals drop off, and it begins to set seed. The leaves continue to expand to eight to ten inches in diameter with deeply scalloped edges. By mid-June, the seeds have ripened inside the two-inch-long pointed pod. When the seeds are ripe, the pods split open, dispersing the seeds. Many of them may germinate where fallen, but others will be carried away by ants for the elaisome attached to the seed. I have plants growing deep in cracks in my stone walls. If you split the pods open to collect the seeds, you will discover that your fingers are red-stained. If not sown immediately, they will lie dormant for a year. Sow them in a light, humusy soil. The year after they germinate, plant them where you want them to grow. Given a rich, humus-filled soil in partial shade, they will spread into larger and larger colonies, surrounded by self-sown seedlings.

I have more than a thousand plants scattered all over my three-quarter acres of woods. Some get the full effect of the spring sun, while others are in deep shade. Although individual plants may bloom for only a few days, I will have bloodroot flowers for three to four weeks. Both Latin and common names refer to the blood-red color of the root, which is a finger-sized tuber. Unlike twinleaf, bloodroot is easy to dig, divide, and transplant. The tuber is easily broken and portions with at least one "eye" will develop into flowering plants. If they need to be moved, dig them up in the fall, break the rhizomes, replant them, and notice your bloodstained hands. Some people classify bloodroot as being ephemeral in both flower and plant. Mine consistently persist until fall when the leaves turn yellow and they die back. If too dry, they do undergo an early dormancy, but they do not fold up their tents and steal away in the normal course.

Spring beauty is in the family Portulacaceae. The genus, *Claytonia*, was named for John Clayton (1686–1773), who was clerk to the county court of Gloucester County, Virginia, from 1720 until his death. He has been described as the greatest American botanist of his day and was one of the earliest collectors of plant specimens in that state. The portulaca family also contains the lewisias, and the flowers of the spring beautys, although less than an inch wide, do clearly resemble the flowers of lewisia.

In prior years, I have spotted the grass-like leaves of spring beauty in late January, when most plants have no thoughts of the approaching spring, but never as early as I did one year on December 10. By the end of March, it is all budded up, waiting for a warm, sunny day to open its flowers. From then into May, it makes a delightful sight wherever it has chosen to grow. The name says it all. It is truly a beauty in spring, with its pink-striped flowers. It has a delicate, fragile-looking beauty that belies its true nature. It is a small plant, growing only three to six inches tall with both basal leaves and a pair of narrow leaves on the stem. The stem terminates in a raceme of small flowers, consisting of five petals that are white with fine pink stripes that vary in intensity. As many as fifteen blossoms have been recorded on each stem. On cloudy days, the stem droops and the flowers close, only to open again on another sunny day. Sunny days bring out the pollinators—all sorts of bees and flies and occasional butterflies. The flowers, when fertilized, produce a capsule, containing a few seeds. By the end of May, it has formed and dispersed its seeds and stored up enough energy for the next year; it decides it doesn't like hot weather and bids a fond adieu. One plant doesn't make much of a splash, but it seeds itself in such profusion to create carpets of pink. Last spring, it covered an area of six to eight square feet. I have begun to transplant it into my lawn and await the spring when there will be hundreds of those delicate pink flowers in bloom. Like other spring ephemerals, Dutchman's britches, squirrel corn, and Virginia bluebells, it takes advantage of the leafless trees in spring to complete its aboveground growth. I have not tried to collect seed but have let it self-sow to make larger and larger patches. I would think one would have to be diligent to collect the seed or bag the flower heads. Its proclivity to self-sow suggests that the seed should be sown fresh. Plants that seed themselves into the path are transplanted.

In correspondence with John Geyer,[11] he wrote,

> Its growth starts again in September when soil temperatures are lower and soil moisture increases. It first produces an extensive root system, which nearly exhausts the energy reserves of the corm. The corm becomes rubbery as the energy reserves are used up. Leaves begin to appear after the energy reserves are half or more exhausted and the corm begins to recover turgor. The growth seems temperature and moisture dependent. Soil temperatures of less than 55F are needed for growth in a good moist soil. Temperatures below about 35F will slow or terminate growth, but do not seem needed to complete the growth cycle.

John also reports growing a yellow-flowered form.

I learned that some of the other common names for spring beauty are *fairy spuds*, *good morning spring*, *groundnut*, *mayflower*, and *wild potato*. The common names *fairy spuds* and *wild potato* allude to the tuber's resemblance to a miniature potato with many protruding eyes. The Algonquins ate the cooked corms like potatoes. Fernald and Kinsey in their *Edible Wild Plants of Eastern North America*[12] state that when boiled in salted water, the spuds are palatable and nutritious, with a chestnut-like flavor. Hundreds of plants would be needed to provide a good sustenance. They further state that the succulent young plants are a possible potherb. I have not tried it, but maybe I will this spring. The Iroquois used a cold infusion of the roots as an anticonvulsive for children. The raw plants were also used as a contraceptive.

It has quite a wide distribution, occurring from Massachusetts west to Nebraska, south to Georgia, and extending into Texas. The New York Flora Association lists it as native to Chemung and Tompkins Counties but lists no reports from Steuben or Schuyler Counties. It is found in a number of habitats, but moist woods with

---

[11] Private communication.
[12] Fernald and Kinsey, *Edible Wild Plants of Eastern North America*.

dappled sunlight are a favorite habitat. One source stated that it will adapt to semishaded lawns if mowing is delayed—another neat thing to try. I have begun to transplant it into my lawn and to await the spring when there will be hundreds of those delicate pink flowers in bloom.

It is one of two spring ephemerals whose common name is spring beauty. *Claytonia virginica* is distinguished from *Claytonia caroliniana* by its narrow leaves. Both can be found in rich woods from Canada to Minnesota and from Virginia to Texas. Elk, moose, and deer eat the flowers and leaves. Sheep and rodents eat the tubers. I can easily imagine that the local deer herd eat some of my plants. After all, it is one of first plants to start growing in the spring and it must be tastier than the ramps that the deer ate one spring. I am sure that after a long, tough winter, both man and beast would relish spring beauty and ramps. Deer have, on occasion, also eaten the leaves of bloodroot and some newly emerging fronds.

Dutchman's britches and its look-alike cousin, squirrel corn, are examples of plants that flower for a long time but go dormant after setting seed. These are relatives of our native fringed bleeding heart and the tall European bleeding heart. Unlike these two, Dutchman's britches and squirrel corn are ephemeral. Dutchman's britches do indeed look like miniature white pantaloons. The foliage of these two are almost indistinguishable, but we have to get to the root of the matter to easily tell them apart. The roots of britches are small white buds, while those of the squirrel resemble little yellow kernels of corn. The ants love the elaisome attached to the seed, and like with bloodroot, they carry the seed away. One of my best plants of Dutchman's britches is one in a wall. They pop up in the most unusual places—one of the joys of gardening.

The Virginia bluebell is another of our spring's here today, gone tomorrow ephemerals. It is among the first of our native wildflowers to emerge from the cold, cold earth. It blooms for weeks, opening pink and changing to that lovely shade of blue. A common name for it is Virginia cowslip, probably named by early settlers for its resemblance to English cowslips. In rich woods, it can form large colonies that are spectacular in bloom. This is what I have tried to emulate on one bank by encouraging the seedlings and by transplanting bluebells to fill in bare spots. It develops a massive carrot-like root system that it uses to store the solar energy that it captures before leaves block the sun. The root system makes it difficult to transplant mature plants, but the small seedlings transplant readily. As my plants have increased, I am starting to plant them on another bank. In addition, individual plants have appeared throughout my woods. In my woods, there are enough other plants like Solomon's seal and ferns to fill in and mask their absence after they go dormant. In a conventional flower bed, their disappearance may present a problem. There is a white form that I had in years past, but it proved too ephemeral and I lost it. Perhaps, I will try again.

Trout lily is also known as dog-tooth violet, adder's tongue, and leopard lily. This is a plant that is very diffident about flowering. The conventional wisdom is that you have to plant them on top of a stone so they cannot burrow any deeper. I suspect that may be true because the roots seem to pull the bulb deep. They are extremely shy about flowering, and after years and years, I am beginning to get more and more flowers each spring as the plants mature. They are not shy about sending out numerous thin rhizomes that seem to pop up in faraway places, forming a nice groundcover in early spring before the plants go dormant. There was one plant just over on our neighbor's lot line that flowered reliably. I was able to transplant this into my erstwhile bog. It has developed into a robust plant with three flowers in 2005 and eight in 2008.

Trilliums Spell Spring

Trilliums spell spring and make a great addition to the garden. It takes five or six years from seed to a blooming plant, making them very expensive for a nursery to propagate and expensive for the gardener to purchase. A nursery may list them as nursery grown—translation: they were dug from the wild and held in the nursery prior to selling. If the nursery has a large tract of woodland and conservatively harvests, that does not present a problem. But how does the gardener know?

With trilliums, everything occurs in threes: the sepals, the petals, and the leaves. Our large white trillium (*Trillium grandiflorum*) produces one of the most dramatic displays of color in May. One spring, as I was driving up to Potsdam, the displays on both sides of Interstate 81 north of Syracuse were spectacular. Colony after colony of these lovely flowers with hundreds of plants in each made a gorgeous display of white. On the throughway between Syracuse and Geneva and on Route 13 north of Horseheads, there are other colonies that can be seen from the highway. With the expanding deer population, many of these large colonies may well be destroyed.

Early on, I was able to collect a few of our white trillium, and these were planted next to the path in the front woods. I started with about a half dozen plants. Then one spring, I noticed these tiny seedlings—some with one leaf, some with two, and others with three leaves—all surrounding the trilliums I had planted. I then realized why it may take as long as six years for trilliums to flower from seed. The first-year seedling will have one leaf, the next year two, and the third year three. It then needs to store up energy in its tuber to flower and set seed. What some people may not realize is that the color of the petals deepens to rose as the flowers age, giving, in essence, two seasons of bloom. I also learned that fresh seed is the secret to germination, and it should be collected about a week before the pods open. If the seed should dry, it takes an extra year or two for the seed to break dormancy. The seed pod that forms is an inconspicuous green and splits open as soon as the seed has ripened, making it difficult for the seed collector if he or she waits too long. As my plants continued to seed around, I started to transplant them and decided to create a swath that would extend over and around the white pine to meet up with the path. Today this swath contains upward of three hundred plants, and this year, I am transplanting seedlings to other parts of the garden—three here, another three there. Trillium seeds, like those of bloodroot and Dutchman's britches, have an elaisome so that seeds that drop from the pod may be carried away from the parent plant. This is what I expect happened with the clump with more than a dozen stems at the edge of my patio.

The white trillium is only one of four trilliums that occur locally. The red trillium has had bad press, having been dubbed "stinking Benjamin." *Wake robin* is another name given to both this and white trillium. It can grow as large as its white cousin but is not as conspicuous or as spectacular because of its darker color, nor are the petals as large. It has not done as well for me as the white trillium. The prettiest of the tribe is the painted trillium, with its white and red markings. Unfortunately, it is also the most difficult to grow, and I have struck out twice in my attempts. It supposedly requires a cool, acidic site to thrive. These three occur naturally in the areas around Corning. Both the painted and the red trilliums have colored seedpods, red and purple respectively. One of the most unusual is the nodding trillium in which the flower hangs down below the leaves. Its most extensive distribution is north of us into Canada. The prairie trillium is not endemic to our area but is to the west of us. My plant came from my aunt and uncle's farm in Indiana. It has found a home here and propagates itself around. It can be hard to transplant because the bulbs can be quite deep.

Homebodies

(The following plants are those that were indigenous to our lot or in the immediate vicinity.)
In the woodland in spring, before the trees leaf out, most of the native flowers take advantage of the sunlight streaming through the bare branches to flower and to photosynthesize. Two such are foamflower and Bishop's cap or miterwort. Foamflower has similar heart-shaped, toothed leaves, but the foamflowers are much showier, bearing resemblance to a tiara. Indeed, foamflower is also known as false miterwort. It is evergreen, or at least the leaves persist throughout the winter before new growth commences in the spring. It tends to spread by runners and can make an attractive groundcover, given the right conditions. There is a nonspreading form, *Tiarella wherryi*, named for Dr. Edgar Wherry, who discovered this form. In the past few years, there has been a plethora of introductions of forms of tiarella with a range of colors and leaf shapes as well as extended bloom. Both these are related to heuchera (alumroot) and indeed tiarella and heuchera will cross, giving rise to heucherella.

Bishop's cap has heart-shaped, toothed leaves. The flowers on miterwort are much less showy than those on foamflower. The flowers give the plant its common name. The delicate flowers are on a thin stalk and resemble a miter that a Bishop would wear.

Not only is a clump attractive when in bloom, but I find it equally attractive when the seedpods are filled with tiny black seeds. A knowledgeable gardener has been known to dismiss it as of little value. I beg to differ. True, an individual plant is not striking. But the gardener in question never saw my clump with several dozen flowering stalks.

Wild geranium has soft pink flowers and attractive foliage. The beak-like seed capsule gives the plant both its common name, cranesbill, and its Latin name *Geranium*. There are now white forms and forms with dark leaves. It seeds itself around quite nicely, even into my lawn from a particularly handsome specimen in the long stone wall. Lately, I have been digging up the seedlings and transplanting them to the end of the driveway. My plan is to use these en masse as a groundcover beneath the post lamp.

Barren strawberry is another native plant that was indigenous to our lot. It is not too well known. Its leaves bear some resemblance to the leaves of strawberries. It is not strictly barren, as the yellow flowers are followed by a dry fruit. But it lacks the fleshy and tasty fruit of our wild strawberry. It has been recommended as a groundcover, but my plants are shy about spreading.

There was one trout lily that flowered reliably just over our lot line. Not so with the plants I have purchased until many moons have passed. They are extremely shy about flowering. I think they have to bury themselves deep and build up a store of energy. After dozens of years, I am finally getting significant bloom. They are not, however, shy about spreading about and popping up in the strangest places. I have one patch about a square yard in extent that has yet to send up one flower. The narrow, mottled lily-like leaves are the clue to its identity. It is also called "dogtooth violet" from the shape of the white bulb. After two score of years in other patches, I am getting a dozen or more flowers. Maybe in another score, it will be a riot of yellow lily-like flowers. This is one of the ephemeral plants that go dormant in late spring.

False Solomon's seal (*Smilacina racemosa*) is one of my favorites. The rather coarse zig-zag leaves are on a long, arching stalk with the raceme of small white flowers clustered at the end. It comes into its glory in the autumn when the clusters of wine-red berries put on a beautiful display.

The following quote is from Thoreau:

> Reached the Highland Light about 2 p.m. The Smilacina is *just* out of bloom on the bank. They call it the "wood lily" there. Uncle Sam called it "snake corn," and said it looked like corn when it first came up. (Henry David Thoreau, on Cape Cod on June 18, 1857)

The plant is attractive in the spring when its white racemes of flowers are in bloom; throughout the summer with its large leaves and arching stem; in the fall, as well, when the wine-red berries ripen; and still later when the leaves turn yellow, albeit a little ratty. My plants do not form large colonies, nor do they get as tall as I have seen them in Washington and Oregon, but nevertheless, they are an attractive plant spring, summer, and fall.

Mayapple (*Podophyllum pedatum*) cannot be overlooked, with its large, umbrella-like leaves. Only plants with two leaves produce a large hanging white flower followed by a yellowish apple-like fruit, which is edible but not very palatable. In a photo taken before our home was built, there is a large patch in what is now our front woods. Mayapple spreads by underground stolons and can be quite aggressive. When it starts invading my swath of trillium, it gets transplanted. In the northeast back corner of our lot, it is usually free to spread to its heart's content. It has a bad habit of looking ragged and going dormant in late summer, especially if it is a dry summer.

Rue anemone is a delightful, delicate-looking plant that is one of the first of the wildflowers to bloom. It was abundant on our lot and in the surrounding woods but has since disappeared.

Liverwort was also abundant on our lot and in the surrounding woods, and walking up the hill to work was a special treat in the spring. The flower colors range from white to pink to blue to purple. It sets its flower buds in the fall, and at times, I have had a plant in bloom in March. New growth is all wooly and fuzzy, as though to protect the plant from the cold.

Canada mayflower or wild lily of the valley was another abundant spring wildflower. Much daintier than its tame namesake, growing only a few inches tall, it has two or three leaves and white flowers in a short raceme, followed by wine-red berries. It can form little colonies but more often occurs singly. It will sometimes pop up in the middle of a path, having gotten there by underground stolons.

One plant that covered large areas in the back woods for a few years was gaywings, which gives the appearance of a tiny purple orchid. It suffered the same fate as my rue anemone, probably by the same family of voles. The flowers of gaywings do indeed look like a miniature orchid. Other names are fringed polygala and wintergreen. A few years after we built, one entire section of the back woods was covered with the gaywings, forming a carpet of purplish rose. That occurred only the one year, and in the succeeding years, the number of plants has steadily decreased so that none are left. What a tragic loss!

Still another plant native to the property was round-leaved shinleaf. It is a pretty little thing, not at all showy. It is supposedly difficult to transplant, but I was successful in establishing it in the front woods.

There were a few plants of wintergreen (*Gaultheria procumbens*), known as teaberry, that were here originally but disappeared early on. I tried to reestablish them once without success.

Partridgeberry (*Mitchella repens*) was also present and would form large patches. It is still in the woods but not as prolific. I miss seeing the small white flowers in July and the red berries.

Wild sarsaparilla (*Aralia nudicaulis*) is prized more for its foliage and growth habit than for the green umbel of flowers. Growing ten to twenty inches tall, the large compound leaves bear three- or five-pointed ovate leaflets on separate stalks. Like the mayapple, plants having only one stalk do not bear flowers. Also like the mayapple, it can spread aggressively by means of its underground stolons. Unlike the mayapple, I have found it difficult to divide.

Starflower (*Trientalis borealis*) is a delightful little charmer that may well be overlooked. There is a whorl of pointed leaves in summer above which there are small white star-shaped flowers.

One of the most unusual flowers on the property was Indian pipe (*Monotropa uniflora*), also known as ghost plant or corpse plant. Botanists tell us that it is related to the shinleafs. It has lost its chlorophyll and exists on decaying matter in the ground. Indeed, it looks like a miniature clay pipe, but as it matures, the bowl becomes erect and later the plant blackens.

Goldenrods are usually associated with sunny fields, but the blue-stemmed goldenrod is a denizen of rich, open woods and remains quite happy in my woods. Sharing the woods is the white wood aster. Both of these are beginning to spread around.

Downy yellow violet, sweet white violet, and northern blue violet all have, at one time or another, popped up hither and yon.

Not occurring on our lot but on a neighbor's lot was a patch of bunchberry (*Cornus canadensis*), also known as dwarf cornell, as it is a miniature version of our flowering dogwood. I was permitted to transplant a few of them. They have persisted but not really thrived. This plant is quite common in the hills around Corning. It flowers well, but seed set is very sparse, and I have come to the conclusion that it is climate-related, probably because summer nights are too warm. We are at the southern limit of its range. At higher latitudes, it grows, flowers, and sets seed in abundance. On a train trip to Alaska on the *Midnight Express*, the roadbed between Anchorage and Denali, for mile after mile, was strewn with plants bearing red berries.

CHAPTER 5

THE WILD ONES

A Baker's Dozen

In the woodland in spring, before the trees leaf out, most of the native flowers take advantage of the sunlight streaming through the bare branches to flower and to photosynthesize. If you have a wildflower garden, you have to have jack-in-the-pulpits. Who says you have to be pretty to be popular? It can grow two feet tall or taller, and each of the three leaves can approach a foot in length. Young plants start out as male, but in following years, as they build up their reserves, they will become female and produce that large clump of attractive red berries. It self-sows readily, and I have found dozens of seedlings at the base of a plant. It is oh so easy to grow from seed. Jack-in-the-pulpit seems to be a favorite of everyone. It is also known as Indian turnip, but the roots had to be cooked and cooked to remove the oxalic acid to keep from burning one's mouth. It is a curious plant. There is a spadix with the flowers at the base. It is either "Jack" for male plants or "Jill" for female plants. The preacher is in his pulpit with the canopy overhead. The curiousness extends further because the plant can change its sex. Young plants are all bucks until they build up enough reserves. They then become female and can produce a big bunch of bright-red berries. Often these will fall at the base of the plant, producing 30 or more seedlings that can be transplanted. A flowering plant will have two stems, each with three leaves. Unlike trillium leaves, which are equally spaced, those of jacks will have two directly opposite and the third at 90 degrees. They often will have prominent veins. There also is a lot of variation in the color and striping of the stem and pulpit. Unlike our ephemeral plants, Jack is a slug-a-bed, not rising until May. In a favorable site, it can be impressive. Years ago, I had one three feet tall with a four-foot wingspread. Another native in the same genus is *Arisaema draconitum*, or dragontail, named for its long spadix. The Far East is home to a vast array, usually referred to as cobra lilies.

Solomon's seal (*Polygonatum commutatum*) is a majestic plant growing four to five feet tall. The creamy bell-shaped flowers hang from the arching stems with their large leaves. The flowers, when fertilized, produce dark-blue berries. I was down visiting my dad years ago and took a walk on the hill behind the house where I used to bird walk. There was an area shaded by an elm tree. There was a clump of Solomon's seal, and I took a few of the rhizomes, brought them home, and planted them in the front woods. They have done nicely and add greatly to that area. Being members of the lily family, they seem to be a favorite of deer. In years prior to my fence, I saw my tall Solomon's seals stripped bare of leaves, leaving just a yellowing stalk. They have spread by seeding and from spreading of the rhizomes. You often see it in large clumps, but mine must be antisocial because they grow by themselves. The solitary form I have works better in a woodland setting and the clumping form in a garden setting. I think that they must be separate clones, as I was just given some clump formers and planted them in areas where they can clump to their hearts' content. I divided the clump that my friend gave me into dozens of plants, and I think every one of them survived the transplanting and the trauma of division. Another friend gave me a goodly number of the variegated Solomon's seal (*Polygonatum odoratum variegatum*). This grows about three feet tall, spreads nicely, and makes a nice companion to our native. The darling of the lot is the dwarf Solomon's seal (*Polygonatum humile*). This hails from Eastern Asia and grows only six or so inches tall. It has small, shiny leaves and small, tubular flowers. It spreads nicely in moist, humusy soil in the shade. Like the others, it is easily divisible to share with others or to spread around in your garden.

Our native wild columbine (*Aquilegia canadensis*) is known to almost all. It is among the first native plants to begin growth in the spring. The scarlet and yellow flowers with the long, protruding stamens make a lovely sight when the flowers are dancing in the breeze. It is a favorite of hummingbirds and butterflies, with its sweet nectar. It has happily seeded itself into one of the rock walls. There is a named dwarf form, "Little Lanterns," that grows only a foot tall. It is on my want list. There is another form with orange flowers and other dwarf forms. It will hybridize with other columbines.

Our dwarf crested iris (*Iris cristata*) with flowers of blue, purple or white is a delightful charmer. Although blue is the typical color with orange falls, the white form is much more vigorous, at least in my garden. It is one of the earliest of the wildflowers to green up in the spring to take advantage of the light before the trees leaf out and create shade. It only grows a few inches tall and spreads outward. This is a mixed blessing because if planted next to a path, it wants to grow into the path. It can by propagated easily be cutting apart the rhizomes and planting them in a suitable mixture. A few plants can easily make a dozen or more. One fall, I divided the rhizomes and had dozens of plants in the spring. Half a dozen or so named forms have become available in the past few years and are worth seeking out.

Merrybells (*Uvularia*) come in three flavors, tall, medium, and short, and three shades of yellow, bright, medium, and pale. Large merrybells (*Uvularia grandiflora*), the largest and brightest yellow, are also the most aggressive, forming extensive clumps. Merrybells are easily divided by digging up and carefully separating the intertwined roots. A clump makes an impressive sight. The next in size is perfoliate merrybells (*Uvularia perfoliata*). They have softer yellow bells and are a tad shorter. The stem comes up through the leaf, hence the botanical name for the species. Wild oats (*Uvularia sessifolia*) are dainty little plants with pale-yellow flowers. Compared to their big brothers, they are barely noticeable but are little charmers.

Spikenard (*Aralia racemosa*) is of the same genus as the wild sarsaparilla that came with the property. The species name both for this and the false Solomon's seal notes that the flowers are in a raceme. I saw a magnificent six-foot specimen in a Minnesota garden, which put it at the top of my wish list. I have seen it again in Canada, making an impressive sight in a woodland setting. This is a new and welcome addition to my woods. It is a tall plant, up to five feet, making it hard to miss. The leaves divide and redivide, and the flower stalks carry the flowers in umbels. I have not succeeded in germinating the dark-purple berries. A friend tells me that she also has trouble germinating the seeds of this plant. How I would love to have a half dozen plants, some grouped and some as individuals, throughout my woods. Wouldn't that make a statement?

Unfortunately, the pink lady's slipper (*Cypripedium acaule*) is difficult to grow. They are abundant in the woods around us, and I was able to rescue a couple of them. They grew, persisting for perhaps twenty years, never increased in size, and then failed to flower and finally disappeared. The large yellow lady's slipper (*Cypripedium parviflorum*), unlike its pink sister, is easy to grow. I have two in different sites, and both are doing well but as well as I have seen in other gardens, which have clumps with a dozen blooms. It is easily divisible, and I would divide my clump long before it got that size. I am told that the Kentucky lady's slipper is *the* one to grow. It is adaptable and has a larger pouch. There are also Asian lady's slippers, and there are many hybrids coming on the market. With the advent of tissue culture, they are readily available but with a price.

Many gardeners are familiar with the European ginger and use it as a groundcover for a shady site. Not as well known is our native wild ginger (*Asarum canadensis*). I have come to appreciate it more than its immigrant cousin. It is not evergreen, but who cares when the entire woods is covered with snow? It grows low to the ground, can cover large areas, can tolerate a fair amount of sun, and in a prime site, can have leaves the size of a small plate. Neither the European nor our native is grown for its flowers. The jug-like flowers that open in the spring lie flat on the ground, providing easy access to ants for pollination. When the seeds are ripe, the seedpod opens, discharging the seeds. One day, it can be closed, and the next day, the seeds are all gone. The ants have gotten their reward. Ants have taken the seeds back to their nest. They then eat the elaison attached to the seed. I have plants growing from deep inside walls thanks to the ants.

Goatsbeard (*Aruncus dioicus*) is related to the garden astilbes and like them has tall plumes. Large, established plants can be as tall as seven feet. The white flowers can be two feet in height, with male and female flowers differing in form. Those on male plants are showier than those on female plants. When in bloom, they make a dramatic display, male or female. It is a spreader and if left undisturbed will form large clumps. But I am impatient, and from my original three plants, I have been dividing them to form a long border and now have a couple dozen. I guess it's about time to let them do their thing. If the deer get in, this is one of the plants they head right to.

My woodland phlox (*Phlox divaricata*) was a gift from a friend. I planted it in the backwoods under some pretty heavy shade. It grows there, but the ones I transplanted to the front woods above my stone wall and at the border of the rock garden and woods do quite well. In April and May, the blue (or white) flowers are held a foot above the foliage. The plants spread nicely from the leafy shoots and are very easy to divide to increase the spread. I keep dividing mine and planting it to increase its spread.

Ginseng (*Panax quinquefolia*) is the *sang* of Chinese medicine. The name *ginseng* is an Americanization of the Chinese *jin-chen*, meaning "manlike." The root does bear a resemblance to a person, and this resemblance increases as the plant ages. The genus name *Panax* means "panacea" or "cure-all." The species name describes the five leaflets. There is a dwarf ginseng with three leaflets. Ginseng has been used for centuries as a tonic in the Orient and is reputed to cure everything from high blood pressure to impotence. The demand from China almost drove our native plant to extinction. Today, it is usually cultivated for export and to supply the American market. I grow mine not to be harvested but for the attractiveness of the foliage and for the bright-red berries in the fall. The flowers I find insignificant, but those red berries are a different matter.

Allegheny spurge (*Pachysandra procumbens*) is North America's answer to Japanese pachysandra and wins hands down, with more attractive flowers and more interesting mottled, almost evergreen foliage. Why is it not more widely used? I know not. It is reputed to be deciduous in our area. Indeed, the first winter after I planted it, it did lose its leaves. But in the dozen or so intervening years, it has kept its leaves, staying green throughout the winter. The old leaves are dark green and mottled, but the new leaves are a bright, handsome green. And oh the flowers! There are dozens of small staminate flowers and a few pistillate flowers on countless spikes, making a very attractive display, together with the fresh new leaves.

Baneberries are included with a little trepidation if you have young children. The very word *bane* spells danger, but it could be a learning experience for them not to eat attractive berries. Is this why I put them thirteenth on the list? But they are attractive plants with stunning berries. They are very similar in foliage and flower, but oh so different in fruit. Those of red baneberries are bright red and ripen early. Another common name for the white baneberry is "doll's eye" for the resemblance of the fruit to the porcelain white and black eyes of dolls of a bygone year. Still another name is "summer cohosh." The red cohosh is also called "red cohosh." The red berry ripens early in the summer, but its white-berried friend waits until fall. It has the more striking fruit; the white berry is carried on thick red stems and has a black spot, leading to its moniker of doll's eyes. Nothing is ever black (red) or white in nature. There is a form of the red baneberry that has white fruit and of the white baneberry that has reddish fruit. This survived for a number of years in my garden.

Double Bloodroot

Sanguinaria canadensis multiplex(us) "perplexus."

A number of years ago, my neighbor called my attention to a low-growing white flower along the line separating our two properties, just behind a row of rhododendron that I had planted. It was a good-sized clump of double bloodroot that was subsequently divided and planted along his driveway. At the time, I made several inquiries as to how this might have gotten there. None of those queried had reported any similar occurrence. I was convinced that I had not planted it. Why would I have planted it in such an obscure spot? I have raised the question sporadically in the intervening years, with no more success than my original inquiries obtained. I raise the question again at this time, because another double is blooming in an even more unlikely location. It was about fifty feet farther on back than the original discovery, almost to the back of my property, in a little thicket. I do not transplant double bloodroot, except to proscribed locations. Bloodroot grows so well from seed that I have no need to transplant it. Rather, I will strew seed where I want additional colonies. So there is no way it could have arrived at its present location by any effort on my part. Do squirrels and chipmunks eat the root? Could this be the result of a mutation like the one that produced the original multiplex plant? Has anybody else had a similar experience? How can one determine if this is a separate clone from my other hundred doubles?

Indian Pipes

I can still recall finding a clump of Indian pipes (*Monotropa uniflora*) in dark woods nearly seventy years ago as a scout. A strange and curious plant living like mushrooms on organic matter in the soil and found usually in the shade of conifers. When it first emerges, the flower hangs down, giving the appearance of a small, white clay pipe—hence the common name. As it ages, the flower becomes more and more erect until it is perfectly so. When growth is complete, the seed ripens and disperses. Then, having completed its function, the plant dies and turns dark. Although inconspicuous at this stage, they can be found throughout the winter and spring. I am fortunate that they have found favorable conditions in my woods. The first year, they were five or six clumps. They persisted for several years, but finally failed to appear, presumably having depleted their source of nourishment and the seeds failing to find suitable conditions. In some forests, they are exceedingly abundant. Years ago, when a new friend and neighbor, seven-year-old Adam McNeil, and I were touring my woods, we found some pipes. His family spent a week in the Adirondacks and while there went on a nature walk. Guess what they found and guess who knew what they were. Though lacking chlorophyll, it is a plant and not a fungus. In fact, it is an ericaceous plant, related to wintergreen, blueberries, rhododendron, and laurel. Somewhere along the line, it lost its ability to make chlorophyll, depending entirely on extracting its food from the soil. In dense shade, the light energy is low, so at some time in the distant past, it gradually came less and less to depend on light and more and more on decaying matter in the soil. Although rare, it is widely distributed, being found in Asia, Europe, and North and South America. Leonard

Wiley, in *Rare Wild Flowers of North America*,[13] says he knows of no one who has been able to grow this plant or to propagate it from seeds. Although seed is produced in prodigious quantities, the seeds are so minute that they contain little food. His own experiments have been met with failure. I have not even tried.

White Stars in a Green Sky

This is what a large, solid patch of partridgeberry reminds me of when in bloom in July. To continue the analogy, when the stars burn out, they become red giants (the red berries). A widespread native plant, its range extends from Florida and Texas to Quebec, Ontario, and Minnesota. It is named for John Mitchell, a Virginia doctor and botanist who died on the eve of the Revolutionary War at the age of sixty-two. Partridgeberry is a neat and elegant plant that can make a delightful low groundcover beside a path or under acid-loving plants. It is also a choice plant for a terrarium. The size of the leaves and the branching habit will vary from plant to plant. Some are very densely branched, while others send out long, straggly runners. The sweetly scented flowers are borne in pairs in June or July. When fertilized, they begin to form berries in late July. These grow into plump, waxy, brilliant scarlet berries by September. The berries persist through the winter and spring. The fruit is edible but not particularly tasty—hence one of its colloquial names, "squawberry." The appellation *repens* is Latin for creeping, which is as descriptive of this plant as it is of trailing arbutus.

Cohosh, Cohosh, Cohosh, Cohosh

Blue, Black, Red, Summer

Cohosh is an Algonquin word, referring to black snakeroot and related plants, which were used medicinally by the Indians. They are members of the buttercup and barberry families

---

[13] Wiley, *Rare Wild Flowers of North America*.

Bugbane, black snakeroot, black cohosh, and fairy candles are but a few of the common names given to this stately denizen of the woods The genus name, *Cimicifuga*, is the translation of bugbane into botanical Latin; *cimi* meaning "bug" and *fuga* to put to flight, as in fugitive. It is a native plant, ranging from western Massachusetts through southern Ontario to Minnesota south to Missouri and Georgia. Last year, Marion and Andy Rasmussen spotted one growing on the bank alongside Powderhouse Road. I've had it for ... I don't know how many years. It is well established and seeding itself around. The foliage is strikingly similar to that of the baneberries, also in the Ranunculacea family. I had accepted it as a welcome addition to the woods garden for its summer blooming period. But the other morning, while eating breakfast on our sun porch, I gazed down into the back woods as the morning sun came through a break in the canopy and lit up the candelabras on two of my plants. That play of light and shadow made a very dramatic and impressive effect. The next evening, while I was having dinner, again on the sun porch, the western sun streamed through in like fashion and relit the candelabras.

Black cohosh can grow to six and even eight feet. One of mine measured out at seven and a half feet. The number of racemes on a stalk can vary from one to four or more. And a plant can have multiple stalks. One of mine has three stalks with three or four racemes per stalk for a total of eleven racemes. Each raceme can be up to sixteen inches long. The small white flowers start blooming at the bottom, and as they become pollinated, the sepals and petals fall, leaving the lone pistil. The other day, I watched a fly of some kind flit from one flower to another. Unfortunately, I did not have my camera at the time.

One of my gardening books says that it prefers more sun than most wildflowers. Not so. My plants are growing in deep shade and thriving. In my lower woods, there are trees to the east, south, and west, so that the shade is almost continual. All my other books list it as a plant for shade. However, at Wylatt and Mary's garden, their plants were growing in full sun. The conclusion: bugbane is adaptable from full sun to deep shade, provided it has rich, moist soil, or as another describes it, it is "undemanding." Because of its height, I am using it to screen my work area and compost heap. I use it also as a background plant and as specimen plants. Recommended transplanting times are usually given as spring or fall, and one book states that it is difficult to transplant. I am glad I moved three of my plants last week before I read that statement. Two of the transplants were over six feet tall. I also potted up two small plants for our August plant sale. It is a great plant for background if you have the room for it.

Another native bugbane is *Cimicifuga americana*, growing to three feet tall and ranging from Pennsylvania south. Other species are *dahurica*, *elata*, *japonica*, *foetida*, *laciniata*, *rubifolia*, and *simplex*. Two selected forms are *simplex* "White Pearl" and *simplex ramosa atropurpurea*.

Red cohosh and summer cohosh refer to our two native baneberries, *Actea rubra* and *Actea pachypoda*, red and white, respectively. Whenever you see *bane* in a plant's name, *beware!* Berries of both of these are poisonous. But they are such attractive plants in flower, foliage, and fruit that you should not be deterred from using them. I've even seen the white baneberry used in a perennial border most effectively. I have trouble telling these two apart and both of them from the black cohosh simply by the leaves. All have toothed and divided leaves that, with my lack of any formal botany, baffle me. I've seen summer cohosh in the woods in our area, and I assume red cohosh could also be found. The flowers are white and feathery and carried in a short raceme (there's that word again). From the difference in the racemes, I am able to distinguish between the two at the flowering stage. As the flowers fade and the berries begin to develop, the differences become even more pronounced. The berries on red cohosh are carried on slender stalks and soon develop into large berries that slowly turn to a brilliant red as they mature. The berries on the summer cohosh give this plant its other common name, "doll's eyes." They are born on thick red stalks and are white with a black spot, bearing a striking resemblance to the porcelain eyes in old-fashioned dolls. Both of these will thrive in the same conditions as black cohosh.

The leaves of blue cohosh, *Caulophyllum thalictroides*, of the barberry family, bear a closer resemblance to the meadow rues than to the other cohoshes. Each leaf is divided into three smaller leaflets, similar in appearance to the meadow rue and the rue anemone (*Anemonella thalictroides*). It forms a handsome shrub-like clump two to three feet tall. Intriguing to me are the dark-blue, almost black stems that push up in early spring. As the plant matures, the color of the leaves fades to an attractive soft gray-green. The yellowish-greenish-purplish flowers are small and insignificant as flowers go. But these are followed by blue berries, which according to the botanists, are not berries at all. My original plant has spread into a clump six feet in diameter, truly a handsome bush throughout spring, summer, and fall. In a dry summer, it tends to get a little ratty and dies back, but the blue berries persist. All four cohoshes—red, white, blue, and black—grow happily under the same shady woodland conditions. All will self-sow and all can be divided in spring or fall. All are worthy additions to a woodland garden.

Green-and-Gold—a Novel Use

Chrysogonum virginianum has become one of my favorite plants. Green-and-gold and gold star are two of the common names for this delightful plant. I think I acquired it about thirty-five years ago, and it languished in the site chosen. About twenty-five years ago, I moved it to another site, and it proceeded to thrive. This site was on the north side of the house in the vicinity of a series of an oak trunk that had been sliced to provide stepping stones. When the oak rotted, I simply mixed up some concrete and poured it into the round hole that the oak had left. I needed a few more stepping stones and made a form out of a sheet of aluminum. All in all, I have forty-two stones that range from twelve to fifteen inches in diameter and that stretch seventy-five feet from the lawn in the front of the house to the rear lawn. A few years ago, the *Chrysogonum* was doing so well that I decided to divide it and plant it around the stones. It is filling in more and more, and by next year, I expect it to make a solid carpet of green and gold over the entire seventy-five feet of path. What a sight to behold this time of year when it is blooming. I calculated that my carpet would be twelve square yards in area. Many gardening books state that it reblooms. For years, I doubted this to be true in general. With such a vast number of plants, I do find that a few will bloom later in the summer and, in fact, will still be yellow when winter comes. But I would not call it a reliable rebloomer.

Anemones

Here is another case where the common name, windflower, and the Latin designation, *Anemone*, have the same meaning. The Greek word, *anemos*, means wind or breath. Aphrodite and Adonis were lovers, and on the death of Adonis, legend reports that red flowers sprang from his blood. It is said that the wind that blows the blossoms open soon blows the petals away.

Native anemones are Canada anemone, wood anemone, thimbleweed, and long-fruited anemone. Another closely related native is the rue anemone. European anemones include *Anemone blanda*, *Anemone ranunculoides*, *Anemone nemerosa*, and *Anemone sylvestris*. There are three Japanese anemones: *Anemone hupehensis*, *Anemone vitifolium*, and *Anemone tomentosa*.

The ones I am currently growing are *Anemone virginiana*, *Anemone nemerosa*, *Anemone ranunculoides*, and *Anemone hupehensis*. Rue anemone was indigent on the property and in the surrounding woods. Rue anemone is a delightful, fragile-looking, early blooming native that has a long period of bloom. It is only five to six inches tall with leaves resembling the wood rues, hence the species name, *thalictroides*, resembling thalictrum. In fact, there has been a recent name change for the species and the current name of the genus is *Thalictrum*. But to this aging gardener, it will always be anemonella, little anemone. Thirty some years ago, it, trailing arbutus, and hepatica would come into bloom often on the same day. Now rue anemone blooms later than its earlier companions. In the spring, it is hardly noticeable until suddenly, it is there and in bloom. Its seeming fragility belies its true nature. It is generally white, but pink forms are available, as are a couple of double forms. One of these, called Schoaff's Pink, is widely available, but it is too artificial and the color too gaudy for my taste.

Thimbleweed and long-fruited anemone are taller plants than their small cousin, and they are not particularly showy and not readily available or grown. Perhaps the distinguishing feature of each of them is their fruit. Needless to say, but I will say it anyway, *Anemone cylindrical*, as both its Latin and common names signify, is in the shape of a cylinder while thimbleweed's fruit resembles a thimble.

Both the European wood anemone, *Anemone nemerosa*, and

the buttercup anemone (*Anemone ranunculoides*) are showy, easily grown, spread rapidly, and can even be weedy. Maybe I should rephrase that and say that they are aggressive and do become weedy. The foliage generally dies down by summer, and I doubt that the tubers interfere with other plants. Besides, they do make a great floral display in the spring, covering large areas. The fragile-looking tubers can easily be uprooted if the plants become too invasive. The roots lie barely below the surface and spread rapidly through the humus-rich soil. The wood anemone can be white or blue, and the flowers can be single or double. The anemones are in the buttercup family, Ranunculoides, and it is not too difficult to surmise that the flowers of *Anemone ranunculoides* are yellow.

The fall-blooming Japanese anemones are tall, reaching two to two and a half feet, and may require staking. Two of these, *Anemone hupehensis* and *Anemone vitifolium*, have been hybridized, and a dozen or more forms are available. Colors range from white to pink with doubles and semidoubles among them. The fall-blooming season extends from September into November, making them a welcome addition to the shade garden. Why do these anemones flower in the fall, so unlike those from Europe and North America?

Allium in the Family

All I um, I owe to my family, of which the onions, garlic, leeks, and chives are but a few of a large family, which includes lilies, tulips, asparagus, narcissi, and trilliums.

Ramps (*Allium tricoccum*) is a native onion, growing in moist woodlands from Newfoundland down to Georgia and west to Iowa and Minnesota. Its common name might be three-seeded onion (tricoccum). But to the mountaineers, it is *ramps*. It is also known as wild leeks. The Appalachian name "ramp" comes from the British Isles, where a related plant, *Allium ursinum*, grows wild. As one version has it, the English folk name "ramson" (son of ram), referred to the plant's habit of appearing between March 20 and April 20, during the sign of Aries. Another source indicates that the folk name was "ramsen," the plural form of an Old English word for wild garlic, "hramsa." The similarity between the two in taste, appearance, and growth habit led early English settlers of Appalachia to call the latter by the English folk name, which later was shortened to "ramp." Ramps are one of the first plants to show green in the spring, sending up smooth, broad leaves that in the mountains of Appalachia gave rise to ramp festivals. These wild leeks provided the first "greens" and were much sought after. I have even seen deer eating this after a long, hard winter, in spite of its pungent odor. Like other ephemerals, such as Virginia bluebells, the foliage dies down in the summer, having stored up enough energy to survive another year. Unlike the bluebells, however, it does not flower in the spring but waits until late summer before sending up a flower stalk, bearing white, onion-like flowers. Then the three black seeds are produced, providing a third season of interest. The stalks bearing the seeds may persist into late fall. Why this particular onion developed this habit of sending up leaves in the spring, dying back, and then sending up a flower stalk months later, I do not know. Certainly, those broad leaves capture a lot of sun during their brief moment in the spotlight. Are the seeds viable for only a short time and this life cycle a reflection of that? Although not as showy as trillium, nor as interesting as jack-in-the-pulpit, it does earn a right to be included in the wildflower garden, even though you might not partake of its culinary bonus. It will thrive even in a drier site than its native habitat of wet woods.

The other native onion is *Allium cnernum*. Here the common name, nodding onion, is taken from the Latin generic name. Or is it the other way around? Next time I see Linnaeus, I will have to query him. This onion is better behaved than its American cousin, sending forth leaves in the spring and flowers in the summer without doing a disappearing act. It is a dainty little onion with delicate, nodding pink flowers. It will grow happily in a variety of sites and will increase slowly.

There are two more native onions, wild onion (*Allium stellatum*), which occurs from Missouri to Ohio, and wild garlic (*Allium canadense*), occurring from Minnesota to southern Quebec south. There is also an alien species, field garlic, that is widespread in the east.

Winsome Weeds

There are two jewelweeds, or touch-me-nots, members of the *Impatiens* genus—the spotted jewelweed and the pale touch-me-not. When the seeds are ripe and the seedpod is touched, it explodes, discharging the seeds. Whether true or not, legend has it that where there are rattlesnakes, there you will find jewelweed because the juice from the stem will counteract the poison. The pale jewelweed was prevalent in my garden and would pop up almost everywhere. I became so familiar with it that I recognized its seedlings immediately. Venus's looking-glass is a pretty little annual with a single tall stem. Small heart-shaped leaves clasp the stem with dainty blue flowers in the axils. This is a distinctive and pretty plant. The other common name is whorled loosestrife, referring to the whorl of leaves. Small yellow flowers on long stalks arise from each leaf axil.

Indian tobacco is a poor relative of cardinal flower. The small light-blue or blue flowers are in leafy racemes. When setting seed, the calyx inflates, hence the species name.

Tick trefoil is one plant that I would not recommend for planting. As you might surmise from its name, the ticks stick to one's clothes. It has pretty little flowers that I could do without. Another weed that keeps popping up is panicled hawkweed. It is not very showy but has a certain attraction to it. For years, it popped up sporadically, but lately, it has threatened to overtake the garden.

Naturalized Citizens

One of the—if not the—earliest flowers to bloom on the roadside, signaling that spring is here is coltsfoot. Its bright-yellow dandelion-like flowers, which appear before the leaves, are a welcome sight. Later in the year, when one comes across large, coarse leaves, it is difficult to relate these with the flowers that bloomed in April.

The other conspicuous nonnative that blooms in profusion along the roadsides is dame's rocket. It is a handsome plant that is often mistaken for phlox because of the white, purple, and blue flowers. The easy way to remember it is that phlox has five letters in its name and five petals, whereas dame's rocket has but four petals. In the east, this has escaped from gardens and is so widespread that it truly is a naturalized citizen. In the Northwest, particularly in Washington, its counterpart is foxglove, and it dominates the roadsides there.

Two other émigrés are Queen Anne's lace and chicory. Queen Anne's lace is also called wild carrot and bird's nest. It is a very attractive plant with a four-inch umbel of florets. The center floret is usually purple. After fertilization, the umbel curls up in the shape of a bird's nest. Chicory or cornflower, with blue flowers, is a plant of roadsides, fields, and waste places.

Butter-and-eggs is welcome to pop up whence it will. It is a pleasant little annual, having flowers of pale yellow, the color of butter, and bright yellow, the color of a yolk, and is aptly named.

The helleborine orchid has an interesting history. It hitchhiked over from Europe and was first sighted in the Syracuse area in 1879. Since then, it has become quite widespread. It is now found throughout eastern Canada and states east of the Mississippi and as far south as South Carolina. It has also spread to our west coast and Vancouver Island. It is a small, inconspicuous, and easily overlooked plant but has a certain charm. In my garden, it pops up all over the place. When it shows up in my seed frames, I will pull it up. It pulls up easily, but the roots must be quite deep because I never get any of the root.

Bouncing Bet, also called soapwort, blooms in the summer with pink or white flowers.

Garlic mustard has a slew of common names: garlic wort, garlic root, mustard root, poor man's mustard, hedge garlic, jack-by-the-hedge, jack-in-the-bush, and sauce-alone. It was introduced as a culinary herb in the 1860s, and the leaves have a mild flavor of both garlic and mustard. Deer do not eat it, preferring native plants. It is out-competing our native plants and is difficult to eradicate from natural areas.

Worts of All

The etymology of the word *wort* is Middle English from Old English *wyrt*, meaning root. It refers to an herb or plant, usually used in combination. It is a name formerly given to plants used for food or medicine. When used as a suffix, it often just means "plant."

One of my favorite worts is our hepatica, commonly called liverwort, which, according to the Doctrine of Signatures, was useful in treating hepatitis. So was the Latin name of the plant derived from the disease, or does the name of the disease come from the plant's name? There are two native hepaticas, round-leaf and acute-lobed. I have a round-leaf hepatica at the south-facing base of a white oak. With direct sun in spring and reflection from the oak, this is the earliest of my native plants to bloom. Colors for hapaticas range from white to blue to an intense purple. The leaves persist through the winter but wither when the new fuzzy growth emerges. It blooms, photosynthesizes, and sets seed by June. In the wild, the two most common locations for it to be found are at the base of oaks and next to rocks. The acute-lobed hepatica is reported to prefer a less acidic soil, but I have not found any such preference. I have a beautiful soft-pink-flowering form given to me by a friend. I once had a semidouble, also given to me, but over the years, it has vanished.

Birthwort refers to any of several herbs or woody vines of the genus *Aristolochia*, having showy, malodorous, purplish-brown to yellowish flowers with peculiar or unusual shapes. The European species was used as a folk medicine to aid childbirth. Our two native species are snakeroot and Dutchman's pipe. Note that the Latin name for snakeroot is *serpentaria*. Another name for our wake robin is also birthwort.

Feverwort is also called fever root and horse gentian. Other names are boneset, agueweed, crosswort, eupatorium, Indian sage, sweating plant, teasel, thoroughwort, vegetable antimony, and wood boneset. It has a wide geographic distribution, the names reflecting local usage.

Milkwort is a genus of plants of many species. The common European milkwort was supposed to have the power of producing a flow of milk in nurses. It includes any of various plants of the genus *Polygala*, having variously colored, irregular flowers with two petaloid sepals. Our native fringed polygala or gay wings is a delightful, low-growing plant that looks like a tiny purple orchid.

Nipplewort is a European composite herb, having a milky juice and small yellow flower heads formerly used as an external application to the nipples of women. It is also called dockcress. It has naturalized in eastern North America.

Pilewort is a perennial herb native to Europe but naturalized elsewhere, having heart-shaped leaves and yellow flowers resembling buttercups. Its tuberous roots have been used as a poultice to relieve piles. Synonyms for the plant are lesser celandine, small celandine, figwort, and smallwort.

Pipewort refers to any plant of a genus *Eriocaulon* of aquatic or marsh herbs with soft grass-like leaves. Our common pipewort has translucent green leaves in a basal spiral and dense, button-like racemes of minute white flowers.

Ragwort is any of several plants of the very large genus *Senecio* in the composite family, having yellow flower heads, especially golden ragwort of eastern North America. They are also called squaw weeds. Golden ragwort is a common plant of wet meadows and marshes.

Sandworts are any of numerous low-growing herbs of the genus *Arenaria*, having small, usually white flowers often grouped in cymose clusters, such as the mountain sandwort.

Soapwort gentian is a common plant of the pink family, so called because its bruised leaves, when agitated in water, produce a lather like that from soap. Other names are bouncing Bet, soaproot, latherwort, Fuller's herb, bruisewort, crow soap, sweet Betty, and wild sweet William. The dried roots and leaves are used to yield soap.

Spiderworts are any of various New World herbs of the genus *Tradescantia*, especially Virginia spiderwort, having three-petaled blue or purple flowers with six hairy stamens. Presumably, the long, narrow leaves resemble a spider's legs. Dayflower is a common name.

Spleenwort is the name for ferns of the genus *Asplenium*, some species of which were anciently used as remedies for disorders of the spleen, dating back two thousand years or more. Pliny and Dioscorides, the fathers of pharmacy, gave it its name (*a-* meaning without, and *splen*, meaning spleen). Ebony spleenwort and maidenhair spleenwort are two of our native spleenwort ferns.

St. Johns wort's, Latin name *Hypericum*, is derived from the Greek and means "over an apparition," a reference to the belief that the herb was so obnoxious to evil spirits that a whiff of it would cause them to fly. There are over a dozen herbaceous species and four shrubby species, all having golden yellow blooms.

Stitchwort is from the Middle English and Old English *sticwyrt*, *stice*, or *stich* (from its alleged ability to cure sharp pains in the side). It encompasses any of several low-growing plants of the genus *Stellaria*, having opposite leaves and small, white, star-shaped flowers. Again we have the Latin, *Stellaria*, for a plant having star-shaped flowers. Stitchwort is a member of the chickweed family, but it is even more aggressive than the common or mouse-ear varieties. This perennial spreads by long, creeping, square stems that take root and give rise to new plants.

Toothwort is in the genus *Dentaria*. Pepper root and crinkleroot are common names for the cut-leaved toothwort. The roots are fancied to resemble teeth, as might be surmised by the common name.

Woundwort is the name for any one of certain plants whose soft, downy leaves have been used for dressing wounds, such as the kidney vetch and several species, including hyssop, hedge nettle, and marsh hedge nettle.

I hope all of this was *wort* it!

The Bells Are Ringing

Virginia bluebells are among our spring ephemerals. It is ephemeral in that the plant dies back after setting seed but certainly not ephemeral in bloom; it blooms for weeks, often opening pink and changing to that lovely shade of blue. A common name for it is Virginia cowslip, probably named by early settlers for its resemblance to English cowslips. In rich woods, it can form large colonies that are spectacular in bloom. It develops a massive root system that it uses to store the solar energy that it captures before leaves block the sun.

Merrybells or bellworts comprise three native bellworts. Large-flowered bellwort is the tallest and showiest, as the name implies, growing twelve to sixteen inches tall with bright-yellow hanging bells. Next in size is perfoliate bellwort in which the stem comes up through the leaves, thus the descriptive Latin name *perfoliate* for the species. It is a few inches shorter, with flowers of a medium yellow. Wild oats is the baby of the family, still sowing its oats. It is about six inches tall with small, pale-yellow bells. All will spread and form clumps, but grandiflora is the most vigorous in forming large clumps, as large as two to three feet in size. The merrybells are one of the easiest of plants to propagate by division. Just dig up a clump, pull apart each individual plant, and pot it up or transplant it. Bellwort was sometimes used to cure throat problems because, according to the Doctrine of Signatures, it was thought that the blossoms looked like the uvula, that pink appendage that hangs down the back of the throat.

Fairy bells or yellow mandarin is one of my favorite native plants. The flowers are not that showy, but oh the bright orange-red berries that adorn the plant in the fall are striking! In my garden, it is a vigorous plant, spreading both by stolons and by seed. If you decide to dig up a clump, have a good spade handy. The roots are so intertwined that it might give you a bit of trouble. To propagate, carefully disentangle the roots, and you will probably have at least six new plants. It grows several feet high, and its spreading habit makes a wonderful bush-like plant.

Fairy bells is also the common name for *Digitalis purpurea*, whose other names are common foxglove, fingerflower, and finger-root. It is a tall plant with clusters of tubular pink-purple flowers along the stem. Its leaves yield the drug digitalis.

Carolina silverbell is a medium-sized tree, having large white or pink bell-shaped flowers followed by large angular-shaped seed pods. Other common names are snowdrop tree and opossum wood. American snowbell is a small understory flowering tree with small bell-shaped white flowers that literally cover the tree in spring. It is also called storax. Swamp sweetbells is a bushy, deciduous shrub with upright branches, while mountain sweetbells is smaller and more spreading.

Harebells *are* the bonnie bluebells of Scotland, with a circumpolar distribution. This is a small, slender plant with blue, or sometimes white, bell-shaped flowers. The round basal leaves last but a short time, disappearing before it flowers.

"E'en the light harebell raised its head."
—Sir W. Scott

Indians Are Still Here

There are at least a dozen native plants that refer to Indians in one way or t'other. Probably the best known are Indian turnips, more commonly known as jack-in-the-pulpits. Another well-known plant is Indian pipes, those white ghostly plants that can be found in dark woods.

Indian cucumber root is a very distinctive-looking plant of the lily family. It has one whorl of leaves near the middle of the stem and a smaller whorl at the top with its greenish-yellow flowers that hang down. The dark-purple berries are held above the leaves.

Indian cup is member of the composite family and is a large plant, reaching eight feet, with egg-shaped leaves united at the base to form a cup.

Indian currant, also known as coralberry, has bell-shaped greenish or purple flowers in summer, producing coral or purplish berries.

Indian hemp is one of the dogbanes. The species name, *cannibis*, refers to hemp. The long fibers were indeed twisted and used to make cordage.

Indian paintbrush, as its Latin name *coccinea* suggests, has scarlet-tipped bracts, hence the common name, as though a brush was dipped into red paint. It is also called painted cup.

Indian pipe—who has not stumbled upon this ghost plant on a walk through a dark woods and not marveled at its whiteness? It indeed resembles a small clay pipe. Related to rhododendrons, it has lost all chlorophyll and gets its nourishment from decaying matter.

Great Indian plantain can grow to nine feet. One heap big Indian. Pale indian plantain has whitish flowers while the sweet-scented indian plantain has sharply-toothed, arrow-shaped leaves.

Indian poke, which is also called false or white hellebore is a denizen of swamps or rich woods. It is a coarse, large-leaved plant whose roots are very poisonous.

Indian physic, *Gillenia trifoliatus*, is also known as American ipecac, Bowman's root, and Fawn's breath. It is a powerful emetic, hence two of the common names. Confusion arises over its other common name. One suggested a corruption of Beaumont but offered no clue as to who Beaumont was. The other suggestion is that Bowman referred to native Americans. The Latin name is also controversial. Gillenia honors a German botanist, but Porteranthus has also been proposed. Nevertheless, it is an attractive, bushy plant with an airy look.

Indian tobacco is a poor relative with light-blue flowers of the showy cardinal flower. It appeared in my woods but then disappeared, not to be seen again.

Indian turnip is our familiar jack-in-the-pulpit. The Indian turnip does not have beautiful flowers, but it is almost everyone's favorite wildflower. The Indians did eat the root, learning to cook it several times to rid it of oxalic acid. It is a very curious plant. Small ones have male flowers. When they get big enough and have enough energy stored, they have a sex change, producing those brilliant red berries. Exhausted, they go back to being a male the next year. The other common name refers to the spathe, which looks like the canopy over a pulpit in those New England churches. My question is "Do we call the female flowers jill-in-the-pulpit?"

Squawroot is a very curious plant. It looks like a pine cone with its brown scales. It is a parasite, feeding on tree roots, preferring oak. Squawroots are also called ragworts, a name that we have already met as a common name for another plant. Was it used for food by the native Americans?

Tres Bane Not Tres Bane

Bane is from Middle English, meaning *destroyer*, from Old English *bana*. Bane means destruction, from Anglo Saxon, *bana*, meaning murderer.

Baneberry has berries that are attractive but poisonous. For years, the genus name was *Acteae*, but it has been changed to *Cimicifuga*. Red baneberry is also known as red cohosh. It and the white baneberry, or summer cohosh, are almost indistinguishable in foliage; the most obvious difference is in the flower stalks. Red baneberry fruits earlier, and the berries may sometimes be white. White baneberry is also known as doll's eyes. Indeed, the berries resemble the porcelain eyes seen on dolls in years past. The white berry has a purplish center as a pupil and sits on a bright-red stalk.

Just as the red baneberry is sometimes white, *Actea pachypoda* has a form, *rubracarpa*, with light-red berries.

Monkshood, or wolfbane, contains some very easily grown plants. The common monkshood is one of the most poisonous, yet it is one of the most handsome of hardy plants. In the past, the root was now and again mistaken for horseradish and eaten with fatal results. The juice from this European monkshood was used to kill wolves. Wolfbane is not native, but we do have two native monkshoods.

Dogbane's common name refers to the plant's toxic nature, which has been described as "poisonous to dogs." It's Latin moniker, *Apocynum*, means "Away, dog!" and the genus name *cannabinum* means like hemp, in reference to the strong cordage that was made by weaving together the stem's long fibers. Dogbane is also called Indian hemp, amyroot, bitterroot, and rheumatism weed. Other common names are Bowman's root and Indian physic, illustrating the fact that the same common name can refer to two or more plants. They are attractive plants with small pinkish or whitish flowers. The slender pods are borne in pairs and the milky juice is the poisonous part of the plant.

Fleabane refers to any of several North American plants of the genus *Erigeron*, having daisy-like flowers. Synonyms are horseweed and Canadian fleabane. The fleabanes have small but numerous purple rays and yellow flower heads. The dried plants supposedly repelled fleas, hence the common name. Starwort is another common name. After all, it is in the Aster family. The most widely used common name, fleabane, is shared with related plants in several other genera.

Berries Are the Berries

There are not many of the woodland flowers that bloom in the fall, but many make up for it by their colorful berries in shades of red, white, and blue. Perhaps the most familiar, because they persist throughout the year, are wintergreen and partridgeberry, the red berries contrasting with the evergreen leaves.

The dogwoods, viburnums, hawthorns, crab apples, and hollies are shrubs or small trees that bear colorful and edible berries relished by birds and mammals. The berries of the crab apples, haws, and holly are red; those of the dogwoods and viburnums are red, white, or blue. The dogwoods' berries range from the scarlet of the flowering dogwood and bunchberry to the white of the gray dogwood and the blue of the pagoda dogwood. Of all these, the fruits of the latter are most relished by birds and squirrels and are usually eaten as fast as they ripen. The bunchberry is like a miniature flowering dogwood in leaf, in flower, and in fruit. Unfortunately, at the southern edge of its range, fruiting is sparse for some reason, either climate or the lack of a suitable pollinating insects.

Two of the most dramatic of the red-fruiting wildflowers are jack-in-the-pulpit and false Solomon's seal. Jack's or rather Jill's fruit is a globular scarlet cluster atop a stout stalk. The clusters can be three inches tall, containing three to four dozen berries. False Solomon's seal has a large terminal cluster, bearing several dozen wine-red berries. A third plant with bright scarlet berries is ginseng, which is heavily exploited for the supposed aphrodisiac properties of its root. It is easy to grow and self-sows readily. Another attractive red-berried plant is the red baneberry—it's attractive but poisonous.

One of the few white-fruiting wildflowers is the spectacular white baneberry. The white, black-spotted berries are borne on red stalks, giving rise to the common name of doll's eyes.

The true Solomon's seal, sometimes reaching six feet, has small clusters of blue berries dangling from the leaf axils all along the stem. Clintonia or bluebeads have several blue berries on a foot-high stalk, while Indian cucumber root bears a few berries above a whirl of leaves. Blue cohosh rounds out this discussion of berry nice plants.

Fall Bloomers

Goldenrod

> And trembles on its arid stalk
> The hoar plume of the goldenrod.
> —Whittier

Goldenrods have had a bad press. They have been accused and convicted on circumstantial evidence of causing hay fever, but they have a foolproof alibi. They have been accused because they are so abundant and so showy that people suspect they must be the culprit. They certainly have the opportunity, but they do not have the means. Hay fever and other like allergies are caused by wind-borne pollen. Such pollen is generated, appropriately enough, by wind-pollinated plants, such as oaks, pines, and grasses. When was the last time you planted any of these for their flowers? Wind-pollinated plants don't need showy flowers. The very word *goldenrod* conjures up a twenty-four-carat image of bright, shimmering yellow. Just as they attract our eyes, so also they attract the eyes of the butterflies and the bees. The Spencer Crest calendar will feature the words of Henry David Thoreau in his essay on bee-hunting. Thoreau had this to say:

> By the roadside ... we saw a large mass of goldenrod and aster several rods square. ..., We found it to be resounding with the hum of bees. Here were bees in great numbers, both bumble-bees and honey-bees as well as butterflies and wasps and flies.

And later, he adds,

> All the honey-bees we saw were on the blue-stemmed goldenrod. It is not in vain that the flowers bloom late too, in favored spots. To us they are a culture and a luxury, but to the bees meat and drink.

So that, dear friends, is why it's a calumny to blame the goldenrod for the sins of the ragweed. Paul and Grace Graham have identified some nine species of goldenrod at Spencer Crest. Goldenrod is mostly an American plant and mostly a plant of the northeast. It is so common that it is seldom cultivated in our gardens, but it is a great favorite in England and Germany for the cultivated border. For those cultivating a meadow, it wouldn't be a meadow without goldenrods and asters. And in a meadow, their beauty does not end with their flowers. One last quote from Thoreau follows: "Withered goldenrod is no failure."

There is something like one hundred species of goldenrod. *Newcomb's Wildflower Guide*[14] lists thirty. In my youth, I could identify most of the common ones in the Poconos. There is one that grows in salt marshes, some that grow in dry woods, and some that grow in bogs and swamps, but most of them grow in open woods, fields, and roadsides. The one growing in my patch of woods is the blue-stemmed goldenrod, also known as wreath goldenrod. And not all are golden; there is a silverrod.

Asters

Asters, along with goldenrods, are the shining glory of the Northeast in the fall. Taxonomists have decided to rename our northeastern asters, but this old dog is too old to learn new names, so to me they will still be asters. New England aster is one of the showiest and one of the most widespread, occurring from the Great Plains to the coast of Maine, but New England gets to claim it as its own. In contrast, New York aster is restricted to the mid-Atlantic, New England, and eastern Canada. As with goldenrods, asters have adapted to almost every niche. They thrive not only in fields and roadsides but also in dry woods, rich woods, bogs, swamps, and sandy shores. The white wood aster was and is widespread in my woods. Another aster I recently acquired is the great-leaved aster.

Other Late Bloomers

Cardinal flower has the most intense red of any flower and is guaranteed to attract hummingbirds, as it blooms in late summer and fall. Great blue lobelia is a first cousin and although not as spectacular makes a nice companion. On rare occasions, a mutation occurs and produces a cardinal flower with white flowers. Plantsmen have propagated this, and it is available from nurseries. Why not grow the three together to have a red, white, and blue floral display? Many, if not most, of these late bloomers are sun-lovers, and I cannot

---

[14] Newcomb, *Newcomb's Wildflower Guide*.

enjoy them in my own garden. But like the New England aster and goldenrods, I enjoy them in their natural habitat. Among these are the sunflowers and the Joe Pye weeds. One that has occasionally appeared out of nowhere is the great mullein with its tall spike of yellow flowers and soft, velvety leaves. Spreading dogbane is prevalent out at the nature center, and it would be great to establish it in my shrub border. Bouncing Bet is yet another of these late-blooming plants that would be nice to provide color in late summer and fall.

But these are natives. What about the nonnatives? Most astilbes bloom in summer, but the delightful, low-growing *Astilbe chinensis pumila* is the exception. Then there are the Japanese anemones available in a large range of colors with single and double flowers. There are three species and a host of named cultivars and hybrids. A dramatic addition to extending bloom in the garden are two related Asian plants, *Kirengeshoma palmata* and *Kirengeshoma korean*. The common name someone has given them is yellow wax bells. I think I will stick with Kirengeshoma. It has a pleasant ring to it. The plants grow up to six feet tall with yellow tubular bells. At Cornell Plantations, they make an impressive display on Comstock Hill. Another group of fall-blooming Asian plants are the toad lilies in the Tricyrtis genus.

Before leaving, I would be remiss in not mentioning plants that are in bloom spring, summer, and fall. They are *Corydalis lutea* with yellow flowers and the white-flowering *Corydalis ochreleuca*.

Patio Plants

Our flagstone patio is laid on a deep bed of sand. Nothing has ever been planted in the cracks. But seeds have a way of finding their way into a crack and the sand makes an ideal site for germination and for sending roots down in search for moisture. Plants do so at their own risk. They may be allowed to stay, but weeds like dandelions, grasses, and others that I consider weeds are not welcomed and are rogued out. If the plant is desirable, but too big, it is removed, usually by lifting a stone or two to dig it out. Some of the good guys that are more than welcome to stay are wild strawberry and European ginger.

One of the plants that I found growing in a crack was a violet, which I identified as Selkirk's violet. For years and years, I had that lone violet. Then one year, it went bonkers and was found in almost every crack. A specimen was taken over to Cornell, and it was determined that it was not Selkirk's violet but probably a Japanese violet. You figure it! Another violet that is happy growing in the cracks is our Labrador violet. I have another mystery plant I know not whence it came. It is a little alpine plant with a small rosette of leaves and a tiny white flower on a stalk about an inch high. An *Astilbe chinensis pumila* has firmly established itself in one corner of the patio and refuses to leave. It would take a major effort to evict it. At the other end of the patio, a bishop's cap has established residence. I am inclined to accept his residency. A number of winter aconites have started to find their way onto the patio. Their bright-yellow blooms are most welcome in late winter and early spring. In a few months, their foliage will have died back and a spring or summer visitor will have nary a clue as to their existence. Following them in bloom is my bloodroot. My bulblet fern is another patio invader, as is the Japanese painted fern.

A Plethora of Plants

Help! I am being overrun by bloodroot and a host of other plants. After almost fifty years of gardening on the same three-fourths acre, the one to three plants of bloodroot I started with now number three thousand and are increasing yearly. Truly, it is a glorious sight in early spring when everywhere one looks, one sees drifts of white flowers. And I am intrigued each April when they emerge from the ground with the leaves wrapped around the rising stem and flower. However, as the season progresses and the leaves get as large as dessert plates, it seems almost all I have are bloodroots. Seeds even germinate in my walls, in the cracks in my patio, and in my paths and are starting to spread into my neighbors' yards. Many a time, I have just yanked some up when they are crowding the path or detracting from some of my other plants.

Not to be outdone, twinleaf is also threatening to take over my woods. It had a later start than the bloodroot, so its numbers are considerably less, but it is struggling to make up for lost time. The flowers, even more ephemeral than those of bloodroot, do not make the floral display that bloodroot makes, but the wine-colored new foliage is attractive in its own right. However, a dozen flowers in a single clump make for a pleasant display. The large, wing-like leaf and the curious seedpod make a stunning display from April into June when the pod opens and spills its seed. I would not be without it, but I do not need any more. Unlike bloodroot, which is easy to dig up and divide, twinleaf forms a massive and fibrous root system that requires real effort to dig out. Even small seedling plants rapidly develop an extensive root system.

Wild ginger is yet another plant that keeps spreading and spreading and spreading, forming mats three or more feet in diameter. It keeps those ants busy distributing the seed. It has soft green leaves, which are much larger than those of European ginger. Some can be as broad as eight or nine inches. It thrives in the shade, but I have one patch that gets hot afternoon sun in a dryish site where it is perfectly content.

The European ginger is, if anything, more prolific. It seeds and germinates so readily; I am continually amazed at the nursery prices. I must have given away hundreds of plants over the years. I gave a neighbor some years ago, and in the narrow space between the garage and the walk, it makes an ideal groundcover. It performs the same function for me in various sites. It is another plant that likes the cracks in my flagstone patio. The dark, glossy green foliage is attractive throughout the year, and I would not be without it. However when it spreads into the woods garden, it is going too far and it does so at its own risk. For some unknown reason, I lost almost all of my plants. One year, they were forming a solid carpet, and the next year, they were gone. I still had a few scattered individual plants popping up hither and yon. Whatever the cause, it did not affect my neighbor's plants.

My dad had *Epimedium rubrum* in his garden, and when I began to garden, I naturally had to have some. I may have started with a dozen plants. Shortly after, I discovered Walter Kalaga and Mayfair Nursery and acquired a yellow-flowering epimedium as well. These were planted along the entrance paths to the front woods. They continued to multiply, rubrum more so than the yellow epimedium.

As the *E. rubrum* multiplied, I divided it and planted it along both sides of the driveway and the length of a neighbor's garage. It also forms the backdrop for a planting bed off the patio as well as the edging for the garage flagstone walk. Along the paths and the driveway, it continues to increase in girth, and I could easily halve the girth and come up with a gazillion plants.

My ramps are one of the first plants to emerge in the spring. Even the deer browsed upon the leaves after one hard winter. It forms huge patches in the back woods and is starting to spread from its allocated site. These ramps are the basis for ramp festivals among the mountaineers as they are the first greens available in spring. They are a curious plant. In late May, the foliage dies, and in June, the flower stalks begin to emerge. After flowering, the tiny black seeds form and make an attractive display in their own right.

Another prolific seeder is our native jack-in-the-pulpit. It comes in various color combinations. The tube and spadix can both be green, or both may be purple, and they can be different colors as well. In my garden at least, the pale form emerges earlier in the spring than the dark form. I have some with distinct veining on the leaves and some where two of the leaves are subdivided, giving the appearance of five leaves. Many times, they have seeded themselves in improbable locations, such as in one of my stone walls. Often, seedlings are so thick around the parent plant that they need to be lifted and transplanted. The largest one this year is thirty inches tall with a wingspread of twenty-five inches, but one year, I measured one forty-eight inches tall with a wingspread of thirty-six inches.

Three Golden Poppies

The Japanese wood poppy (*Hylomecon japonicum*) was given to me as a gift from a fellow gardener. That is one of the best ways to acquire special plants. It was probably in a four-inch pot. In a year, it had grown considerably, and by the second year, it made a huge clump. I split the clump and planted them. Each clump kept getting bigger. I don't know how many times I've dug them up, divided them, and repotted them for plant sales. It blooms early and makes a nice display in early spring. No reblooming for this baby. Once it's done, it's done, as it puts all its energy into getting ready for next year.

Our second golden poppy is the Welsh poppy (*Meconopsis cambrica*). This is a slug-abed, not emerging and flowering until mid-May. The plants I have are a nice soft yellow, but I've been trying to get the seed of the orange form. It seeds itself around nicely. It quickly develops a long taproot, making it difficult to transplant. It has a nice bloom period in the spring and some rebloom in the fall.

The third in this trio of golden poppies is the greater celandine poppy (*Stylophorum diphyllum*), our very own wood poppy. This doesn't form clumps, but it seeds itself around with abandon. I am trying to restrict it to the patio level, but it persists in popping up in my back woods. Unlike the Welsh poppy, it is easy to pull out the seedlings and the mature plants. There is a Chinese celadine poppy (*Stylophorum lasiocarpum*) that is much more restrained in its behavior. It differs from its American cousin in the more pointed, long, bean-like seedpod.

CHAPTER 6

WHAT WOODST THOU?

Woodies of the Understory: Shrubs and Subshrubs

Cornus-copia

The shrubs and subshrubs of the dogwood clan, with one exception, do not have the showy bracts of our native flowering dogwood or the Chinese dogwood (*Cornus kousa*). Nonetheless, they are a valuable addition to the garden for their flowers, for their fruit, for their autumn color, and for providing food for the birds and other animals. Fruit color ranges from white to blue to black, and the fall foliage ranges from yellow to red to shades of purple. Birds and the twigs relish the berries by rabbits and deer.

Red osier dogwood (*Cornus serrica*) has a wide range, from Labrador to the Yukon south to West Virginia and west to Iowa and New Mexico. Its distinctive feature is the bright red stems that add a bit of unexpected color to the winter landscape. Drive along almost any of our roads, and you will see large colonies of the red-stemmed dogwood. Since it is stoloniferous (i.e., spreads by underground roots (stolons)), chances are that what you see is one plant. It grows six to eight feet high and bears creamy white flowers in May and June; the dark-purple drupes are short-lived, being eaten by birds and other animals. It has no disease or insect problems and is easily transplanted. It grows in shade, but colors better with sun. It is tolerant in its growing conditions and even thrives in moist sites. All in all, it is an attractive, colorful plant for the shrub border. Many cultivars or selections are available. In 1990, the cultivar Silver and Gold received the Pennsylvania Horticultural Society Gold Medal. There are many other varieties of possible interest. Another native plant with red twigs is silky dogwood (*Cornus ammomum*), also known as redbush, squawbush, swamp dogwood, and blue-berried dogwood. This is a late-blooming dogwood, not flowering until mid-June. As suspected, this grows particularly well in damp soils. It grows to nine feet tall and is more tree-like than the other red-stemmed shrub dogwoods.

Gray dogwood (*Cornus racemosa*) is another widely planted native, growing to fifteen feet tall. It is a vigorous grower and can be used as a barrier planting by cutting back harshly and maintaining it at six to eight feet in height. The small, creamy-white flowers are borne in flat clusters mid-June, followed by white berries on red stalks. Birds relish these early berries, and the red stalks remain, providing interest throughout the seasons. The narrow leaves' color is purplish autumn. I particularly like this because of the white, red-stemmed berries.

Round-leaved dogwood (*Cornus rugosa*) is a medium-sized shrub with nearly round leaves. The twigs are greenish or red-brown. A distinguishing characteristic is the purple-blotched stems. The flat-topped flower clusters in June are followed by light-blue berries in September. It does well in shade.

Cornus alba, the Tartarian dogwood, is native to Siberia, hence the other common name, Siberian dogwood. The greenish twigs turn bright red by fall, and the red twigs and branches provide winter interest. The yellow-green leaves turn red in the fall. The cultivar Sibirica has coral-red twigs, providing even more color. If you like variegated plants, look for *Cornus alba*, "Argenteo-marginata." It has red branches, and the leaves, up to five inches long, are edged with white. The overall effect is a striking green-and-white shrub. The foliage of the cultivar Gouchaultii ranges from yellowish and pink to red, or it can be yellowish white and pink or red, in streaks. The cultivar Spaethii has five-inch-long leaves, which are yellow green, bordered with brilliant greenish yellow. Kesselringii's distinguishing feature is its very dark-purple—nearly black—branches.

How to classify *Cornus canadensis*, the dwarf cornel or bunchberry? Is it an herb or a subshrub? I've always liked Harriet Keeler's description in her book[15] *Our Northern Shrubs*: "The Dogwood makes a very attractive family group which consists of herbs, shrubs and trees. The trees are small and sometimes play at being shrubs; the shrubs now and then try to be trees; and the herbs are woody at base and apparently hope some day to be shrubs." Or maybe because none of the shrubs have bracts, perhaps its hopes are grander—to be a tree. It truly is a dwarf flowering dogwood, albeit only a few inches tall. The whorl of typical dogwood leaves is topped by flowers with four bracts, very like its big brother. Its range is circumpolar, extending from Greenland and Labrador to Alaska and Eastern Asia. A related form occurs in the Scandinavian countries. Southward it can be found in West Virginia and in New Mexico and California in the west. The flowers are followed by bunches of bright-red berries. Other common names are puddingberry and crackerberry. It is native to our area. I know of one colony down by the Gazebo at our nature center and of other colonies in our hills. One of my neighbors had a patch in his woods that is the source of my plants. Unfortunately, my plants do not set abundant fruit. There are several likely causes. My plants are clones and do not self-pollinate so pollinating insects are required, or pollination is climate-sensitive. I suspect the latter because the poor fruiting seems to be associated with the southern extent of its range. In the Adirondacks or Maine or Alaska, it fully lives up to its name, bunchberry. I will never forget riding the Midnight Sun Express from Anchorage to Fairbanks and seeing bunchberry on either side of the tracks, brilliant red fruit mile after mile.

Apologia

While writing an article, "Cornus-copia," for our local nature center magazine, I decided to look up the etymology of "cornus." My *Random House* Dictionary reports it derives from Vulgar Latin, thence to Middle French and Middle English. I have to confess that I was not as clever as I thought when I came up with the title for these

---

[15] Harriet Keeler, *Our Northern Shrubs and How to Identify Them* (New York: Dover Publications, Inc., 1969).

articles. I discovered that the word derives from *horn*, referring to the hardness of the wood. The common name for cornucopia is "horn of plenty," a literal translation of the Latin (*cornu*, meaning horn, and *copia*, meaning copious).

Good Vibes

The viburnums are one of the best flowering shrubs and come in a wide variety of shapes and sizes. They have attractive flowers and the fruit usually goes through color changes as it ripens. Some of the exotic species can be very showy. There are many native species, and these are the ones I tend to grow. One native not generally offered is the maple-leaf viburnum. It is the least showy of the tribe of vibes, but it has the advantage of growing in dense shade. Another plus is the beautiful wine-red fall foliage. This was one of the native shrubs that were endemic on our lot, and I have come to appreciate its many qualities. Hobblebush was another endemic viburnum and forms thickets, hampering one's passage through woods where it is abundant. One of the tallest of the vibe tribe is the plum-leaf viburnum. I attempted to espalier them on either side of the sliding doors to the patio. They grew well enough, but with the east-facing site, they did not fruit well or color up in the fall. I have recently planted one in my shrub border. Its common name is the plum-leaf viburnum, another reason for growing it. As you might expect, cranberry viburnum has bright-red fruits lending color to the fall and winter. The *viburnum nudum*, Winterthur, is a selected form that fruits better and colors more intensely than the type. The small white flowers are followed by large clusters of blue fruit, while the foliage turns color, ending in a brilliant red.

Three Favorite Azaleas

One of the native azaleas in the woods around us is pinxterbloom. There was one in our back woods, growing in dense shade and not flowering well. There were others alongside the road, unappreciated by my neighbors, and they soon fell to the ax. Its name comes from the Dutch settlers because it flowers at Pentecost with aright pink flowers, reminding them of the descent of the Holy Ghost upon the early Christians. One of the first of the native Azaleas I bought was the pinkshell azalea (*Rhododendron vaseyi*). This is very limited in its native range, occurring in only four counties in North Carolina, along the Blue Ridge Parkway, but is adaptable throughout the Northeast. It makes a tall shrub. (Mine is eight to ten feet tall.) It blooms in the middle of May with—you guessed it—large, pink flowers making a stunning display. In all the years I have had it, it has not failed to bloom. There is a white form available, but mine is too young to flower. The third on my list is *Rhododendron prunifolium*, the plum-leafed azalea. In the wild, it is restricted to a narrow band, straddling the border between Georgia and Alabama. But despite its narrow range, it is hardy and adaptable far north of its natural range. It makes a stunning display with its orange flowers in the middle of August, long after other azaleas have bloomed.

Mountain Laurel

June is the month for mountain laurel (*Kalmia latifolia*), and Spencer Crest is the place for laurel. The state flower of Pennsylvania and Connecticut, it ranges from Mississippi, Alabama, and the panhandle of Florida to Maine, extending west into Ohio and Southern Indiana. In our climate, it is a shrub, growing slowly to a height of six to eight feet. The tallest specimen on record, located in northern Georgia, is twenty feet tall with a spread of thirty-eight feet with one trunk four and a half feet in circumference. The genus is named for Peter Kalm, a Swedish botanist who explored Pennsylvania, New York, New Jersey, and southern Canada for useful plants. Since he reached Niagara Falls in his explorations, he may well have passed through the Chemung Valley. Bog laurel and sheep laurel are more northerly shrubs, bog laurel barely extending into Pennsylvania and sheep laurel into Delaware.

Mountain laurel must rank as one of the more perfect shrubs, native or exotic. It is hardy, evergreen, grows in either sun or shade, and has a great floral display, both in bud and in bloom. It can be pruned drastically to reshape it or to use for greens, but do it only on your own plants. It is a protected plant, and you could be fined for collecting it or cutting it on public land or on private land without permission.

The most exciting development in recent years has been the use of tissue culture to clone selected varieties. Laurel can be grown from seed, but the seedlings will vary in growth habit and flower color. Propagation by rooting cuttings is possible but difficult and limits the rate at which cultivars can be reproduced. However, the advent of tissue culture has caused a revolution in the propagation and dissemination of distinctive cultivars at reasonable prices.

Most of us are familiar with the white or pinkish flowers of laurel. The pink coloring shows up most dramatically in the buds, and there is one colony at the south end of the high meadow that is spectacular in mid- to late June. When opened, the flowers show only a slight tinge of pink. There are today dozens of cultivars that differ significantly in color, banding, size, and shape of the flower and in the size of the leaves and even of the plant. Colors range from bright red to pink to maroon. The banded flowers are stunning, both in bud and in bloom. There are dwarf varieties with small leaves as well as small size. There are some that have been selected for compact growth habits.

Not only is laurel beautiful; it also has a fascinating technique for getting pollinated. The anthers are held under tension in pouches in the corolla. When a bumblebee lands, the anther is released, projecting the pollen onto its body to be transported to the next flower.

To grow laurel, provide the same site and soil preparation as for rhododendrons. Choose a site with some shade, avoiding low spots. Mix plenty of peat or leaf mold, and in our clay soil, a substantial size hole is recommended. Provide an inch of water each week during the first growing season. Once established, they should take care of themselves, but if the summer is extremely dry, give them a good soaking once a week until the rains return. Be moderate in fertilizing; too little is better than too much. A mulch of pine needles or oak leaves is beneficial. Pruning is best done in early spring before growth starts. Second best is immediately after flowering. A little pruning each year will keep the plants from getting too leggy. If they have gotten away from you, sacrifice a few years' of flowers and cut them back to within two to three inches of the ground. It sounds drastic, but if the plants are healthy, they will resprout and form a dense, multistemmed bush.[16]

Great Laurel

Rosebay rhododendron (*Rhododendron maximum*) is referred to as great laurel because it is the big brother to mountain laurel. Its range extends from Georgia to Nova Scotia, and it is one of the hardiest species. The flowers are small, opening in late June or early July after the new leaves emerge. Driving in Pennsylvania through the Poconos in July, you will see stretch after stretch of the rosebay in the woods. At my old Scout camp, Camp Acahela, at the confluence of the Lehigh and Tobyhanna Rivers, the plant was abundant. The stands were so dense that it was difficult to fight one's way through. These are referred to as rhododendron or laurel "hells." I recall one hike we took down the Lehigh with both sides of the streams flowing into the river lined with the rosebay. We were not there when they were flowering, but how I wish we were. It would have made a beautiful sight and a great picture. It was also on this hike that we rested under a big old chestnut tree. Even if it had not succumbed to the blight, it would have been killed by the high waters created by the dam on the lower reaches of the Lehigh.   At its northern extreme, rosebay rhododendron may reach four feet after many years, but in North Carolina, it becomes treelike, reaching forty feet in height.

Friends of my dad's had rosebay growing on their property in the Poconos, and he brought up a half-dozen or so. One is planted at the northwest corner of the house and is now about eight feet tall. Others were planted in the woods. Before I erected the fence, the deer killed a couple of small plants in their foraging. One down in the back woods was about seven feet tall and was badly foraged. It survived, but only now is there new growth from the base. It looks a bit odd, having leaves at the base and six feet up. Two other five-footers succumbed to repeated defoliation and have died, despite my attempts at cutting them to the base to save them.

---

[16] *Screeches* 10, no. 2 (Summer 1985).

Deck the Halls

"... with boughs of holly!" This custom dates back thousands of years and was practiced by the Celts, Assyrians, Egyptians, Persians, Greeks, Romans, Chinese, and Native Americans. It continues down to the present day wherever the holly tree grows.

Why this fascination with holly? The Druids, priests of ancient Gaul, believed that the sun never deserted the holly tree and considered it sacred. Bringing it inside in the dark days of winter brought the sun in and provided a refuge for the woodland spirits. The Romans, during their Saturnalia festival, sent holly boughs along with gifts to their friends as tokens of good wishes. Early Christians incorporated these customs and beliefs into the celebration of Christmas. The very name, holly, is thought to be a corruption of the word "holy." In Italy, holly sprigs are used to decorate the manger, and in Germany, holly is called Christdorn, the thorn woven into the crown of crucifixion. The berries, according to legend, were once yellow but have been stained red from the wounds of Christ. The white flowers were symbolic of his purity.

A Brittany legend tells us that a small bird attempted to relieve Christ's sufferings by plucking thorns from his brow. The bird's breast became stained with his blood, and today, it is known as robin redbreast. To this day, it is unlucky to step on holly berries, its favorite food. Holly was hung in the stables as well with the belief that the cattle would thrive if it was hung where it could be seen on Christmas Day. An old English tradition tells us that even the bees must be wished a Merry Christmas. A sprig of shiny green and bright-red holly must adorn each hive.

Superstitions abound as to when the holly should be removed after Christmas. We always left our decorations and Christmas tree up until Twelfth Night, the last day of Christmas. In parts of England, holly had to be taken down before Shrove Tuesday and burned on the same fire on which the pancakes were to be baked. In other parts of England, holly could not be burned but had to be saved until the following year. In colonial America, holly was kept in the churches until Good Friday to prevent the Christmas festivals from being forgotten.

Did You Overuse Yews?

Don't feel too badly because you have a lot of company. Yews are a most useful shrub, but like anything else, too much can be made of a good thing. The nurserymen like them because they are easy to grow and are extremely hardy, but whenever I see a home planted exclusively with yews, I see a lack of imagination—at least as far as plant material is concerned. Oddly enough, these same people may show great imagination in their interior decorating. In addition, they probably went out of their way to find something different in furniture or decor. But when it comes to planning their exterior decoration, they rely on others rather than on their own taste and good judgment.

The aim of decorating is to create interest and diversity with an overall unit. Things need not match, but they should complement rather than conflict. The same is true of landscaping, but when a home is planted exclusively with yews, all neatly sheared, the effect is antiseptic. There is no interest and no diversity unless you call the use of low, medium, and tall yews interesting rather than diverse. Even worse is when yews are used in locations where something else would be much, much more suitable.

All this is very well and good, you may say, but what would you recommend? I would reply that there are hundreds of plants to choose from, both green and nonevergreen. One of my favorites happens to be Japanese holly (*Ilex crenata convexa*), which will eventually form a large shrub, but it can be pruned either to a formal or informal shape. It somewhat resembles box, with its small, shiny evergreen leaves, but does not have the obnoxious odor of box. Low-growing forms, such as Green Luster are available. The junipers are always good, but make sure you know the ultimate size or you will have a fight on your hands to keep them within bounds. There is growing interest in dwarf evergreens, and there are many dwarf junipers and dwarf spruces that would make good foundation plants. Our lovely native hemlock grows too big for the foundations, but there even dwarf forms of these available. Many of these will grow no taller than a foot or two.

For a protected location, the Japanese andromeda (*Pieris japonica*), commonly called lily-of-the-valley bush, is truly one of the best plants that one could hope for. Its glossy green leaves make it attractive throughout the year. The new growth is tinged with pink or red, adding additional interest in the spring. The flower buds form in the fall, giving interest during the bleak winter. The drooping racemes open in early spring, forming delightful bell-shaped flowers. Oregon grape holly is a good evergreen but cannot stand winter sun. Rhododendrons are always good, and there are low-growing varieties as well as small-leaved ones. Hardiness is extremely important in choosing rhododendrons.

But whatever plants you choose, try to blend their foliage and textures so as to create interest. If you use something in your foundation planting, tie it in with similar plants elsewhere on your grounds. If you are in an established neighborhood, blend your plantings with your neighbors' to create a sense of unity. Remember though, that is just as bad to overuse anything as it is to overuse yews.

So what are the alternatives to yews? We chose to go with the Japanese holly, *Ilex crenata*. It is evergreen with small leaves somewhat similar to boxwood.

Rhodo-mania: Favorite Rhododendrons Described

One of the first rhododendrons I bought was a hybrid named Windbeam. This is a small-leaved, semidwarf that is extremely hardy (to -25 degrees F). It has not failed to bloom in fifty years, and when it does in late May, it is smothered in small trusses that open white and turn to a lovely soft pink. It will eventually grow four feet tall in a very attractive, informal habit. It makes a lovely foundation or patio plant in an entrance garden or along a driveway. It is one rhododendron all nurseries should carry, but few do.

Another plant that I bought early in the game is the Dexter hybrid Scintillation, and it does scintillate in late May or early June with its clear, vibrant pink blossoms. The flowers are large in an attractive truss, but even without lovely blooms, it makes a striking plant. The foliage is large and a deep, glossy green. The plant will grow about five feet in ten years. Unfortunately, it is a bit on the tender side, but mine has done nicely on the north side of the house. In the five years it has been blooming, it has a better blooming record than my forsythia. This and Windbeam were used in the Corning Free Academy courtyard. Hybridizers cross plants to produce a plant that is superior to either parent. With *Rhododendron yakushimanum*, they have a difficult task because many knowledgeable plantsmen consider this species to be the perfect rhododendron. Yak is a plant that is native to Yakushima Island in Japan. In growth habit, it makes a low, densely foliaged mound-like bush. The leaves are of good color and substance, covered on the underside with a thick velvety indumentum. The new leaves are covered with a white powder, giving the appearance of silver candles. Even without blooming, it would be a favorite landscape plant. But the flowers are something else again. The buds are a deep pink, and as they open, the color softens until the opened blossoms are pure white. With the buds on a plant in various stages of bloom, it makes a striking display. Its one drawback is that like any species, it takes years for it to bloom. Our plant, bought seven years ago, had one bloom last year and only three flower buds this year. But with all its other assets, it seems a small price to pay.[17]

Requirements of Rhododendrons

Rhododendrons will not survive well in open, exposed positions so that the selection of the planting site is very important. Being evergreen, they lose water throughout the winter and must be protected from fall sun and drying winds. An antidesiccant sprayed on in the fall will offer some protection. Tall deciduous trees will provide broken shade even in winter. In a wooded area, an open site may provide the best conditions. Rhododendrons, with their shallow roots, are easy to move so that if one location doesn't suit them, another can easily be tried.

Many rhododendrons today are grown and sold in pots containing artificial soil or a peat mixture. This is great for the nurseryman but

---

[17] *Corning Leader*, Thursday, May 29, 1975

can be bad for the buyer. If you buy such a plant, make sure you thoroughly break up the soil ball. Take a knife and hack away at it until it is practically in ribbons. This sounds drastic, but it is necessary so that the roots will grow into your soil. Even if the plant has been grown in soil I like to break up the surface of the ball to provide better contact with the soil.

In planting almost any plant, a generously prepared hole will pay off in vigor and growth of the plant. Although rhododendrons are shallow-rooted, an eighteen-inch-deep hole will provide added protection during cold winters. Be generous with the peat in mixing the soil. One third each of soil, peat, and sand makes a good growing medium. Rhododendrons should be planted at the same depth as grown. If you have poor drainage or your soil has a high pH, raised beds can be built.

A very necessary and often neglected final touch is good deep mulch. Many gardeners prefer a bare soil kept weed free by cultivation. Such a practice is almost always fatal to a rhododendron. I prefer a ground cover under the rhododendron. Myrtle and rhododendrons get along very nicely. Some growers in Michigan like an herbaceous ground cover, and their favorite is sweet woodruff. This is a delightful plant for a shady spot even if you don't grow rhododendrons.

If you want to fertilize your rhododendrons, fine, but go easy and don't fertilize after June. You will cause continued growth that will not have time to harden off. Rhododendrons like a moist but well-drained soil. When established, they can withstand an amazing amount of draught, if well mulched. For the newly planted rhododendron, a good soaking weekly should be sufficient. A good test as to whether they need water is if their leaves fail to perk up after sunset on a hot, dry summer day. They should not be watered in late summer or early fall unless they really need it, as described above. If the fall weather is dry, a good, deep soaking around Thanksgiving is necessary to carry them through the winter.

I provide no artificial protection for my rhododendrons. Why buy an evergreen and then hide it six months of the year with some contraption or other? Choose your site carefully, plant it properly, mulch it well, and enjoy it.[18]

---

[18] *Corning Leader*, Thursday, May 15, 1975.

CHAPTER 7

WHAT WOODS THOU II

The Understory Trees

The genus *Cornus* is a plenteous tribe of which our native flowering dogwood (*Cornus florida*) is only one of many shrubs, shrublets, and trees native to North America, Europe, and Asia. This native tree blooms in late May and early June with inconspicuous flowers but showy bracts, the same type of transformed leaf appendage that provides the floral display for the Christmas poinsettia. When young, the bark is smooth, but as it ages, the bark resembles alligator skin, so that one can always tell a dogwood tree by its bark. Another distinctive feature is the flower buds, which appear at the end of branches in the shape of a crown. When blooming, these flower buds gradually open and the bracts expand and whiten into the cross-shaped "petals" with a tinge of red at the tips. One legend has it that this was the tree Christ was crucified on, hence the color and shape of the bracts. This tree is native to eastern North America, ranging from southern Maine and southern Ontario as far west as Kansas and Texas and south to Florida. When buying, it is best to buy locally grown trees, as they will be better adapted to the local climate vagaries. It is one of the prime understory trees in the eastern forest, blooming best at the edge of a clearing. Bright-red berries, relished by squirrels and birds, follow the flowers. One winter, a pileated woodpecker came in to feast on the fruit. A seedling may take fifteen to twenty years to flower, but over the years, individual clones have been selected that bloom when the tree is quite young. Unfortunately, the anthracnose fungus has been spreading, wreaking death and destruction in its wake. The trees most affected are those in deep shade, which allows the fungus to spread and do its dirty work. Trees out in the open are much less susceptible to the fungus. Pruning out dead and diseased branches is always good practice but especially in this case. Garden catalogs may list a dozen cultivars—pink or white bracts, variegated foliage, yellow-fruited, dwarf varieties, and more.

An Asian relative, *Cornus kousa*, blooms weeks later with bracts that are pointed rather than blunt. There are a number of cultivars of this genus selected for color and blooming period. It is found most often grown with multiple stems. As it matures, the brownish bark flakes, providing winter interest. It too has red fruit, but the fruit is pulpy, resembling raspberries. It is resistant to the anthracnose fungus. Dr. Orton at Rutgers University has crossed *C. florida* with *C. kousa*. The plants are listed as *Cornus x Rutgersensis*, Rutgers hybrid dogwoods. They bloom midway between that of their parents and are resistant to the dogwood borer and the anthracnose fungus. Either of these makes substitutes for our native flowering dogwood where anthracnose is a problem. If you do buy the native dogwood, plant it in an open location with good light and air circulation to minimize losing it to the anthracnose fungus.

Another native dogwood tree that is underappreciated is the pagoda dogwood (*Cornus alternifolia*). Most trees have alternate branches, and an acronym to remember which ones have opposite branching is MAD (maple, ash, dogwood). But if you are not careful, this tree will trip you up. The smooth leaves with the distinctive veined pattern are a sure giveaway. It too is an understory tree and derives its common name from the fact that the layered structure of the branches is likened to a pagoda temple. There may be a foot or more between successive adjoining branches. The scientific species name means alternate foliage, if you have not guessed it already. Its range extends further north into Newfoundland and Manitoba but only to northern Florida. It does not have bracts and thus is not as showy as *Cornus florida*. The flowers, although relatively inconspicuous, produce berries that change color as they ripen. They are relished by birds and squirrels and are usually eaten as soon as they ripen and turn blue. This tree seems to be relatively short-lived but is an excellent tree for a habitat planting. In colder climes, it is *the* dogwood to grow. It was endemic on our property so it holds a special place in my heart.

Another great nonnative dogwood is the cornelian cherry. It comes in two varieties *Cornus mas* and *Cornus officianalis*. *Cornus mas* is a native of Central and Eastern Europe and western Asia, whereas *Cornus officianalis* is a native of Japan. The only obvious difference to a nonbotanist is that *Cornus officianalis* blooms earlier than *Cornus mas*. The flowers are yellow, and they bloom early in the spring when forsythia, also yellow, is blooming. But unlike forsythia, it has attractive and edible fruits, hence the name, cornelian cherry. They are said to make excellent jam, but as with all dogwood fruit, they are relished by animals other than *Homo sapiens*. It too has distinctive bark, differing both from *Cornus florida* and *Cornus kousa*. Corning is a Sister City of Lviv in the Ukraine, and a cornelian cherry was chosen to plant in the Peace Garden.

The West Coast has a dogwood that rivals our native. It is *Cornus Nutallii*, the mountain dogwood. It grows to seventy-five feet with four to seven white or pinkish petal-like bracts. It is not hardy hereabouts. This has been hybridized with our native, the result being Eddie's White Wonder. It may be hardier than *Cornus nutalli* and might be worth the gamble to plant. Another of the dogwoods to consider is the giant dogwood (*Cornus controversa*) with picturesque wide-spreading branches, small creamy flowers, black fruits, and red fall color. An added attraction in the winter is its rich-red young wood. *Cornus macrophylla*, large-leaved dogwood, is a medium tree, growing to twenty to forty feet. It grows not in layers like its brethren but in a round shape. It blooms in midsummer, with large, flat-topped panicles of flowers.

There was one flowering dogwood on our property when we bought it as well as several pagoda dogwoods. One of the first trees in our initial planting was a flowering dogwood, and this tree is now fifteen feet tall, overhanging the woodland path in the front woods. Two other flowering dogwoods are on either side of the front walk, one with white flowers and the other with pink bracts. Two other good-sized trees border the patio in back, one being a fastigiate (upright-growing) variety. Two smaller dogwoods are at the northeast and northwest corners of the house. The one on the northwest corner is suffering from the aforementioned anthracnose. Another two dozen are scattered across the front, back, and side yards. All of my trees are limbed up (i.e., the lower branches are removed to give headroom for both us and our other plantings).

I have one magnificent specimen of Kousa dogwood off the back patio. The flaky bark provides year-round interest, but in late June, its floral display is outstanding. The only drawback is that from below, one does not fully appreciate its beauty. This is best seen from the second-floor bedroom.

I purchased and planted three cornelian cherries early on, one by the front border, one off the driveway, and one in the back. Although of the same age, the one in front is the tallest and most prolific bloomer, since it gets considerably more sun. The tree off the driveway is next in size because of its shadier location. The third one in back is only about five feet tall compared with twelve to fifteen feet for the other two. Its location is not as favorable and its growth habit has led me to do a lot of corrective pruning, which has kept it small. A few years ago, a friend in Ithaca gave me some small plants of *Cornus officianalis*. These have been planted about but are still too small to provide an evaluation. The same can be said for the *Cornus controversa* and *Cornus macrophylla* that I bought two years ago. What prompted me to try these two was the nice specimen of the giant dogwood in a friend's garden.

The Care and Feeding of Dog(Wood)s

The gardener's best friend is the dogwood, from its splendiferous floral display in the spring to the bright berries that follow, to its fiery red foliage, its distinctive bark, its horizontal branching habit, and its four seasons of interest. The flowering dogwood, whereof I speak, is the showiest of the breed, but they are thoroughbreds all, ranging in size from four inches to four hundred inches.

Bunchberry or dwarf cornel is like a miniature dogwood carpeting the forest floor. It occurs in several locations at Spencer Crest and can be found throughout our area.

Unfortunately, the flowering dogwood can be a shy bloomer. I'm frequently asked, "Why doesn't my dogwood bloom?" Usually it's a failure to set buds because of youth. Seedling trees may take up to twenty years to reach maturity. A trick that I have not tried is to make shallow cuts the circumference of the trunk. Supposedly, this will fool the tree and cause it to set buds that year. Some of my trees that I planted almost that long ago are finally setting a few flower buds. Many flowering trees bloom in alternate years since so much energy goes into producing berries that none is left over for setting flower buds for the next year. We are close to the northern limit for flowering dogwood, and the flower buds can be killed in the winter by low temperatures or in the spring by a late, hard frost. The wrong combination of moisture, sun, and warmth in late summer can inhibit the formation of flower buds. The flowers are not always white, the leaves are not always green, and the berries are not always red. However, named varieties, like Cloud 9 and Appleblossom, start flowering at an early age and bloom more consistently than unnamed seedlings. The return on your investment is much greater. Trees in sun will set more buds and set them more dependably than those in shade.

The pink dogwood has been around since colonial days, arising as a chance seedling. Over the years, better pinks, whites, and reds have been selected and introduced. Now there are some four dozen cultivars. These generally have larger bracts and flower more profusely and at a younger age. A number have variegated leaves of yellow and green or purple and green. Fall color ranges from yellow or soft orange to brilliant reds or shades of maroon and purple. There is a yellow-berried form, one with double flowers, one with a weeping habit, and a dwarf variety. For the extra it costs to purchase these named varieties, the return on your investment in terms of more extensive bloom and greater enjoyment is worth it.

Dogwoods are susceptible to borers, canker, and fungal disease. Dogwoods in the northeast are showing symptoms of decline because of the anthracnose fungus. It starts with brown blotches and small purple-rimmed spots on the leaves. Small twigs on the lower branches die, waterspouts appear on the trunk, and branches with cankers develop at the base of the spouts. The lower branches begin to die, and the disease progresses upward until the entire tree dies. Anthracnose can be controlled by spraying with a fungicide when the leaf buds break and at seven- to ten-day intervals until the leaves are fully out. Zineb, benomyl, maneb, or mancozeb will probably be effective. In addition to spraying, removal of dead leaves and pruning of water spouts, dead twigs, and branches will decrease the source of the spores. This type of pruning should be done on all trees as a matter of course. Watering and fertilizing as noted above will mean a healthier tree and healthy trees, like healthy people, can better fight off infections.

Barking Up the Right Tree

When the flowers fade and the leaves fall, there is a dearth of color until spring. Six months of the year, 50 percent of the time, the garden can be pretty drab. But it doesn't have to be. With a good choice of shrubs and trees and their proper placement, the garden can be interesting twelve months of the year. Choose your trees and shrubs not only for their flowers, which last such a short time, but also for their form, their autumn color, their fruits, and their bark.

All the birches provide interesting bark. The white birch, also called paper birch and canoe birch, is a favorite of many and for good reason. The black triangles and its white bark are very attractive and distinctive. Either singly or in a clump, it stands out in the garden. Unfortunately, it is subject to leaf miner, can be short-lived, and has a shallow, spreading root system. River birch, despite the inference in its name, will grow in moderately dry soils as well as damp soils. Heritage river birch is a selected form that has pinkish to bronze peeling bark. It is widely used, planted usually as clumps, and can be a great addition to the garden. Consider yellow birch for its yellow bark, which can get quite shaggy, adding interest throughout the year.

Beech, either American or European, has an attractive, smooth, light-gray bark. It needs lots and lots of room and gives such dense shade that little can grow under its canopy. It retains its leaves throughout the winter, adding interest. It is the tree of choice for lovers to proclaim their undying love. Blue beech is not a beech. Its other names are musclewood or ironwood. It is of interest for its sinewy gray trunk. It is a small understory tree often found near streams. Another small tree with light-gray-striped bark is the shadblow, a native tree and the first to bloom in the spring. It has dainty white flowers and good fall color. An unusual tree with greenish-striped bark is moosewood. It is abundant at Spencer Crest. Has anyone chosen it for his or her adopt-a-tree?

Other trees have bark that flakes off. Sycamore and London plane trees are good examples. Their use by the Glass Works in Houghton Park provides year-round interest. Two trees from the Far East come to mind. Paperbark maple, with its reddish-brown shredded bark, is a small tree. The leaves are small and turn a beautiful shade of orange in the fall. Mine is in a protected location and is late to show its true colors. The other is Chinese dogwood. In addition to its attractive light-orange shedding bark, it has white-pointed bracts, which open a month later than our native dogwood, fruit that looks like a raspberry, and good fall color.

Of our native forest trees, shagbark hickory is the most distinctive, with its long strips of shaggy gray bark. Its leaves turn yellow early in the fall, and its nuts are relished by humans as well as by squirrels and chipmunks. White oak is one of our great native trees, and its rough whitish-gray bark is most attractive. Red maple and sugar maple are other excellent choices. The fall color of the maples can range from yellow to orange to red. It is best to buy a nursery tree in the fall to be sure you get the color you like.

Another criterion for your choice should be the tree's form or shape. Dogwood has everything going for it—foliage, bark, form, flowers, fruit, and fall color. Its horizontal branching habit is distinctive. The pagoda dogwood has a similar habit. Dogwood and crab apples tend to sucker, and the suckers need to be pruned out before they destroy the shape. Of the trees already mentioned, all have good form.

Maples that I would avoid are Norway maple, box elder, and silver maple. Many Norway maples develop a poor shape. Their shallow roots and dense shade make it difficult to grow anything under them. They seed prolifically, and you will be forever contending with seedlings. Box elder, another maple, tends to be weedy. Silver maple, while fast growing, is easily splintered in a storm. Its shallow roots can play havoc with a lawn.

Then there are the evergreens. I like natives, especially eastern hemlock and white pine. Pitch pine is scrubby, and Scotch pine is too coarse for my taste. A mature white pine is a majestic sight to behold. Like many mature people, it has lots of character and individuality. Presumably red pine was abundant on our hills during the logging era. Twice, I have attempted to grow red pine without success. Hemlock is one of the easiest evergreens to prune and makes a beautiful hedge as well as a majestic tree if grown singly. The spruces and firs provide a formal look, if that is your desire. The blue form (*glauca*) of Colorado spruce tends to be overused, and all too frequently is planted too close to the house. They look great for fifteen to twenty years but then become overpowering. Added to that, when lower branches die, they lose most of their charm. Remember, they are forest trees and require a lot of room.

Planting some interesting trees can add interest to the garden throughout the year.[19]

Hackmatack, the Nonevergreen Evergreen

Driving up to Rochester recently, I could not help but notice scattered groves of pyramidal trees aglow with yellow foliage. Most of the other trees, save beech and oak, had lost their leaves, so that the hackmatack, known also as tamarack and eastern larch, stood out. One other fall, driving over to Ithaca, I observed many other groves of larch on the hillsides. I don't recall seeing any at the nature center, but if it does occur there, it would be one that I might want to adopt. There are other trees that are easy to identify from the highway— white pine, beech, hemlock, red maple (especially in the spring when it is in flower), white birch, dogwood, red cedar, and shagbark hickory, to name a few. But in the fall, the tamarack really stands out. The pines, firs, spruces, junipers, cedars, and hemlocks are all close kin of the larches. But unlike the other conifers, the tamarack sheds all of its needles every year. I may have been aware, but not consciously, that pines shed needles every year, retaining needles for three growing seasons. The three-year-old needles turn yellow and

---

[19] Vol. 10 no. 4 (Late Fall 1985).

drop before the broad-leaved trees drop their leaves. As a gardener, I would have arranged for them to hold on to their needles until all the other leaves had fallen. We are near the southern limit of the tamarack's range, which extends northwestward to the Yukon and Alaska. At the southerly edge of its range, it more commonly occurs in swamps and sphagnum bogs, but around here, it is found on our hillsides.

Both *hackmatack* and *tamarack* are words of Algonquin origin. The Indians used the slender roots of the trees to sew together the strips of birch bark for their canoes, while the colonists used tamarack "knees" in boat building to join the deck timbers to the ribs. It is a tough, durable wood, resistant to rot, and has been used for telephone poles, railroad ties, and mine timbers. Not only does it provide color in the fall but also the soft, light-blue-green needles make an exceptional and distinctive display in early spring. Unfortunately, it is subject to insect attack, which can defoliate and kill the trees.

I have since realized that the trees along the highways are not our native tamarack but a European species planted in the 1930s by the CCC. Nevertheless, our native tamarack is well worth growing.[20]

Death of a Tree

One of my favorite trees at the nature center was that majestic old white pine between the building and Amelia Pond. In a way, trees are like people; they develop more and more character as they age. That is especially true of our native white pine. Just as one's skin gets more and more wrinkled with age, the bark gets more and more furrowed. Whereas we may get more stooped and bent over, the white pine seems to stand taller and straighter. As with people, its character is shaped by the struggles and difficulties it encounters throughout its long life. It loses its lower branches and many of its upper ones, just as we may lose the use of our limbs. A hundred-year-old white pine is surely a sight to behold, standing a hundred or more feet tall, towering over its neighbors or alone on a windswept hill. Each one

---

[20] Vol. 18 no. 3 (Holiday 1993).

is an individual. Each one is distinct and molded by the elements. It is easy to form attachments to them, as to a favorite grandparent or revered older friend. That is how I felt toward that big old pine and why I grieve over its demise.

It's been there well over a hundred years. Why did it die this particular year? Did we hasten its demise? The building was built ten years ago. Has it been on a slow decline since then? Perhaps we did; perhaps the extra drainage of rainwater from the building slowly overwhelmed its ability to adapt. Certainly, drainage is a likely culprit. When you drive to Bath, have you noticed how many dead trees there are in the median strip? Surely these have suffered because of the change in drainage caused by the construction of the highway. When did it die? Six months ago? Nine months ago? It is hard to tell. Did it put out new needles this past spring? I can't recall. But my Christmas tree was cut in December and its needles look fresh and green these three months later.

Interestingly enough, Jennifer Fais painted this tree and donated it for the auction, and Linda Manuel outbid me.[21]

Haw Haw

A vast and confusing tribe that seems to get the last laugh on anyone trying to sort them out are the hawthorns. They are relatives of roses and share with them thorns and hips. They were one of the understory trees on our lot and grew so thickly that many of them were removed. But many still remain. There are some good hawthorns for the home garden, as they are tough, adaptable plants. In fact, I chose to add two other species to the one endemic on our lot. The cockspur hawthorn was one such. In the wild, this is found in roadsides, abandoned fields, and hedgerows from Quebec to Maryland. The common name refers to the spur on a rooster's leg. Being curious, I wondered what the species name, *crus-galli*, translated as. *Crus* means lower leg, and *galli* comes from the species name for chicken—a virtual word-for-word translation. It was a good choice. It has a handsome form, white flowers in the spring, and red

---

[21] Vol. 16 no. 1 (Spring 1991).

fruit in the fall. For the more timid, there is a variety, "intermis," that lacks the spurs. The other haw I purchased is the Washington haw. The site I chose was not a good one, and lo these many years, it is still struggling to show its character.

Iron(Wood)

Two trees are commonly called ironwood. I had only known the blue beech as ironwood, and even now, I find it hard to think of hop hornbeam as ironwood. How did two dissimilar trees get the same common name? They are both hard and strong woods, but there the similarity almost ends. And why blue beech and hop hornbeam? Musclewood is another name for the blue beech. And both these names are easily explained. The trunks and branches are a blue-gray color, and the leaves bear a resemblance to beech leaves. Not only are the limbs blue-gray, but they look like human limbs—like forearms or upper arms in shape. They do indeed look sinewy—hence "musclewood" as a common name. But why "hop" and why "hornbeam"? The *hornbeam* comes from its use as yokes for oxen. *Hop* comes from the seed pods, which resemble the hops used in beer making. In the early years, we saw ruffed grouse feeding on the hops. Both are good understory trees for a woodland setting.

Moosewood

Striped maple is another common name for *Acer pensylvanica*, a small maple with large leaves and interesting green-and-white-striped bark. Note that there is only one "n" in the genus name. That is how it was originally written, and that is the way it stays. According to the nomenclature rules, priority takes precedence over any correction. It is an attractive tree with its striped bark, the only native maple with similar bark, although there are many Asian striped-bark maples. The other unusual feature is the size of its leaves, rivaled only by the big-leaf maple of the Northwest. The leaves turn a bright yellow in the fall. I had planted a red striped-bark variety in the back woods, which was growing nicely. I root-pruned it one spring and in the fall transplanted it to my front plantings so I could enjoy it when its bark turned a brilliant red in winter. It would make a fitting contrast to the paper-bark maple across the path. Come spring, it did not send out new growth. I have yet to find a replacement. But why is it called moosewood? I presume because moose will browse on the young shoots as deer do on the shoots of red maple. It seems all members of this family—deer, moose, and elk—have an affinity for trees of the maple family.

Oaks from Acorns

Everybody knows that mighty oaks from little acorns grow, but how many can tell a white oak from a red oak? These are the two main groups of oaks. The white oak clan have rounded lobes while the reds are pointy. The bark of the whites tends to be light and that of the reds dark. The acorns of the whites mature in a year, but those of the reds will have both last year's and the current year's acorns on the branches. Acorns of the white oaks are sweet and edible. Red-oak acorns are bitter, but the Indians were able to process them. Acorns are a favorite food of turkey, deer, and bear. Squirrels, blue jays, and woodpeckers cache the acorns. If it doesn't get eaten, a weevil can deposit its eggs in an acorn, and the larvae will feed on the nutmeat. Some of the buried acorns will send a shoot deep into the soil, the nut providing the energy. Only then will it send up a leaf shoot. Of all those that germinate only a few will survive to adulthood and produce acorns to perpetuate the species. In some years, there will be a large crop of a couple thousand. Having expended a tremendous amount of energy producing such a crop, it may be four years or more until another bumper crop is produced. Oaks are among those trees that rely on wind pollination. In the spring, the remains of the flowers come wafting down out of the trees.

Two of the most common oaks in our area are the white oak (*Quercus alba*) and the red oak (*Quercus rubra*). They derive their names from the color of the bark and that of the leaves in the fall, respectively. The red oaks, with the exception of the pin oak, drop their leaves in the fall while the white oaks tend to retain theirs until the new growth in the spring. Chestnut oak (*Quercus prinus*) occurs at Spencer Crest, and I am familiar with it from our backyard in Wilkes-Barre. The shape of the leaf is that of the chestnut, but the teeth are rounded rather than sharp. All of these are upland trees.

The white oak and the red oak are big trees. In the woods, they will grow straight and tall. The white oak is a slow grower, the red oak a more rapid grower. In an open field, they will grow out, forming a wide canopy. The Wye Oak in Maryland finally succumbed in 2001. It was the champion of champions, holding the title for a white oak for more than sixty years. The Wye Oak had a girth of 382 inches, a height of 96 feet, and a spread of 508 feet. It started life as a little acorn in the 1500s and survived more than 450 years—not as long a life as the giant sequoias nor Methuselah, but for an oak, that ain't bad. It has been propagated both by cuttings and by acorns so that its progeny live on. May some of them last 500 years. The Maryland state tree is the white oak, and the Wye Oak was the honorary state tree, until its destruction by a violent thunderstorm on June 6, 2002. There is a red oak in Monroe County that scored three points higher than the Wye Oak. It was not as tall with a smaller spread but had a bigger girth.

Paw Paw

Where O where is Ginny?
Way down yonder in the paw paw patch
Picking up paw paws
Putting 'em in a basket
Picking up paw paws
Putting 'em in a basket
Way down yonder in the paw paw patch.

Paw paw is not indigenous to the southern tier, but I remember it from my boyhood days in Pennsylvania. And years ago, when I visited my aunt and uncle in Indiana, I saw it again. I brought back three plants. One did not make it, but the other two, after a long period of getting established, are doing well and have flowered ever since but have not set fruit, which is a big disappointment. I suspect that the trees I have are clones and need to be pollinated by another plant. Another possibility is that I have no pollinators attracted to the flowers. I cannot do anything about the latter, but I have recently purchased other plants in case my first hypothesis is correct. We will wait and see. Another characteristic of paw paws, alluded to previously, is that they form colonies by sending out roots that then form new trees. My trees have started to do this, and I have had several trees pop up yards away from the parent trees. It is a tropical-looking tree with its large leaves and banana-like fruit. I am hoping mine will fruit so I can savor it.

Sassafras

Sassafras is a native tree that is sadly neglected in the nursery trade and seldom found or used by the homeowner. It makes a very handsome, small ornamental tree with yellow flowers in the spring, a beautiful fall color, and interesting and distinctive bark throughout the year. As a tree, it can reach thirty to sixty feet with a trunk diameter of eighteen inches. Autumn color is a rich red and orange. The bark is rough and reddish. It is upright growing, with short branches giving a pleasant appearance. Frequently, it will form shrubby thickets, spreading by root suckers. It is difficult to transplant except when young, which may explain its scarcity in the nursery trade. If you can find it, buy it. I transplanted a small specimen some twenty years ago, and it is now about 20 feet tall. It occurs throughout our woods, and a rather large tree is to be found at Spencer Crest. One of my neighbors has a beautiful specimen at the edge of the woods.

Its very name is Indian in origin, and the Indians and early settlers used it extensively. The aromatic twigs and roots are used for making sassafras tea. It provided one of the preartificial flavorings for root beer, and the extracted oil has been used for scenting soap. At one time, its bark was thought to be a panacea for our ills. Its leaves are used today by the Cajuns of Louisiana to make filé. This, I learned most recently, is a powder made by fine-grinding the leaves, which are then used as a thickening agent in gumbo. So all you Cajun cooks out there can collect your own leaves and make your own filé.

Almost everything about the tree is unique. Like the paw paw, its closest relatives are tropical trees. The leaves are the most obvious feature, being shaped like mittens. The mittens (leaves) may have a right thumb, a left thumb, both right and left thumbs, or no thumbs. The yellow flowers in the spring are followed by blue fruits on red stalks and are relished by songbirds, bobwhite, wild turkey, and black bear.

Some trees will have all male flowers, some all female, and some will have both male and female. The male staminate flowers have valves or lids, which lift, as if hinged, to allow the discharge of pollen. The twigs are browsed by rabbit and deer. Its leaves are favored by those two invaders, gypsy moths and Japanese beetles. It is reputed to being one of the favorite hosts for the beetles. All I know is that I find them on the sassafras and the blueberries.[22]

Shad

This is a tree story not a fish story. The shad I am talking about is also known as shadblow, serviceberry, and juneberry. It is a member of the rose family and is found throughout our region. It can grow in shade but is most often noticed at the edges of woods when it flowers in early May—one of the first of our native trees to bloom. More often than not, it is found bordering streams and rivers, and a trip to Elmira on the old river road in April will open your eyes. Because it blooms along streams and blooms in spring when the shad (fish) are migrating up the rivers and streams, early settlers named it shadblow, *blow* being an Old English word for blossom. Because it bloomed in the spring when parsons were making their rounds after winter, it attained the name serviceberry. It blooms early, and its fruit ripens early, giving rise to its other common name, juneberry. Its early bloom is welcome after a long winter, and its fruit is welcomed by birds and other animals when not much else is available. I have read that it makes a delicious jam, if you can harvest the fruit before the robins gobble it all up. It comes in a variety of shapes and sizes from the running serviceberry, which is only a few feet high, to forty- to fifty-foot trees. There are a number of hybrids and cultivars available—truly worthy candidates for the home garden.

---

[22] Vol. 17 no. 1 (Winter 1992).

Treeeeee-Mendous[23]

What is the biggest tree? Is it General Grant or General Sherman? The formula used by the American Forestry Association adds the circumference in inches (at four and a half feet above ground) to the height in feet and one-fourth of the average crown spread in feet. Based on this formula, General Grant beats out General Sherman. The National Park Service measures size by volume, and here General Sherman beats General Grant hands down. In 1980, its volume was calculated to be 52,508 cubic feet. Sequoias take five hundred to seven hundred years to reach their ultimate height. General Sherman reached this height about the time of the birth of Christ. Since then, the growth has been in its girth and crown spread. At 75 feet, it is not the tallest tree. That honor goes to a coast redwood in the Humboldt National Forest at 363 feet. The General's girth is 998 inches, a diameter of 26.5 feet, whereas the redwood has a girth of 638 inches, a diameter of 17 feet.

The third largest tree species is a western red cedar with a girth of 732 inches, followed closely by the Sitka spruce. The respective total scores for these four giants are 1300, 1183, 924, and 910.

What about big trees in our neck of the woods? Up in Dansville, there is a black locust with a girth of 280 inches, a height of 96 feet, and a crown of 92 feet for a respectful score of 399. Rochester has the biggest red oak at 458. I don't think of hornbeam or hop hornbeam as big trees, but there is a hornbeam in the Catskills with a girth of 95 inches and a rating of 178 and a hop hornbeam in Michigan scoring 217. A scarlet hawthorn in Oneida scores a 98. Even nonnative trees can be declared champions. A Norway maple in New Paltz has that honor, with a girth of 35 inches and a height of 137 feet.

The biggest species in the east is a sycamore in Ohio at 737 (girth: 582, height: 129, crown: 105). The Wye Oak, a white oak, in Maryland is 60 percent smaller with a girth of 374 inches for a score of 479. Other oaks are not far behind: red oak at 458, black oak at 416, scarlet oak at 392, and chestnut oak at 379. Would you believe that the silver maple is the largest maple with a score of 461? A red maple in Michigan is next with 431 and a sugar maple at only 382.

---

[23] National Register of Big Trees.

Nassau County has the largest striped maple. It's twenty feet taller than the sugar maple but scores only 134.

Following in rapid succession are a weeping willow (Michigan), a black walnut (Oregon), a red maple (Michigan), a white ash (Palisades, New York), a basswood (Pennsylvania), a green ash (Michigan), and a white pine (Michigan), all scoring over 400 points. The champion white pine has a circumference of 200 inches and height of 180 feet for a score of 400. In colonial times, the white or Weymouth pine was prized for ship's masts. The Royal Navy documented trees over 200 feet in height and over seven feet in diameter (a girth greater than 264 inches). Such trees easily topped 500 points. (My biggest pine has a girth of 100 inches and is close to 100 feet tall and over 100 years old, a mere youngster.) The largest hemlock has a girth of 24 inches but is only 123 feet tall. Of the birches, the yellow birch and the paper birch are in a virtual tie with 351 points and 346 respectively. Likewise are the river birch at 293 points and the sweet birch at 280 points. The gray birch is a short-lived species and only scores 166. A white ash in the Palisades rates a 420 and a green ash in Michigan 403.

Other high-scoring species are the weeping willow, 460; basswood, 395; beech, 366; black cherry, 351; sassafras, 346; and shagbark hickory, 299. Although the black walnut and chestnut are native to the East, Oregon boasts the largest black walnut at 443 and Washington the largest American chestnut at 366.

There are champions even among the smaller trees. A flowering dogwood in Virginia scores 154, and three shadblows tied at 140 from North Carolina, Virginia, and Michigan, sharing championship status. The staghorn sumac weighs in at 116, the witch hazel at 95, and a recently crowned pagoda dogwood in Michigan with a score of 71. Up here, we don't think of mountain laurel or the rosebay rhododendron as trees, but a laurel in North Carolina has a girth of 58 inches and a height of 25 feet for a score of 90 while a rhododendron is higher at 40 feet, but with only a 25-inch girth and a score of 71.

The West Coast has thirteen species with scores over 500, compared to the East's one species, the sycamore. There are four cedars, including the West Coast cedar, scoring greater than 500 at Port Orford, Incense, and Alaska. Among the firs, the Douglas fir (not really a fir) leads with 782. The true firs scoring above 500 are the noble, Pacific, silver, and red firs. The western juniper, aged 4000 years, scores 581. The Rocky Mountain juniper, aged 1500 years, rates a 292 but is only 40 feet tall with a 21-foot crown. Sitka spruces in Oregon and Washington tie at 910, and a blue spruce in Utah has a girth of 186 feet and a score of 317.

Florida leads with the most champions with 104, many of them not indigenous. Texas has 81, Michigan 76, and California 74 champion trees. New York trails badly with only thirteen.

CHAPTER 8

A YEAR IN THE GARDEN

Late Winter to Early Spring

This year, we had snow and cold. The snow protected the perennials from feeling the cold. Other years, we have open winters where the ground can thaw and freeze and thaw again, wreaking havoc with newly planted perennials that don't have their roots firmly implanted in the soil. A snow cover or a thick mulch is needed to protect our plants from frost heaving. Some winters get cold and stay cold. This is the best kind. When the temperature fluctuates and plants start to break dormancy only to be blasted with cold Canadian air, it is hard on marginal plants.

There is not much to do in the garden but enjoy it from the inside looking out. With a good snowfall, my wall gets buried, but as the sun shines and the temperature warms, individual rocks appear. Rocks in the northwest wall are the first to poke out of the snow, then those in the east-facing and finally the north-facing walls. After every snowfall, we get a winter wonderland with snow outlining the branches. Then there is the alligator-like bark of our flowering dogwood, the flaking bark of the Kousa dogwood and the paper-bark maple, the shaggy bark of the hickory, and on and on. This year, I did not do any pruning, but this time of year is a great time to prune your trees. The leaves are off, and you can see the skeleton of the tree. It is also a good time to cut flowering branches—forsythia, witch hazel, dogwood, and so on—bring them indoors, and enjoy a foretaste of spring.

Some years, in late January or early February, the snowdrops push up and on warm, sunny days, open up, bringing out the pollinators. Other winters, such as this one, it is late March or early April before we see signs of life. Then a week or two later, the bright-yellow winter aconites emerge and open up, and a horde of bees descend upon them on a warm, sunny day. In my perennial/ shrub bed, the hellebores send up their flower buds, opening their blossoms of white, pink, or purple. Each year is different. It is what makes gardening fascinating. We yearn for spring, but it comes in its own time.

April

What a glorious week this has been, albeit a trifle warm to my liking, but it has made the garden literally burst into bloom. The snowdrops and aconites have long since faded and are setting seed. Chiondoxas, glories-of-the-snow, which provided masses of bloom in the front woods and are now spreading lustily into the front lawn, were a sight to behold a week ago. The dozen varieties of daffodils are in full bloom, with some already spent and some just opening up. Hyacinths, grape hyacinths, and squill add more color to the front bed. The growing collection of hellebores provided a half dozen plants in bloom with twice that number waiting for next year.

There are a dozen rhododendrons in bloom right now, with others showing color. Colors range from white to peach to pink to purple. Both the Japanese and mountain andromedas are in flower, with their white panicles of bell-shaped flowers. The cornelian cherry, actually a dogwood, is past bloom, but the shad opened this week and my white redbud is showing color.

In my walls, arabis, aubrietia, candytuft, and saxifrage are blooming. Growing up in the cracks in the patio are violets, European ginger, ferns, and assorted other opportunists. Both the European ginger and the native ginger are growing and spreading lustily. Off the patio, my trout lilies, white and yellow, are in bloom. The clumps grow bigger, and seedlings appear each year. The wood anemones—white, blue, and yellow—form masses of bloom and green hither and yon throughout the garden. Along the driveway, paths, and borders, epimediums, ranging in color from white to yellow to pink, will continue to spread and provide interest now and throughout the year.

In the woods, spring started with my ramps and wild leeks, providing an early green carpet. The bloodroot came into bloom about ten days ago, and although each flower lasts but a few days, the thousand scattered through the woods provide close to a month of bloom. The double bloodroots opened this week with their miniature white peony-like flowers. Since they are sterile, the bloom will persist longer. More ephemeral in bloom than bloodroot is twinleaf, named in honor of our third president. Spring beauty, which sent up its grass-like leaves in January or February, came into its glory this week with its small, delicate pink flowers providing a pink carpet on the forest floor. My first trillium opened a week or so ago, but now at least a half dozen varieties are in bloom. One section in the back woods is filled with masses of Virginia bluebells, reminding me of a similar sight in Pennsylvania last spring. Another plant forming large colonies is mayapple, which needs to be restrained from invading areas where it is not wanted. It is one of my favorite weeds. And dozens of ferns are uncurling their fronds, the first being the dainty fragile fern, soon to be followed by its cousin, the berry bulblet fern.

I wish we could share our garden with each and every one of you sometime in the next two months, as these flowers fade and others take their place, as the ferns come into their glory, and as the native and Chinese dogwoods spread their colored bracts overhead.

It is hard to get work done, to take time from just enjoying the garden. To stroll through the garden in the early morning or at twilight is one of my greatest pleasures.

May

The dogwoods and the trillium are the shining glories of the May garden. Two dogwoods, a pink and a white, frame the front entrance while four more light up the patio and surrounds. Several more are in the front and back woods, most alas too young to flower.

Complementing those in the front garden is our white-flowering redbud, a more pleasing color than the normal "not quite red" color of the flowers. Not as spectacular as the flowering dogwood is the unassuming pagoda dogwood, with its distinctive shape and its profusion of clusters of small white flowers to be followed by blue berries, which are devoured as soon as they get ripe.

The other stunning display in May is the swath of white trillium, containing three hundred plus plants, starting at one part of the front path and sweeping around to the path as it curves around a big white pine. The swath is the result of self-sown seedlings, and seedlings continue to pop up in unexpected places. One big clump, having a dozen blooms, has seeded itself at the edge of the patio, making a dramatic statement. Scattered throughout the woods are small clumps of white trillium around every corner. The prairie trillium that I acquired from my aunt and uncle in LaPorte, Indiana, has made itself at home in this eastern garden, seeding itself throughout the garden. The yellow trillium and the snow trillium do not wait for May to bloom, but a dozen other trillium species light up my May woods, including the nodding trillium.

As May ends, the Dutchman's britches, spring beauty, and Virginia bluebells have stored up enough of that solar energy and go into dormancy until next spring—or, as in the case of spring beauty, until January or February. The seed pods on the bloodroot are nice and fat as are the intriguing seed capsules on twinleaf. The jacks-in-the-pulpit started emerging four weeks ago, and a few have just recently emerged. Jacks are one of my passions, and in addition to literally hundreds of the native jacks, I have a growing collection of the Asian jacks, including the dramatic *Sikokianum* and the one-meter-tall *hederophyllum*. Almost everywhere I look in the garden, there are jacks, including in my stone walls. Some are very pale green, and some are dark purple, with various combinations in between. The foamflower and miterwort have similar foliage to each other but vastly different flowers. One is foamy, and the other has small white cap-like flowers up and down a tall stalk. The red and white baneberries have similar flowers and foliage, and I find it difficult to tell them apart until they set seed. The mayapple is threatening to take over the entire woods and has to be moved, a truly great weed!

Windbeam, my favorite of the small-leaved rhododendrons,

beamed through most of May. One specimen next to the driveway is thirty-five years old and six feet tall and has bloomed every year even after temperatures 25 degrees F below. That and the other small-leaved rhododendrons have finished blooming, and now it is the turn of the big guys. In the waning days of May, boule de neige is snowballing. David Gable on the north side of the house makes a great contrast in pink with the pinkshell azalea, just a few feet away on top of the wall. Rosy is looking rosy, Scintillation is scintillating, and Janet Blair is showing her pink ruffles.

Some of the fern fronds are still unfolding, and they will be the glory of the summer garden when the spring blooming flowers have passed. They range in size from the three-inch oak fern to the three-foot Goldie's fern. Some have ferny fronds, some not. Some are evergreen, some not. Some spread, and some clump. I would be hard put to choose which is my favorite. It would probably be a toss-up between the native evergreen Christmas fern, the delicate and attractive maidenhair, and the lovely Japanese painted fern with fronds in shades of green and wine red.

We had our garden party the first Sunday in May, and the day was perfect. It was sunny and in the mid-70s, the company was great, the wine and cheese were enjoyed by all, and eighteen-month-old Rachel was the hit of the party. As one of our friends wrote, "Rachel was the prettiest flower." We have not had as nice a Sunday since then. May, in general, was ideal for gardening, cool and rainy. I indulged in exterior decorating, dividing and moving plants to fill in here and there. As someone has remarked, "A garden is never finished."

June

June is the month for mountain laurel, the state flower of Pennsylvania and Connecticut. What a great plant this is. It is one of America's greatest contributions to the world of horticulture. It has so much going for it. In a sunny site, it forms a compact, rounded shrub. In a shady site, it is more open, presenting an informal aspect. In the wild, it can form extensive colonies, giving rise to the expression "laurel hells" because it is almost impossible to get through the tangle.

Ah, and what an imposing sight it is in full bloom. Most laurel have white or pinkish flowers, but in nature, there are always odd balls. One of the first nonstandard laurels we acquired was Otsbo Red, a variety with red flower buds, opening a soft pink. Then along came Richard Jaynes, a researcher at the University of Connecticut, who started looking for the oddballs. He then made crosses between his selections and came up with dozens of varieties with a range of colors, flower types and growth habits. Now it is hard to find a non-Jaynes laurel for a woodland setting where one wants an unassuming laurel. The original laurels we planted are now about eight feet tall, but the lower foliage is sparse because of deer browsing prefence.

Summer in the Garden

It's been a brutal summer, hot and dry. From July 1 until the third week of August, my garden received only an inch and a half of rain and in the fourth week a like amount. As a result, the ground is bone dry, and although I did not water the lawn or the well-established shrubs or trees, I did water plants that showed stress. Unfortunately, some newly planted shrubs died despite my efforts. Many of my native plants went into early dormancy, such as mayapple, blue cohosh, and bloodroot, so for the past month, the woods garden has been looking a bit shabby.

Fall in the Garden

Spring is the season of rebirth, but fall is when plants start to prepare for that rebirth. The warm days, cool nights, and shortening daylight are signals for plants to harden off and get ready for the coming winter. Many plants have already produced seeds that birds and other animals have relished, which may well become new plants. Leaves are losing their chlorophyll and preparing for putting on their fall foliage display. The asters and goldenrods have waited until now to flower, providing pollen for bees, flies, and the myriad other insects that pollinate the flowers in return. It may not have been designed for us, but we humans glory in the fall flowers and the brilliance of the fall foliage.

The Garden in Winter

This Sunday morning, I came home from church. I made myself a cup of tea and laid a fire in the fireplace. The radio was on, bringing me *St. Paul Sunday* as I sat in my blue chair and started working on the *New York Times* Sunday crossword puzzle. Our Christmas tree was still up, not to be taken down until Twelfth Night, and the poinsettias on the hearth made a lovely indoor setting. As I worked on the puzzle, I would occasionally look at the roaring fire and through the sliding doors to the patio and the back woods. What a beautiful sight, what with the recent snow outlining every limb on every tree and bush in the woods. On the patio, the wrought-iron chairs and table had a lovely blanket of snow. A dwarf boxwood had a dome snow hat that was quite enchanting. A small beech tree in the woods still retained its leaves, and the brown seed pods still hung on the silverbell tree. Off to the right of the silverbell was the Kousa dogwood with its attractive flaking bark.

After putting down the puzzle, I meandered out to the family room and gazed out the window to the front yard and woods. With icicles starting to form on the gutters, the scene of snow-laden trees was repeated in the front woods. Every truss on my six-foot-tall Janet Blair rhododendron had its own hat of snow, as did the Japanese hollies. Looking across the ribbon of lawn, I saw only a few of the stones in my wall were visible, but as the days go by and the sun returns, they will reappear. First to emerge from their blanket of snow will be where the snow is not so deep or where the sun is stronger. I note with pleasure the varying textures of the bark on the trees—the alligator-like bark of my dogwoods; the dark, furrowed bark of the pines; the smooth bark of the maples; and the dark and light barks of the red and white oaks, respectively. Surpassing them all is the reddish flaking bark of the paper-bark maple. My snow-covered sitting rock, backed by rhododendrons, makes a lovely accent along the path. Beyond that, in the row of shrubs in the front hedge, the bright-red berries of the spicebush cling tightly to each branch.

Looking toward the driveway, I see the Serbian spruce is a thing of beauty, standing tall and narrow with its pendulous branches. Although I cannot see them from the window, I know the row of hemlocks make a picture of green and white on the south border. Although still in winter's grip, I know that beneath the blanket of snow, plants are stirring. Already we have ten to twelve minutes more of daylight at the end of the day. In milder, snow-free winters, the snowdrops would have emerged and might even have been in bloom. If I looked harder in such a winter, I could find a few grass-like leaves of spring beauty.

CHAPTER 9

THIS AND THAT

Green Thumbs and Dirty Fingernails

When people remark that I have a green thumb, I reply, "No, I have dirty fingernails." The following essays are a collection of articles on gardening in general.

Some Favorite Tools

One or two trowels of different sizes are essential. My favorite is an indestructible trowel, a Wilcox ALL-PRO 102. The blade is stainless steel and two inches wide, with a seven-inch pointed blade. It has a cushioned red plastic handle grip. It has not rusted. The width and pointed end of blade make it useful for digging and transplanting. The red handle makes it easy to find if misplaced (Source: Smith & Hawkins). It is also available in a larger size. I also have a narrow trowel that has a semicircular blade with a pointed end and a simulated wood handle. It's great for digging out seedlings (Source: unknown).

In addition to the trowels, I have two stainless-steel spatulas available from chemistry supply houses. One has a semicircular shape, which is useful for digging out small seedlings. The other has flat blades—one end rounded, the other pointed.

My favorite spade is my poacher's spade. It has a narrow, rounded blade. The rugged design, narrow blade, and rounded end make it useful for digging plants and for transplanting (Source: Lee Valley).

Also from Lee Valley is a stainless-steel fork. This is just the right size for digging holes and loosening soil. I love it, and it is in constant use. So what if a tine gets bent out of shape? What's to be expected? When you don't dig holes, you remove rocks. For heavier work, I have a larger garden fork, which is sold in hardware stores.

In my early gardening days, when I was doing a lot of digging in our rocky soil, I used a pick mattock almost constantly. This is a great tool for heavy digging in rocky and clay soil. The pick breaks up hard soil and dislodges all but the largest rocks. The mattock end chops roots and tills the soil. In thirty-five years, I've only worn out one handle.

I hardly go anywhere (in the garden) without the trowel and the pruners. You never know when you might need them.

The Shady Character

Who would trust a shady character, or who would not delight in someone with a sunny disposition? Good is associated with light and evil with darkness. In a sunny garden, one could grow corn, tomatoes, and zucchini. In a shady garden, I would not be able to grow lilacs, phlox, roses, asters, chrysanthemums, or any of the scores of annuals and perennials that must have sun to grow well and to flower. But shade and all its nuances is so much more interesting than a sunny, shadowless garden.

They are now telling us that people suffer from lack of light in the long, dark winters. Plants lacking chlorophyll must get their energy from decaying matter. But nothing is ever black or white. Our sun may be necessary to life, but with the discovery of life at the hot vents and in the depths of the earth, that too is questionable. With the concern for skin cancer, we must guard against too much exposure to the sun. Still, people curse the darkness and moan that nothing will grow in the shade. How wrong they are, both in their attitudes and their beliefs. If I had my druthers, I druther have a shady garden than a sunny garden. If that sounds heretical, hear me out. True, I would give up the ability to have a vegetable garden, except for some leafy vegetables, but the gains outweigh the losses.

Challenges of Growing Plants in the Shade[24], [25]

All gardening is a challenge, if you try to grow a plant where it doesn't want to grow. The trick in any kind of gardening is to adapt your gardening to your particular situation, whether you have sun or shade, whether it is wet or dry or has a northern or southern exposure. Do you have morning sun, midday sun, or afternoon sun? Do you have thin shade, high shade, open shade, dappled shade, part shade, or full shade? Shade will vary with the time of year. Think oaks and maples and the time of year, especially in the spring before they leaf out. Think the length of the day. Alaska has such long days that that they have phenomenal crops. Think the time of day since the intensity of sunlight changes with sun elevation. Morning sun is a lot gentler than afternoon sun.

The height of the branching affects the shade below. High pruning is desirable both for providing a more open shade and for improving air circulation. By pruning high, you allow for more plants to be grown. My woods, patio, lawn, and south-facing walls get winter and spring sun. In summer, the woods, lawn, and east-facing stone wall receive morning sun. By midday, the front lawn, patio, and areas to the north of the house are in sun. In the afternoon, the front border is sunny. Sites that are shady all day are the woods to the north, south, and east, including the east- and south-facing walls. And this is fairly dense shade. My perennial bed off the patio is where I am looking for plants that will bloom during the summer and fall in the limited amount of sun they receive. This bed receives dappled morning sun and full midday sun, and then as the sun gets farther over the yardarm, the house casts shade.

What exposure do you have? A southern exposure warms up in the spring and is ideal for bulbs. The soil temperature will be greater for a southern exposure and in a sunny location as opposed to a shady site. Soil temperature has a greater effect on the blooming of bulbs and perennials than does air temperature. A northern exposure

---

[24] Morse, *Gardening in the Shade* (New York: Charles Scribner's Sons, 1967).

[25] George Schenk, *The Complete Shade Gardener* (Boston: Houghton Mifflin Company, 1984).

warms up much more slowly and can be weeks behind in bloom. It is also not subject to fluctuations in temperature.

The latitude of the garden determines the amount and intensity of the solar radiation, Alaska and the Equator being extreme examples. Generally the farther north the garden, the more sun a plant can tolerate or may require.

Knowing the microclimates of your garden allows you to grow plants that ordinarily would not grow in your zone and allows you to extend the blooming season by growing the same plants in different exposures. Drainage, wind protection, distance from the house, mulching, exposure, sun, and shade all will affect the microclimate.

Evergreen trees provide year-round shade, deciduous trees summer shade only. Most woodland plants bloom before the trees leaf out, and some like Virginia bluebells, Dutchman's britches, and spring beauty die back after flowering and setting seed.

Woodland and shade plants prefer a rich, humusy, acidic soil. Shady sites are more retentive of moisture. The more sun a shade plant has, the more moisture it may require. A woodland soil usually has good drainage; if the soil is very heavy clay, it needs to be improved. Avoid trees with surface roots. Root competition, along with dense shade, is an almost impossible growing situation. Norway maple is one of my least favorite trees because of this. If you are growing plants under shade, additional fertilization may be necessary to provide enough nutrients for the plants and the tree.

Another focus for your garden should be the nonflowering aspects, such as form and structure of the shrubs and trees, bark texture, the color and texture of the foliage, berries, and fall color. Flowers aren't everything. A plant may be in flower for a day, a week, or a month. There are days, weeks, or months when it is not in bloom. How does it earn its keep the rest of the year?

The beauty of the year-round garden can be enhanced by choosing trees with good growth habits and pruning them to reveal their branching habit. Japanese maples are a popular ornamental tree. They provide texture and color. But sometimes pruning is neglected and they look like just a mass of foliage. How much better to open up the tree by judicious pruning so as to see the structure of the tree. I prune all my ornamental and flowering trees, such as dogwood and crab apples, to provide a pleasing silhouette not only when in foliage but also after the leaves have fallen.

There are many textures to choose among, from the fine foliage of golden locust to that of basswood, from the delicate maidenhair fern to the coarse fronds of the ostrich fern. There are many shades of green; use them to advantage. Seasonal interest can be provided by variegated foliage. New growth is often more intensely colored than mature foliage, and the fresh green of new foliage is refreshing. Foliage on evergreens is present 365 days in the year, but older leaves and needles will turn color before dropping. If it is a broad-leaved evergreen, do the leaves turn color in the winter? PJM rhododendrons turn purple in the winter and attain their best color in a sunny location. Leaves of the small-leaved rhododendrons will turn red before falling. The tamarack is a deciduous conifer. The new needles in the spring are a soft green and then turn a delightful yellow in the fall. Choose trees and shrubs with good fall color. The color on flowering dogwood ranges from yellow to orange to red to purple. The sugar and red maples have gorgeous color. The yellows of the ash, hickory, and witch hazel provide a nice contrast. My enkianthus turns a delightful orange. The last of my trees to color is my paper-bark maple, turning shades of red and orange. The viburnums all have good fall color.

Berries are a bonus in providing color in the fall after the flowering season is winding down. Jack-in-the-pulpit has bright-red berries, as does Italian arum, ginseng, and red baneberry. The berries of fairy bells are a glowing red-orange. False Solomon's seal has more subdued red berries, while the true Solomon's seal has blue berries. Another plant with blue berries is blue cohosh. The white berries of doll's-eye make a dramatic statement. Among the shrubs, dogwoods and viburnums produce berries, ranging from white to red and purple. In the case of viburnums, berries on the same bush will exhibit a range of colors. The flowering dogwood produces red berries, but those of the pagoda dogwood are blue.

The bark of trees can provide another element of interest throughout the year. Birch, beech, maple, shadblow, dogwoods, pine, hop hornbeam, and hickory all have interesting bark. The white birch is a popular clump-forming tree, but the yellow and river birch also have interesting bark. The smooth gray bark of the beech is unusual; in addition, the leaves persist throughout the winter. Moosewood is a native maple with striped bark. There are striped-bark trees among the Asian maples, as well. But can anything equal the reddish peeling bark of the Japanese paper-bark maple? The shad has an attractive grayish bark, while that of flowering dogwood has been likened to alligator skin. That is why you can always tell a dogwood by its bark! White pine has a rough, dark bark. The bark on the hop hornbeam is shred-like, and that of the shagbark hickory is, well, shaggy.

Plants in shade tend to grow taller and be sparser in foliage. Plants may do well in the shade but not bloom. Mountain laurel is found in nature in woods. Flowering is poor, but when moved into the open or if it gets additional exposure through the defoliation of trees by the gypsy moth, bloom will increase dramatically. Dogwood is often found growing not in the woods but at the edges and so gets some direct sun during part of the day and shade the rest. This is where it will do best in the garden. Rhododendrons, especially the large-leaved varieties, are ideal plants for shade. Other evergreens for shade are andromeda and leucothoe.

Putting the Garden to Bed

In the spring, I am frequently asked, "Have you planted your garden?" and in the fall, "Have you put your garden to bed?"

For me, these questions are meaningless and if repeated frequently can get somewhat annoying. I don't have a vegetable garden, not that I have anything against vegetable gardens, but they do require a bit more sun than I have at my disposal. So there's no garden, as such, to plant in the spring. And Mother Nature sort of takes care of the beddie-bye in the fall when the pine needles and the fall leaves come a-tumbling down. Oh, I plant things in the spring. I may order some fern or some wildflower that I don't have, and I will certainly dig up some of those favorite weeds and pot them up for a sale or for the wildflower garden of some lucky bidder at the nature center auction. Spring is a busy time of year, as I am moving plants around and removing some leaves from here and there. Fall can be busy, but there's not much in the fall that can't be put off until spring. If I have time to do it, okay; if not, okay. I did get some new bulbs in this fall. I like the so-called minor bulbs, such as the scillas, chiondoxa, and leucojums, as well as the narcissi. I do not rake up leaves from my small plot of grass. Instead, I run the lawnmower over them and let them lie. NYSEG did some trimming and left me a big pile of chips, half of which went into my compost pile and half of which were just spread hither and yon. Aside from that, I can't think of anything that has to be done.

Weather or No

As a skier, gardener, and sailor, I have a different perspective on the weather than the golfer, the water-skier, or the sun worshipper. It bugs me when a weatherperson or announcer speaks of "good" weather or "bad" weather. Whether the weather is good or bad is in the eye of the beholder.

In the winter, the skier, downhill or cross-country, welcomes the snow. For the gardener, it has been termed "the poor man's fertilizer." It makes welcome mulch, and nothing is harder on plants than a cold, open winter without a snow cover. A deep snow can make the difference between life and death for plants. Plants that are newly planted do not have their roots firmly established, and thaws and freezes can lift them out of the soil. The January thaw might be a pleasant respite from the cold, but if it gets too warm, lasts too long, and is followed by a sudden drop in temperature, it can mean the demise of many plants. They break dormancy, buds start to swell, and when the temperature plunges again, the buds are nipped in the bud. Likewise, abnormally warm weather in spring followed by a frost can kill flower buds on grapevines, fruit trees, and flowering shrubs and trees. I've had fresh growth nipped by a late frost, just as the leaves were beginning to expand. Nonnative plants are more susceptible to this type of damage than our native plants. The latter know that just as a single drop of water doesn't make a shower, a few warm days does not mean that spring has arrived. Early in the year, those bright, sunny days in March qualify for "good" weather for us humans, but with the ground frozen, it is "bad" weather. Evergreens can replace the lost water from the still frozen ground and can be desiccated and die.

In the summer, too many "nice" sunny days can be too much of a good thing, for the gardener and for the farmer. The drought in the southeast last summer attests to that. After all, by some meteorologists' definition of *good*, the Sahara has good weather all year round. It may be a nice place to visit, but I would not want to live there.

A warm, sunny day might be ideal for golf, a picnic, swimming, sunbathing, or water skiing, but unless there's a breeze along with it, it is not good weather for the sailor. Many a day, we've started a race only to sweat and swelter, becalmed in the middle of Keuka Lake. However, when the wind gets above twenty knots, it can be great fun on a sunfish or a sailboard but can lead to broken masts and capsized boats on the bigger sailboats. In certain cities, such as Cleveland or San Francisco, the weather reports include wind velocities as a regular feature but not in our area.

As the poet Ruskin put it,

> Sunshine is delicious, rain is refreshing,
> Wind braces up, snow is exhilarating,
> There is no such thing as bad weather,
> Only different kinds of good weather.

Perhaps if our weather was like that of the mythical kingdom of Camelot, we all would be satisfied.

> The climate must be perfect all the year
> July and August cannot be too hot,
> And there's a legal limit to the snow here,
> The winter is forbidden until December,
> And exits March the second on the dot.
> By order, summer lingers through September.
> The rain may never fall, 'til after sundown.
> By eight the morning fog must disappear.

Then there are the adages:

> "Every cloud has a silver lining."

> "It's an ill wind that blows no good."

> "Red sky in the morning, sailor take warning,
> Red sky at night, sailor's delight."[26]

Plants and Frost Dates

A fascinating bulletin[27] from Cornell lists frost dates for New York State. When is it safe to plant in the spring? When can we expect the first killing frost in the fall? What plants are most susceptible to freezing, and how can plants be protected? These and other questions are answered in this Cornell miscellaneous bulletin No. 33.

Would you believe that one year we did not have a spring frost after April 9? Would that happen every year? The latest recorded spring frost was on June 10. These are the extremes, and most gardeners hesitate to set out plants earlier than Memorial Day. About once every ten to fifteen years, they risk a frost. If you're a gambler and plant on May 18, two out of three years, you will be okay. Toward Elmira, the chances of frost are even less, but our friends in Addison can expect frost two weeks later than Elmira. Up in the hills, frost comes later in the spring and earlier in the fall.

In autumn, we can expect a frost any time after September 10, and one year out of two, we will have frost after October 4. One year, believe it or not, we went all through October and into November before we had a frost.

A light frost might not hit all areas on your lot. Slopes provide air drainage, but low areas act as pockets into which cold air flows. The slopes of Lake Keuka offer protection in yet other ways. The cold air

---

[26] Vol. 12 no. 1 (Winter 1987).
[27] *Spring and Fall Freezing Temperatures in New York State*, College of Agriculture, Cornell University.

from the lake retards growth in the spring, and the warm water in the fall moderates temperatures, thus reducing the danger of a late frost.

If a frost is expected, plants can be covered for protection. The homeowner does not usually have heaters or smudge pots, but if the garden is small, sprinkling can afford protection. The heat released when the water freezes serves to keep the plants from freezing. Root crops can withstand frost temperatures, but tomatoes and beans, as most gardeners know, are among those tender plants that are killed by a freeze.

Spring May Be a Little Late This Year

But it will come. Just this past week, the winter aconites and the early crocus have emerged. On the first warm, sunny day, they will open up, and the bees will search them out and be buzzing about. The snowdrops are already out, but they are a week later than they were a year ago, and at this time last year, my aconites and crocus were already in bloom, but then it was 60 degrees F and sunny on March 10 last year. By the end of the month, lots of things were in bloom—lots more crocus, witch hazels, Daphne, heath, scillas, and chiondoxa. I even had three native species blooming by the end of March. These were the dwarf snow trilliums, spring beauty, and the first bloodroot. I had first detected signs of spring beauty at the end of January. By early April, more of the natives had bloomed. The first hepatica opened up on the fourth, followed shortly by rue anemone and trailing arbutus. Twinleaf and Dutchman's britches weren't too far behind and colt's foot with its yellow bloom brightened the roadsides in early April to be followed in the summer by huge leaves.

Thoughts on the Hot, Dry Summer

Three years ago, I transplanted a tulip tree at Spencer Crest that was donated by a friend. It was pruned back severely and for the first two years seemed to be well established. It leafed out well this spring, but by August, the leaves had withered and dried. My normal gardening practice is to baby a new plant through its first year or maybe two, and then it should be on its own. Summers like this past one can throw a monkey wrench into such noble plans. Some astilbes and azaleas were just getting established and had to be watered. The bluegrasses and fescues are attuned to dry summers, go dormant, and recover with the fall rains, so they were left to fend for themselves. Between the heat and lack of rain, some rhododendrons that I have had for twenty years showed signs of stress and required watering. If the leaves remain curled up after sundown, that is a sign they need watering. All of my dogwoods, mountain laurel, and other native shrubs survived the dry summer. The lawn has become a status symbol, and people will water to keep that dark-green image. Me, I do no supplemental watering of my lawn. I let it go dormant and wait for the fall rains and cool weather to revive it.

Was the past summer a foretaste of things to come as the greenhouse effect makes its presence known, or was it simply a normal fluctuation in the weather, which will average out over the long run? Whichever it was and whether the winter will be warmer or colder than normal, it reinforces my belief that as a gardener, I should, to a large extent, grow plants that are adapted to dry summers. In the past few years, xeriscaping has come into prominence to reduce or eliminate the need for artificial watering. I am content that most of my rhododendrons came through without additional watering. Of the ferns, the interrupted and the maidenhair seemed most susceptible to the lack of moisture. Some of the wildflowers simply went into an earlier dormancy. My Turk's cap lilies only grew five feet tall instead of six feet plus. What saved the plants was the heavy rains we got the last two weeks of July. If it had continued dry, my losses would have been more severe.

My final observation is that it is not the normal climate that determines the local and area distribution of our native flora but the extremes of winter cold and snow, summer heat and rain, or lack thereof.

Random Thoughts on Hardiness

Cold hardiness cannot be defined by a single number. The survival of plants is not determined solely by the minimum winter temperature that the plant experiences. Fall temperatures and day length, spring temperatures, rainfall, snow cover, duration of the cold weather, depth of the frost, sun and wind exposure, air drainage, microclimates, fluctuating winter temperatures, and mulch all play a role. Each part of the plant will respond differently—from branch dieback to leaf and flower bud blasting, to killing of the roots. The hardiness zones are expressed as average minimum temperatures. But what winter is ever average? Although this rating is useful, it is a simplification, and lately indicator plants have been used to supplement the temperature limits. These indicator plants integrate the factors that determine the hardiness of a plant. For a plant to be successful in the garden, it has to do more than just survive. It has to be happy and do "good." I am also convinced that the duration of cold weather and the depth to which the ground freezes plays an important role in a plant's ability to survive the winter. The fact that a plant rated to zone 6 survives one night of –20 degrees F in one atypical year does not mean that it would survive in zone 5 year after year.

We all try to grow something that is not hardy in our zone. I have long thought useful information would be the five-, ten-, twenty-five-, and fifty-year lows. If, for example, the five-year-low was -10 degrees F and the twenty-five-year low was -25 degrees F, major plantings in your garden should be restricted to plants hardy to -25 degrees F. You might try plants rated for -10 degrees F, realizing that their long-term survival is risky. Even riskier would be trying plants hardy to 0 degrees F. And just because zone 6 gets a -15-degree F low temperature once in twenty-five years or so doesn't make it a zone 5 plant. Donald Wyman,[28] in *Trees for American Gardens*, reports that a giant sequoia reached sixty feet in height at Cornell Plantations above Cayuga Lake only to be killed by the severe winter of 1933–34. However, whether you believe in global warming or not,

---

[28] David Wyman, *Trees for American Gardens* (London: The MacMillan Company, 1965).

the USDA hardiness zones have shifted one-half of a zone warmer than they were fifty years ago.

The hardening-off process is very critical to the hardiness of a plant. The plant, in essence, makes antifreeze, which prevents the rupture of cell walls. And in this respect, timing is critical. There was an article years ago that described studies on *Cornus stolonifera* from southern and northern populations. The southern strain failed to respond to the changing day length in summer by hardening off. It would still be in active growth when a fall frost struck, killing back shoots. I am sure we have all heard the advice to buy plants grown in our zone or colder. This is one of the reasons why. Rhododendron maximum is one of the hardiest of all rhododendrons, the flower buds normally being able to bloom after -35-degree-F temperatures. However, if there is a cold snap in late fall or early winter before the hardening off is completed, the flower buds will be killed.

An open winter is much harder on plants than a deep snow cover. With a dependable snow cover, perennial plants do not experience the below-zero temperatures. The late Lanny Pride, a nurseryman and rhododendron and holly grower from Butler, Pennsylvania, claimed that the American holly (*Ilex opaca*) can survive low temperatures once the taproot grows below the frost line. Good advice for broad-leaved evergreens and evergreens in general is to make sure they go into winter with plenty of moisture in the ground. Water them well in late November, if necessary, and mulch them to keep the ground from freezing as deeply as it would otherwise.

Windchill factors are all the rage these days. Our body heat is lost by radiation and convection. Dead air is an insulator, and in calm air, heat is lost only by radiation. The stronger the wind blows, the more heat the exposed body surface loses. It is most commonly expressed as a temperature, which is the equivalent rate of heat loss per unit area for calm air. It is a subjective measure of how cold it feels. It only applies if the air temperature is above freezing. Windchill factors for humans cannot be applied to plants or to other animals. Your dog, with no bare skin, does not experience the same wind chill as you would.

With plants, the wind causes desiccation. The effect of wind on plants is to remove the dead air layer and to increase the transpiration rate. It may be possible to devise a desiccation factor that would be expressed as the rate of moisture lost per unit area. Just as a dog does not experience the same windchill as a human, a rhododendron would not have the same desiccation factor as a yew. The effect of wind on a plant is to remove that dead air layer and increase the transpiration rate. On humid summer days, we want air movement, but in the winter, strong winds will remove water from plants. The use of antidesiccants serves the same purpose. Those *wonderful* sunny days in March that delight our souls can spell disaster to a plant that has no way to replenish the lost water from the frozen ground. The other factor that causes the demise of evergreen plants is a January thaw followed by a drop in temperature and a stiff wind. The warm temperatures fool our exotic plants into thinking it is spring, and the buds begin to swell. Then when the cold and bitter wind hits them, they are tender and susceptible.

In my garden, I do not have to worry much about additional wind protection because the surrounding woods moderate the wind velocity. Good advice is to avoid house corners and other windy locations. Some people resort to burlap screens to provide protection. My inclination is to use plants that do not require coddling. However, it is good practice to provide protection the first winter after the plants have been put in. If you are planting evergreens in the fall, it would be wise to provide some protection that first year. An alternative to burlap wind screens is the use of antidesiccants, such as Wilt-Pruf for broad-leaved evergreens. Every garden has microclimates within it. A south-facing wall or foundation will be warmer than other areas. But it will also be subject to greater fluctuations in temperature. The north side will be cooler and if also protected from wind will not experience large temperature swings.

Protection from winter sun is also critical for the survival of broad-leaved evergreens. Accordingly, I have planted rhododendrons David Gable and Scintillation on the north side of the house where they are protected from winter sun. The more familiar large-leaved rhododendron hybrids prefer shade but in a site protected from wind will do well. The small-leaved rhododendrons can take more sun and wind than their large-leaved brethren. For low plants, snow is an excellent insulator. Those who live in areas that get reliable snow cover can grow plants one zone warmer. Lacking snow cover, small plants like heaths and heathers can be protected with pine boughs.

Cultural practices can also influence the survivability of plants. Already mentioned is the need to ensure that broad-leaved plants have sufficient water in the ground before the ground freezes and the ability of mulch to moderate the depth of freezing. Plants need time to harden off. The wrong combination of temperature and rain in late summer can delay this process. So can late pruning and late fertilizing. *Ilex crenata* is marginally hardy. I have learned not to prune my Japanese holly in late summer. It will put out new growth that will not harden off. They come from a different climate than ours and respond differently to day length and temperature. It is marginally hardy in zone 5 but has survived for some fifty years. I learned a number of years ago not to prune it in late summer. When I did, the new growth would get killed back. Now I do major pruning in the spring immediately after the first flush of growth and only minor pruning of long shoots thereafter. I was unable to establish the Japanese holly, Pencil. It apparently is not as hardy as *convexa* and was on a site exposed to wind, two strikes against it.

As a general rule, flower buds are tenderer than leaf buds and the woody parts of a plant, which makes sense since a plant can afford not to set seed every year. So a plant that is perfectly hardy, such as forsythia, Japanese andromeda, and certain rhododendrons will survive and flourish, but you will occasionally get no bloom because the flower buds have been blasted. I have cut forsythia in early January to force for the indoors. Later that winter, the temperature got to -20 degrees F, and in the spring, I had no bloom. I remember seeing a photo years ago where the middle of a forsythia had no bloom, but both the top and bottom of the bush was in full bloom. The bottom was covered with snow and protected. The temperature just above the snow was cold enough to kill the flower buds but not so higher up. Also in some years, forsythia and an occasional rhododendron will bloom in the fall. The climate and day lengths are different in their native habitat than in their adopted home, and they get confused into thinking it is spring. The reverse often happens in the spring for nonnative rhododendrons. They respond to lengthening daylight and a few days of warm weather by expanding the flower buds. Then when normal weather returns, the buds are blasted. One year, the Korean azalea, *Rhododendron schlippenbachii*, in full and gorgeous bloom, was blasted by a hard frost.

This past winter was harsh. Any bloom on my forsythia will probably be under the snow line. I doubt if I will have bloom on my *Pieris japonica*. Most, if not all, of the flower buds on rhododendron David Gable will have been blasted and three-quarters or more on rhododendron Scintillation. Windbeam should come through unscathed. I think I have demonstrated some understanding of hardiness in woody plants, but what makes one perennial hardy and another not somewhat eludes me. The hardiness zones are based on woody plants, on trees and shrubs, but I always see listed the hardiness of perennials. Is it the amount of moisture in the soil and hence in the plant tissues? I think that moisture in the ground and in the plant tissue is an important factor, if not the most important factor. Is the depth of frost critical? I think it is for both woody and herbaceous plants. Roots are not as hardy as the aboveground woody tissue. Only after the ground freezes can the soil temperature fall below 32 degrees F. The longer the cold lasts, the colder the soil can get and the deeper the frost can penetrate. That is what I base my contention on that the length of cold temperatures is important in the hardiness of plants.

Mulching helps perennials by reducing heaving of the plants from freeze/thaw cycles. It also helps both woody and herbaceous plants by insulating the soil from the air temperature. With rhododendrons, it moderates soil temperatures not only in winter but throughout the year. A gardener in Minneapolis used heavy mulch and was able to grow many plants in that cold location, because the plants never saw those cold temperatures. It was important to remove the mulch in spring before growth started. It is an extreme method to grow less-hardy plants, but it is effective.

Southern Tier Tier Theory of Gardening

Forgive me, but I cannot resist a pun or an alliteration. This theory is not original. In fact, it is nature's way, but by adopting it, we can make our gardens more carefree and more beautiful at the same time. It allows one to grow the "mostest in the leastest."

The first or uppermost tier is the canopy of the tall trees of the forest. These trees cast only high or intermittent shade and permit the growth of the second tier of understory trees. The second-tier trees either provide flowers, such as the flowering dogwood and the shadblow, or interesting bark, like moosewood and white and yellow birch. Ideally the canopy trees would be the oaks and hickories, which cast a light shade and have deep roots. The red and sugar maples would serve, as would high-branching white pines. These would cast more shade but have proven satisfactory. I open these up by selective pruning in addition to removing branches under about six feet in height. Avoid silver maple and beech, and avoid Norway maple above all. These all have voracious surface roots, and the Norway maple and beech cast a heavy shade. Up to now, we have the topmost stories, the tall trees, for shade and the medium trees for flower and form. The third tier would consist of flowering shrubs, such as azaleas, viburnums, shrub dogwoods, mountain laurel, rhododendrons, and any of our native shrubs. A selection of these would provide a display of flowers throughout the spring and summer, colorful fruit in the fall, and winter and evergreen foliage throughout the year. Below these would be the fourth tier of wildflowers, ranging in height from one to six feet, consisting of the taller-growing wildflowers, such as mayapple, Solomon's seal, trillium, jack-in-the-pulpit, cohosh, and ferns, such as wood ferns, Christmas fern, and the delightful maidenhair fern.

The fifth tier would be comprised of plants under a foot in height. These could include foamflower, bishop's cap, hepaticas, our native pachysandra, and low-growing ferns. Plants such as oak fern and partridgeberry would be among those qualifying for this tier. Below and intermingled will be the forest debris—the needles, the twigs, and the branches that on decomposition form the humus-rich layer that provides perfect conditions for the five tiers of plants above.

Such a garden will provide beauty and pleasure throughout the year. The tall, straight trunks of the oaks, hickories, and pines lend character winter and summer. Red maple is one of the earliest trees to bloom in the spring. Dogwood is handsome year-round, providing flowers in spring, color in fall, fruit in winter, and a distinctive form throughout the year. Shadblow and moosewood have delightfully patterned and colored bark, and shad flowers early in spring followed by berries in June, which the birds love. Witch hazel provides a touch of yellow in fall, both by its foliage and its flowers.

Most of the shrubs will bloom in the spring—some as early as April and some in June like the mountain laurel—or in summer like the summersweet. The deciduous shrubs almost all have good color, notably the viburnums, dogwoods, and enkianthus. Most of the shrubs will provide a bonus of colorful berries that in some cases persist throughout the winter. The vast majority of the fourth tier of wildflowers bloom early in the spring, but a few, like snakeroot and Turk's cap lily, are summer bloomers. There are asters, sunflowers, and goldenrods that will grow under the tall canopy. Many of our wildflowers have brightly colored fruit, like jack-in-the-pulpit, Solomon's seal, baneberry, and cohosh. Partridgeberry blooms midsummer, and the red berries persist into the New Year. The native ferns offer an outstanding variety of color, texture, and form while the new growth of the ferns is a joy to behold. Some, like Christmas fern, are evergreen, while others, like ostrich, produce fertile fronds that provide interest in winter as well. What a contrast to the monotonous look of a lawn!

A recent discovery provides evidence of an unexpected benefit of plants growing under tall, deep-rooted trees. It seems that these trees draw up moisture from the lower depths of soil and make it available to the plants growing under them.

Path-ology

Path-ology. The art and science of constructing paths.

The most important path and sometimes the only one is the path to the front door. Usually it is a narrow concrete walk. We wanted something that would tie in better with the design and setting of the house. Accordingly, we chose a three-foot path of random flagstone. Originally, this was set in sand, but it has since been set in cement. We actually have two front walks. One goes to the front door that opens onto the foyer. The other goes to the laundry door; that is the one most people use. The front stoop and the laundry porch also use random flagstone.

Because I want access to the woods, I have paths wandering through both the front and back woods. These are simply dirt paths, and moss has been encouraged to grow on the paths. It was not always so. For the paths in the front woods, I laid down black plastic and covered this with pine needles. The source of the pine needles, in addition to those from my trees, was the empty lot across the street that had years' of accumulation. This did not prevent seedlings from growing in the path, and I forewent the yearly addition of pine needles. Some people use shredded bark as a surface for paths, but this has the same drawback as the pine needles, in addition to being expensive. So now the paths are just plain dirt. But it is not plain dirt, for moss has been encouraged to grow in the path. Seedlings still come up in the path and are a source for plants for plant sales or exchanges.

Early on, I lost two oaks because of changes in ground level. Having a surfeit of firewood, I asked my tree man to saw the trunk into eight- to nine-inch sections. I then used these as stepping-stones at the north of the house, leading from the front lawn to the back lawn. This worked quite well until the oak started to rot. I then cast stepping-stones in concrete, using an aluminum annular cylinder as a form. Presently, these round stepping-stones lead all the way from the front lawn down into the back woods. The area around the stepping stones was originally grass, but it has gradually been replaced by *Chrysogonum virginianum*, whose common names are goldenstar and green-and-gold. This is a low-growing native plant with bright-yellow flowers. This makes a very dramatic statement. All the grass in the back of the house has been removed, and the path leading off the patio has been replaced with rectangular flagstones, interplanted with wild strawberry, foamflower, goldenstar, and whatever low-growing plants volunteer. The path around the garage is random flagstone, as is the off-driveway parking area. At the back of the garage, rectangular flagstone surrounds the triangular raised bed and flagstone steps extend down the slope to the back woods.

The moss-covered paths through the woods, the random flagstone front walks, the round stepping-stones, and the rectangular flagstones leading off the patio and those leading down into the woods all work well together.

This is a letter to the editor of *Fine Gardening*.

An almost "perfect" discussion, but I must take exception to the statement "In a Woodland Garden," paths covered with shredded bark, wood chips or pine needles are most in keeping with the informal setting." That is true *only* if one is talking about woodland "gardens," but not when one is talking about "woodland" gardens. What is most in keeping with the informal setting of a "woodland" garden are bare paths that emulate trails through a forest. And, if moss grows on the paths so much the better. I have almost 1000 lineal feet meandering through my 3/4 acre "woodland" and if I were to cover the paths with shredded bark, I would need some 26 cubic yards replenished every few years. Then there is the problem about what to do with the leaves that fall on the path. Incidentally, I use irregular flagstones for the paths to the front doors, rectangular flagstones leading off the patio down into the back woods and round concrete stepping-stones that connect the front lawn with the back lawn. These replaced stepping-stones made from an oak tree that had died following house construction.

Stone-Walling

Our lot has a gentle slope from the northwest to the southeast and has a plentiful supply of rocks of all sizes. In addition, the streambed of the adjacent unnamed creek was the source of many collected rocks. The garage is a half-level below the main house, and the contractors built a stone wall between the driveway and the laundry entrance. They also built a stone wall off the patio in the rear of the house. These were the first of many stone walls to be built.

The driveway wall was rebuilt early on and after another thirty-plus years is in need of another reconstruction. There is an eighteen-inch-wide area between the wall and the sidewalk, and this was originally planted with *Cotoneaster horizontalis*. Some twenty years ago, I decided that this planting was not successful and needed to be replaced. It now contains several small rhododendrons, a couple heaths (*Erica*), and a Japanese spirea. Growing in the wall itself are maidenhair spleenwort, aubretia, arabis, and sedum, Autumn Joy. Plants that have volunteered are *Corydalis lutea*, Japanese painted fern, and maidenhair fern. The painted fern will disappear during a drought but reappears after some good rainfalls. This is a south-facing wall, and it pleases me that a sun-loving plant, aubrietia, and a shade-loving plant, maidenhair spleenwort, are growing happily side by side. My explanation is that the aubrietia gets enough sun in spring before it is shaded from the tall trees whereas the spleenwort gets enough shade when the trees leaf out.

There were two oak trees off the patio that soon died because of the change in grade. I took this opportunity to extend the wall encapsulating the stump of one of the oaks. I have planted very little in this wall, but it has become home to a host of plants. This wall faces east but is shaded by trees on my property and on my neighbor's behind me. It gets sun in spring before the trees leaf out, but during the height of the summer, it is in full shade. It contains a big clump of Dutchman's britches that is simply spectacular when in flower. There is a big jack growing out of the wall. Then there are ferns galore.

The wall that is my pride and joy is the one I built that separates the front lawn from the woods. Originally, the lawn sloped up to a red maple at the edge of the front woods. In 1972, after several years of contemplation, I decided the time had come. No more stonewalling. I started at the spot where the path comes out of the woods to the north of the house. The wall starts out only two stones high. As it gets to the front corner of the house, it begins to assume a gentle curve, all the while increasing in height. It then parallels the front of the house, attaining a height of some thirty inches. After about twenty-five feet, the height slowly decreases, and at the end of the lawn, it curves to the east and is only one stone in height. Construction began at the north end. The lawn's slope was reduced, and a trench was dug the length of the wall. This trench was then filled with small stones and construction of the actual wall begun. The procedure followed was that in Linc Foster's *Rock Gardening*.[29] The first row of stone was laid below ground level, and then succeeding stones were placed on top with soil behind the stone and between the

---

[29] Foster and Lincoln, *Rock Gardening*.

layers. During the construction, I had piles of dirt and piles of stone as I worked my way from north to south. Each stone was set slightly behind the one below and sloped inward. This procedure helps to resist the pressure on the wall and allows rain to run back into the wall. The books recommend planting the wall as it is built, but I know few people who would have the plants to carry out such a project.

There is a four-foot drop from the level of the garage to a path that leads to the back woods. What better reason for building another stone wall. Originally, it was more modest in scope. But I needed a parking place for a sailboat during the winter. Consequently, I pushed the wall out to provide the space. This is a shady wall facing south. The most plentiful and prolific plant in the wall is *Corydalis lutea*. If it gets too rambunctious, it gets pulled out. There are a variety of ferns in the wall and a nice dark-blue hepatica.

In the back and to the south of the patio, I attempted to build a rock outcrop. I was never happy with it and decided to build two more walls. There are steps leading from the patio to the garage level. Walls were built on either side of the steps with one wall ending at the end of a screened-in porch and the other opposite it. Then some years later, we decided to close in the porch and I decided to extend the one wall another couple of feet and create a raised bed at the south end of the porch. On the opposite side, a low wall, one to two stones in height was built, giving another planting bed.

The triangular area bordered by the porch and the back of the garage presented a problem. It was too shady for grass to grow and lacked any interest. My solution was to construct a triangular-shaped raised bed for growing some dwarf varieties of plants. The north-facing wall should make a nice home for ramondas. To complete this area, I laid rectangular flagstone on the three sides and leading down the path to the back woods.

Interesting facts: 2,500 stones weighing 60 tons and comprising 750 square feet spanning 500 lineal feet.

CHAPTER 10

PLUMMER'S PRINCIPLES OF PRACTICAL PRUNING

Pruning is just as important to the health and well-being of your plants as watering and fertilizing. The same people who allow their shrubs and trees to get overgrown are often the same people who mow their lawn religiously. The difference is that mowing the lawn doesn't take much thought, but it has to be done on a regular schedule. Pruning takes thought and has to be done on a schedule that is not nearly as rigorous as lawn mowing. Because it takes thought, people put it off, and the need gets worse and worse. Or they butcher their hedge rather than prune it. Pruning is an art. Pruning is fun. Pruning can be learned. And one learns by doing. There are obvious branches on a tree or stems on a bush that need to be pruned. By starting with these, one gains confidence and then can proceed to the pruning that enhances the form of the shrub or tree.

Damage Control

A fellow gardener shares with me the same attitude toward pruning. He has his four Ds; I have my principals of practical pruning. His four Ds are dead, diseased, damaged, and deranged, which, simply put, means that you remove any dead, diseased, or damaged branches. We will get to the deranged later. Dead wood, except on a bonsai plant, serves no useful purpose and usually should be removed. Diseased branches should be removed as soon as they are noticed in order to prevent the spread of the disease to other branches or to other plants. The one recurring problem I have with my rhododendrons is stem borers. The leaves on a healthy-looking branch will start to droop. I will pull my pruners from my hip pocket and cut back to the next branch. If the stem is hollow at that point, I will cut back farther and farther until I come to healthy wood. Alternatively, I will take a metal rod and jam it down the hollow stem until it meets resistance. If not caught in time, the stem borer could kill the entire plant. On more than one occasion, I have had to cut back practically to ground level. The moral is if you see something that doesn't look right, do something

Freak ice or snowstorms and humans can break branches on your trees or shrubs. The one serious problem with arbor vitae is the propensity to bend under snow loads. Rhododendrons can suffer damage from snow or ice. In addition to removing the broken branches, take it as an opportunity to reshape the tree or shrub. It may mean removing other branches to restore the symmetry of the tree. There is not much that can be done in those cases. Spruces and firs are more adaptable to snow loads, pines less so. Deciduous trees can handle snow loads when bare but not when leafed out. Ice loads can cause damage at any time.

To Be or Not to Be

That is the question! How does one decide which branches should be removed after we've pruned out the dead, diseased, and damaged branches? Now we come to the fourth D—*deranged*. My answers would be "Interference!" and "Look to the future!" Two bodies cannot occupy the same space at the same time. One has to go, and you have to decide which branch will contribute more to the future shape of your tree. It takes visualization, but with a little practice, you will soon get adept at it. For long-neglected trees, this will probably mean sawing off some good-sized branches but better late than never. Once you have the worst offenders removed, step back and look at your tree. Where else are there branches growing east when they should be growing west? Are there two adjacent branches growing in the same direction? Are their suckers on side branches growing straight up? Are there a lot of suckers growing out of the same spot or at the base of the tree? If the answer to any of these questions is yes, take your pruners and cut out the worst offenders. Many of the smaller twigs can be removed by breaking them off between your thumb and finger—hence the term *green thumb*. Step back, and look at your tree again. How does it look? If it is still a bundle of branches and twigs, you have some more work to do.

Look Up, Open Up, and Au Naturel

One of my objects in pruning is to bring out the natural beauty of the tree or shrub. Removal of suckers, pruning up, and opening up are three ways this can be done. A lot depends on one's individualistic approach to pruning. But look up, open up, and au naturel form the basis of Plummer's principles of practical pruning.

I am a firm believer in pruning high. Sometimes I may overdo it, but it is nature's way as well. Have you ever noticed the difference between pine trees or oak trees that have grown in a wood as opposed to those that have grown in an open field? Those grown in the woods are straight and tall as they reach for the sky. These tall ones are self-pruning and have lost their lower limbs. Those grown in open fields are big and broad with huge limbs. Both can be majestic in their own way, especially a white oak. But nothing matches the majesty of a hundred-year-old pine that has lost limbs to ice and snow and wind. The older it gets, the more character it has. The same can be said of our hemlocks. If you have acres of land, you can afford to emulate the look of the openly grown oak. But with limited space, up is the way to go.

Another aspect is this: how many times have you walked down a street only to have to duck to avoid branches? Or if you have a tree in your lawn, how annoying is it to duck as you mow the lawn? Pruning high improves the appearance of the tree as a tree and makes practical sense as well. My "look to the future" dictum applies here as well. Say you have a tree with a low-growing branch one inch in diameter. Now imagine what that branch will be like when it is three or four inches in diameter. How far will it extend out? How low will it be? How much lower will the ends droop? If you are happy with that, okay, but if not, 'tis better to remove it when it is small than when it means a major operation.

The other reason I like to prune up is to be able to grow other plants under my trees. By pruning high, I can grow flowering trees under my oaks, pines, and hickories. I can grow shrubs under the flowering trees, and I can grow flowers and groundcovers under the shrubs.

I consider this the best of all possible worlds, as I once described it under the title "Southern Tier Tier Theory of Gardening." Aesthetically, I like the appearance of the forest trees pruned high and the flowering trees pruned for head clearance. It serves a practical purpose as well: it improves air circulation.

"Open up" is another technique that improves both the appearance and the air circulation of trees, especially flowering trees. We have leaves on our trees for six months of the year and flowers for a week. The remainder of the year, we are looking at the bare-bones structure of the tree. Do you prefer to look at a rat's nest of twigs and branches, or do you like to be able to follow a branch from beginning to end? Utilizing this principle takes a bit more thought and imagination than those enunciated earlier.

Au naturel is pruning to enhance the natural beauty of the tree. Have you ever visited a Japanese garden? They have perfected this technique of pruning to enhance the natural form and beauty of a tree's structure. It is an art but an art that can be learned. The fact that the tree or shrub has been pruned is not obvious. Bonsai is this technique carried to its ultimate form. One method of practicing this art is "drop-pruning." This is a means of reducing the amount of branches without sacrificing the shape of the tree or shrub. You select a branch, which has one or more other branches branching out. You follow one of these branches back to where it joins the main branch and cut it off. This reduces the weight on the main branch and increases the headroom because of the decreased load and the removal of the branch. The casual observer would not even realize that the tree or shrub had been pruned. It sounds more complicated than it is. Once you have done it once or twice, you will realize how useful it is.

Whatever you do, don't do it halfway. When a tree has been neglected, the lower branches interfere more and more with our noggins as we try to walk or work around them. The solution so often is to lop off the end of the branch with no thought to the morrow. This result is the entire branch or the end of the branch dying or becoming diseased. The correct and proper way is to cut either back to the trunk or to another branch. It is simple, but then it is the simple things that so often are the hardest to do.

Timing Is Everything

Or almost everything. Someone once asked a French abbe when it was okay to prune. His answer was any day of the year, except Sundays. Most everyone can agree on the principles enunciated so far, but some times are better than others. In general, the best time to prune trees is winter and early spring before the buds break. Some trees, noticeably birches and dogwoods, bleed. Heavy or extensive pruning of these should be avoided in the spring when the sap is rising. Spring-flowering trees or shrubs are best pruned immediately after flowering. Alternatively branches can be cut to bring indoors for forcing. Broad-leaved evergreens should be pruned in the spring after the first flush of growth. Any new growth should not be pruned in late summer. I learned this lesson the hard way with my evergreen Japanese holly (*Ilex crenata*). I was experiencing a lot of winterkill and realized that I was pruning too late in the season; the new growth did not have time to harden off. Since I have ceased that practice, the hollies come through in fine shape. Instead, wait until December and use the branches for holiday greens.

How Much Is Too Much?

Generally speaking, it is not wise to cut back more than one-third. The less you trim in one season, the better. That is the basis of the procedure for pruning flowering shrubs discussed here. But there are exceptions. If a rhododendron is too leggy and it is healthy, it can, with some exceptions, be cut back to the ground. The exception is those rare hybrids that will not break forth new growth. Yews, boxwood, and holly can also survive drastic pruning. They will not look like much for a few years. A healthy tree can also be cut off at the base. I had a silverbell tree on my patio that was leaning in order to get more light. An ice storm caused it to lean to a forty-five degree angle. It is a lovely tree, and I did not want to lose it. I simply cut it off at the base and removed all the suckers but one. It is now a good-looking tree again. Plants want to live, and if they are healthy and have the food reserves, they will.

Evergreens

Hemlocks are one of the easiest of the conifers to maintain at a convenient size. I have a hemlock hedge that is one-third of a century old, and the tallest is only eight feet high. Assume it grows an inch a year; it would have been some forty feet tall if allowed to grow. I have even seen a hemlock hedge that was at least twelve feet high and at least fifty feet in length. Was it ever a beautiful sight.

Pines are the more difficult of the evergreens to prune. We remarked that "timing is everything," and this is especially true when it comes to pines. If you are using pine as a hedge or a shrub, the most effective time to prune is when the candles have started to lengthen. I presume you know what I mean by candles. In case you don't, each spring, a bud will start expanding and form a shoot from one to four inches long before it opens up, displaying the needles. This is the candle. To control the size of the plant, these candles are cut back by two-thirds. For severe pruning, you can cut back a branch, but only if you don't cut back beyond where there are needles.

The same candling technique can be applied to spruces and firs. But they seem to be more forgiving than pine trees. A pine will seldom have adventitious buds that will break and start a new branch. Spruces, however, will often break forth from the trunk or a branch. But again, by proper timing and due diligence, it is possible to maintain a forest tree to a manageable size. The better solution is to find one of the dwarf varieties that puts out only an inch or so of growth a season rather than six to twelve inches.

Flowering Shrubs

Shrubs grow from the base. Ergo, they should be pruned from the base and not given a brush cut. There is no worse pruning sin than to trim forsythia as one would privet. You have not only lost most of the bloom for the following year, you have destroyed the natural beauty of the shrub, which wants to flow like a fountain. To maintain the vitality of flowering shrubs and to maintain control over their spread, one-third of the shoots should be removed each year. Each year, one-third of the oldest canes would be cut off at the base. For shrubs like forsythia, I would do some of my pruning, as noted above, in January and February. Bring the branches indoors to force them and to enjoy a little touch of spring in the dead of winter. Fall bloomers are pruned in late winter or early spring. If you miss a year, it's no big deal.

What often happens is pruning is neglected for several years until the shrubs get too big for their site. Then, instead of being started on the three-year pruning schedule, they are simply lopped off at a convenient height. The result is thick shoots topped by a lot of smaller shoots. The effect reminds me of the pollarding of trees we saw in Italy. If you like that sort of thing, okay, but if it is because you haven't thought about it, think about it. Start the three-year schedule. If the wrong shrub has been planted, whether as a hedge or as a foundation planting, the best thing in the long haul may well be to rip them out and replant something more in scale with the house and the property. Then maintain the pruning schedule and do not allow them to gain control over you.

The rhododendron is another species that requires special techniques—or rather, an amplification of techniques we have already discussed. They can be grown as trees, but they are shrubs and should be treated as shrubs. Most of the common hybrids available can take drastic pruning. I have even seen them pruned as a hedge bordering a driveway. They are spring flowering and in addition are evergreen. Hence they should be pruned as soon after flowering as possible. This will allow them to make their growth and for that growth to harden off before fall. Again, always prune back to a crotch. If they have gotten leggy, they can be pruned way back, even to the ground. This should be done early in the year, even before they bloom. A healthy plant should be able to withstand pruning back to ground zero. So do not worry about pruning too much. They will thank you for it, by becoming denser.

Ideally your rhododendron will put out several shoots from each leaf bud. If only a single shoot is produced, this can be twisted off just as it begins to extend. What this should do is cause several of the dormant buds to start growing and give you a much denser and better-branched shrub.

That's about all there is to it except for dead-heading. You say, "What is that?" It is simply removing the dead and shriveled flowers. This is done for aesthetic reasons as well as for practical ones. It looks better, and by removing the dead flowers, you are removing the means of the plant to set seeds. By not having to put all that energy into producing seeds, it may flower more abundantly next spring. To do this, you grip the flower stem and turn or twist. If you don't get around to it, not to worry. The small-leaved rhododendrons, like PJM, Olga, and Windbeam, can be sheared instead of pruned. I have a couple of PJM rhododendrons at both sides of the entrance and intend to keep them at five feet in height and from not encroaching on the walk.

Tools of the Trade

A good hand pruner is the first weapon in your arsenal. Buy the best you can find. Felco and Corona are considered to be among the best. Felco pruners even come in right-handed and left-handed versions, as well as a smaller version for dainty hands. One I like even better is a German make, a Romulus leichtschnitt gartenschere. I have had mine for twenty-five to thirty years, but I have been unable to locate a source in the States.

Your next weapon should be a lopper, which is a long-handled version of a pruning shear. There are miniloppers, maxiloppers, and ratchet loppers. I have a lightweight pair that I use most frequently, but I also have a monster lopper that can cut through big, tough branches. I even have a ratchet lopper that can tackle the jobs that the monster lopper cannot. For general use, a pair that can cut a one-inch branch might be all you need.

A pruning saw is the third must-have weapon. I have a curved-blade saw that cuts on both the forward and reverse strokes. Again, be sure to buy a good sturdy saw. I have had mine for more than thirty years. This type is great for sawing off thick stems of shrubs as well as for sawing off tree limbs. A bow-type saw is also useful since one can get different types of blades for different purposes. Its disadvantage is that it requires a lot of clearance.

A combination pole pruner and saw is another useful weapon for pruning trees. Mine has a telescoping pole with a detachable saw and pruner. The saw can be used for sawing off limbs from trees. The pruner can cut off smaller branches. I like it for its ability to execute my drop-pruning technique and to cut off high dead branches.

CHAPTER 11

TRIPPING THE LIGHT FANTASTIC!

Clark Reservation: Oneida County, New York

For five years or more, Debby Shanahan has been extolling the features of Clark Reservation, just south of Syracuse, and her difficulty in negotiating its spatial dimensions. Her account of guiding Sean Hogan to the location of the hart's tongue fern in our newsletter was amusing and alluring. Finally, Debby got her chance to show this unusual landscape to our chapter members. Unfortunately, I was the only one to arrive at the meeting place at the appointed time. We waited about ten minutes, and when no one else was in view, we three, Debby, Steve (the naturalist from the nature center), and I—headed off to find the colony of hart's tongue fern (*Phyllitis scolopendrium*). Neither Steve nor I had seen these plants before.

We walked close to the cliff edge, over gaps in the bedrock, skirting *Rhus radicans* and climbing over fallen trees, until we came to a point where two cliffs joined. Then it was down the steep hillside, Debby managing quite well with her foot brace and its clomp, clomp as she walked. The bottom was mucky, so we headed off to the right at the base of the slope, making our way through waist-high vegetation, feeling with our feet where our next step might be and then again over tree trunks. Finally, Debby spotted the first of the hart's tongue ferns. We pushed on, and there was the whole hillside of clump after clump of ferns with fronds ten to twelve inches long, some plants with fronds just emerging, some with fronds lying flat, exposing the rows of sporangia. What a magnificent site and sight! After oohing and aahing, we proceeded to the other side of the creek, stopping to admire a walking fern growing virtually in moss on the side of a boulder. All around grew the marginal shield fern and Goldie's fern. Suddenly, we come upon a magnificent clump of the glade fern, the narrow-leaved spleenwort

Across the creek, the habitat changed completely. We entered a wooded glen with plant after plant of blue cohosh, a few jacks-in-the-pulpit, white trillium, scattered plants of false Solomon's seal, a small clump of bishop's cap, and lots of wild ginger, some with leaves as big as dessert plates. We elected to hook up with the lake trail. Turning over a huge slab of wood, Steve found a spotted salamander and decided to take it back to the nature center. We finally came across maidenhair fern and a small colony of the oak fern.

We arrived at the creek flowing out of Green Lake, and there on the opposite bank were grove after grove of flowering fern, also known as royal fern, in full *flower*. I was sorely tempted to plow through the muck to get a close-up photograph. On the hillside on our right was the most abundant fern on the reservation, the berry bulblet fern, literally covering the entire hillside. Here we also found red baneberry and large colonies of wild sarsaparilla, including, at last, a plant with seeds galore. We spotted one that appeared to be the dwarf ginseng. Taking a low path, we missed the steps up to the top of the cliff. But then we found more walking ferns and could feel the cool rush of air out of numerous small caves. Retracing our trail, we located the ascending trail and began to climb the 182 steps. I did not count them, but Debby assured us that that was the number the CCC built back in the 1930s. Finally, back at the top, we got a cool drink of water and learned that someone had arrived, wishing to join us, after we started. But who that was will have to remain unknown, for he or she has yet to reveal an identity. Whoever it was surely missed a fine field trip!

Mid-Atlantic Fern Foray

When I learned there was going to be a fern foray in the east, my adrenaline started flowing and I immediately sent in my registration. It was billed as the Mid-Atlantic Fern Foray and was sponsored by the Hardy Fern Foundation and the Delaware Valley Fern & Wildflower Society. It was a five-day event, from Tuesday, July 9 through Saturday, July 13. There were eight regulars plus three hosts: Jack and Rose Marie Schieber, who were the foray's organizers, and Otto Heck. Three of the participants were from Seattle: Rob Leitner, Sylvia Duryee, and Sue Olsen (Sue spoke to our chapter several years ago). Catharine Guiles from Maine, John Scott from Pennsylvania, and Nels and Jean Maher from Owen Sound, Ontario, joined us as well. Both Catharine and John were recent contributors to the *Hardy Fern Foundation Quarterly*, and John Scott's Rockland Botanical Garden was on the foray. John was collecting forms of the Christmas fern, *Polystichum acrostichoides*, and I took a corkscrew form down that Toni Wilkinson had gotten from Yuri Orlov. The Mahers lead nature groups in Grey and Bruce Counties in western Ontario and have written three guides on the counties' ferns, orchids, and rare and endangered plants. When we met the Mahers, Jean was wearing a delightful and hilarious T-shirt showing "Nelson talking to the ferns." Depicted were maidenhair fern (*Adora mea*), walking fern (*Bootin alongus*), hart's tongue fern (*Extremis rudeus*), and sensitive fern (*Mucho afraidis*). Nels also had on a T-shirt, "The Canadian Fern Checklist," with thirty-seven of Nels's fern prints illustrated. Not normally a person who goes in for souvenir T-shirts, this was one I had to have. Mike and Sharon Rosenthal, knowledgeable naturalists, joined us for the trips to northern New Jersey and central Pennsylvania, and Jim Montgomery, of Berwick, Pennsylvania, was our guide in that state. Six of us stayed at a motel in Clinton, New Jersey, that thus became the jumping-off point for each day's adventure.

Our first foray was to northern New Jersey, with our first stop at Camp Bernie, a YMCA camp, to search for grape ferns. The Rosenthals, who had marked their location with sticks, made our search easier. Even so, other than the rattlesnake fern, *Botrychium virginianum*, they are small and easily overlooked. We added *B. lanceolatum*, *B. matricariifolium*, *B. simplex*, and *B. dissectum*, and I soon became able to identify them. *Botrichium oneidense* grows at that site, but we unable to find it.

Our second stop of the morning was at Oxford Furnace, an old lime kiln, which provided an ideal habitat for *Pellaea glabella* and *Woodsia obtusa*. At our next destination, the Andover railroad old right-of-way, we examined *Cystopteris bulbifera* and *C. tenuis* (which is very similar to *C. fragilis*, a species that does not occur in New Jersey). We found four of the spleenworts—maidenhair (*Asplenium trichomanes*), ebony (*A. platyneuron*), wall rue (*A. ruta-muraria*), and the walking fern (*A. rhizophyllum, Camptosorus rhizophyllus*), as well as Scott's spleenwort (*Asplenosorus ebenoides*), the hybrid between the ebony spleenwort and the walking fern. We also saw the purple and smooth cliff brakes, *Pellaea atropurpurea* and *P. glabella*, and *Polypodium appalachianum*, which differs slightly from *P. virginianum*, but you could not prove it by me.

Next, it was time for a wonderful picnic at Kittitiny Valley State Park—one of three organized by Rose Marie Schieber that we enjoyed during the week. We then explored the Sussex Branch Trail and the Paulinskill Trail, which was particularly abundant with ferns; more than thirty were recorded. We found a number of hybrids of the wood ferns. It was fun to see the experts analyze the fronds and the position of the sori to determine that one particular fern was a hybrid between *Dryopteris clintoniana* (itself a hybrid between *D. cristata* and *D. goldiana*) and *D. marginalis*.

The last stop of the day took us to the Delaware Water Gap. Some members of the group explored Dunfield Creek Trail while others headed up the Tammany Hill Trail, which offered a stunning view of the gap to the south. Our goal was to find *Cheilanthes lanosa* and *Woodsia ilvensis*. Find them we did, but they were all dried up from the lack of rain. I kidded Otto that he should have come up the day before and given them a good soaking to revive them.

On the second day, we traveled north to New York City and the New York Botanical Garden in the Bronx. We hoped that John Mickel and Robbin Moran, the senior curator and curator, respectively, of the garden's Institute of Systematic Botany, might be there, but they were out of town. Word had it that Robbin Moran was ferning in Costa Rica. The NYBG's native plant garden contains the Gordon Foster Fern Collection, which is also a good place to see *Dryopteris* hybrids, among them *D. x slossonae* (*D. cristata x D. marginalis*), *D. x dowellii* (*D. clintoniana x D. intermedia*), *D. x australis* (*D. celsa x D. ludoviciana*), and *D. x boottii* (*D. cristata x D. intermedia*). Following lunch at the garden's restaurant (which Sue Olsen forewent in order to go through the newly restored conservatory), we journeyed to Tarrytown, in Westchester County, where we saw the Lyndhurst fern garden. This relatively young collection, dating from 1989, grows under a canopy of yellow birch, *Betula alleghaniensis*. The raised beds are bordered with stone, and each bed is devoted to a particular genus—*Athyrium, Adiantum, Dryopteris, Polystichum, Cystopteris*, and so on. Gray Williams, who was our guide there, is responsible for the collection, and he and colleagues from the Taconic Gardeners Club regularly divide the ferns to create a massed effect. The *Polystichum braunii* was particularly striking, as was the clump of *Dryopteris pseudo-mas*. Gray has obtained plants from John Mickel and from the Norcross Wildlife Foundation in Massachusetts. Unfortunately, because John Mickel was out of town, we were unable to visit his own marvelous collection at his home in Westchester County.

On day 3, our group headed to southern New Jersey and the Pine Barrens. Our route was to take us through Fort Dix, but armed guards at the entrance said that civilians, even peaceable fern enthusiasts, were no longer welcome, so a detour was necessary. We stopped first at White's Bog, where our guide for the day, field botanist Linda Kelly, joined us, as well as three DVFWS members, Bill Bondinell, Donna Wilhelm, and Ellen Wilen. There, we found some nice specimens of Botrychium, but Otto, in spite of a noble effort, could not find the walking fern. We also found the adder's-tongue fern, *Ophioglossum vulgatum*. Driving along by the cranberry bogs, we spotted a huge clump of the marsh fern, *Thelypteris palustris*, growing in full sun. And along the roadside, there were sundews and pitcher plants in flower as well as the white-fringed orchid. The two chain ferns, *Woodwardia areolata* and *W. virginica*, were also found in the Barrens, as were *Azolla caroliniana* and two of the Osmundas, the royal and cinnamon ferns. The curly grass fern, *Schizaea pusilla*, was the big find on the boardwalk at Greenwood Forest Wildlife Management Area.

That evening, we drove to the home and garden of Jack and Rose

Marie Schieber in Holland, Pennsylvania, north of Philadelphia, for a delicious buffet dinner. Jack has an impressive fern collection, and his weed is *Dryopteris carthusiana*, which pops up all over the garden. A big expanse of *Adiantum capillus-veneris*, the southern maidenhair, was impressive and unbelievable; this species is rated zone 7 to 10. Equally impressive was an outstanding clump of the holly fern, *Polystichum braunii*. These ferns were grouped around their patio. In the beds in the main garden, there were more ferns. The one that caught my eye was *Arachniodes simplicior* var. *variegata*, with its lustrous dark-green fronds. Hardy to zone 6, it is well worth the attempt to grow it. On the other side of the greensward were *Cystopteris protusa*, the southern fragile fern, and *C. tenneseensis*, a hybrid between *C. protusa* and *C. bulbifera*.

On Friday, joined by John DeMarrais, we traveled to Pennsylvania through the Poconos, seeing *Rhododendron maximum* still in bloom in the woods bordering Interstate 80. Exiting at White Haven, we traveled to the state's newest park, Nescopeck, where park ranger Diane Madl greeted us. Walking down the road, Mike Rosenthal spotted a purple-fringed orchid in a damp locality. (John Scott pinpointed the site using his GPS.) But the Hartford, or climbing, fern, *Lygodium palmatum*, was the real find of the morning—acres and acres of them growing up through low-bush blueberries and even up the stem of a fly poison, *Amianthium muscaetoxicum*. From Nescopeck, we headed to Berwick, where Jim Montgomery joined us. Jim is coauthor with David Fairbrother of *New Jersey Ferns and Fern Allies*.[30] We crossed the Susquehanna and headed upland to Ricketts Glen State Park, which is almost due west of my hometown of Wilkes-Barre. There are twenty-one waterfalls in the park, the highest being Ganoga at ninety-four feet. The five- to seven-hundred-year-old hemlocks, *Tsuga canadensis*, are the other notable feature there. Alas, they are now in danger of dying because of the woolly algedid. A number of windstorms over the past forty years have toppled some of these giant trees. We only had time to walk a few hundred yards up the 3.5-mile trail that follows Kitchen Creek to Lake Jean and to explore the lower waterfall below the highway, but there we found *Polypodium appalachinum*, *Cystopteris tenuis*, and one lone

---

[30] Montgomery and Fairbrother, *New Jersey Ferns and Fern Allies.*

Asplenium rhizophyllum on the damp cliffs above the creek. By not ascending the trail, we alas missed seeing one of the southernmost sites of *Polystichum braunii*. This species, by the way, does not occur in New Jersey.

Instead, we drove uphill to an old railroad bed to see the club mosses, specifically, *Lycopodium obscurum*. Jim informed us that their spores are used in fireworks. We did not see *L. inundatum*, but we did see *Lycopodium clavatum*, *L. digitatum*, *L. tristachium*, and *L. annotinum*. Unfortunately, this area is over 2,900 feet in altitude and is subject to cool nights and even frost on occasion. Our next brief stop was at a lake, where Jim pointed out *Isoetes echinospora* growing in the shallows.

We then headed back by way of Sullivan Falls to see *Cystopteris fragilis*, which is rare in northern Pennsylvania. On the rocky hillside were huge patches of *Polypodium appalachianum*, some drying up from the drought. Sharon Rosenthal spotted *Gymnocarpium dryopteris*, oak fern, to add to our list. Then it was to a diner for dinner. Afterward, we made the long drive back to Clinton; we arrived after ten o'clock. (The last time I was in Ricketts Glen was in 1949 or '50 when a group from college went down for the day. That day, we walked and ran the entire seven miles and have a photo at the three-and-a-half-mile post to prove it!)

Our last jaunt was to the Morris Arboretum in suburban Philadelphia, where we were joined by Delaware Valley Fern and Wildflower members Tony and Carol Carbo and where Donna Wilhelm rejoined. Our guide there showed us the arborctum's Garden Railroad, the rose garden with its rock-garden wall, and their Victorian-style fernery, constructed in 1899 and restored and dedicated in 1994 as the Dorrance H. Hamilton Fernery. For perhaps a half hour, we left the world of temperate ferns and visited the tropics, admiring the fernery's specimens of cyatheas, blechnums, davallias, and other tropical beauties and discussing their care with curator Dianne Smith.

It was then time for lunch, followed by the trek to Mertztown, Pennsylvania (near Allentown), the location of John and Margaret Scott's Rockland Botanical Gardens. After a tour there of three hours, we had only begun to explore the Scotts' nine acres of woodland, let alone get more than a glance at their conifer collection. There were thirty-eight indigenous ferns in the woods, to which John has added sixty additional North American ferns and fern allies and about eighty exotic ferns, including numerous varieties of *Athyrium niponicum*, both painted and unpainted. There were three *Dryopteris* hybrids to which John has added eight more. John also has a collection of variant forms of *Polystichum acrostichoides*, some of which he got from Dr. Edgar T. Wherry with whom he studied. After a delicious dinner prepared by John and Margaret, it was time for the Clinton group to return to their motel and for me to head north for the four-hour drive home to Painted Post.

The author thanks Catharine W. Guiles for her editorial suggestions.

Oregon Gardens

Part of the annual meeting of the North American Rock Garden, hosted by the Emerald Chapter in Eugene, Oregon, was a tour of gardens. We began at the Sebring Rock Garden in the Alton Baker City Park. It is named in honor of Gene and Virginia Sebring, two of Emerald Chapter's charter members, and encompasses six thousand square feet. It was built in collaboration with the city that supplied the equipment to secure and place the giant rocks. It includes seven beds, each one of which is more or less devoted to plants from a specific region. This was a very fitting first stop on our bus tour. Next on our agenda was the garden of Dorothy and Myron Stahl. Situated on a small lot in town, it encompasses Dorothy's perennials, her canary aviary, Myron's rock plants, and two ponds. I have a nice slide of a terra-cotta goat filled with sedums. Maleah Spinell's garden is more spacious. The rock garden itself is quite new, surrounded by older perennial beds, a vegetable bed, and enormous delphiniums. The rock garden itself is a model of restrain, though this may change as the plants become bigger. A feature I admired was a cotoneaster splayed against a rock. She uses dark gravel, and her labels are painted black with the names inscribed, making them very unobtrusive. Scherer Delight was our luncheon stop at Carol and Tim Scherer's. Atop a hill overlooking the Oregon hills, it consists of several contrasting areas. The front garden is more formal, with impressive plantings. The patio garden is tastefully executed, while much of the woods and slope are more natural. Because these first two sites need daily watering, the native madrone, *Arbutus menziesii*, is in decline. They have recently created a dry slope for the madrone. Marietta and Ernie O'Byrne's nursery and garden was the highlight of the garden tours with so many different rooms in their garden it was hard to encompass it in one short visit. Our last stop was the garden of Maxine Rowan, which is completely different from any of the others. In a wooded setting, it is approached up a long driveway and on to a patio overlooking her sunny rock garden. It is completely fenced in to keep the deer from destroying the garden, and she and a friend are the sole gardeners. In addition to being a delightful garden, it abounds with artwork, whimsical birdhouses, and a well-organized work area.

On Sunday, Eve and Len Gottesman were kind enough to invite me to ride with them on the open garden visits. We headed up to Corvallis, an hour north of Eugene, with our first stop at Loren Russell's. His garden is definitely that of a plantsman. Curiously, he has a thing against conifers in the rock garden, but his deciduous shrubs are distinctly out of character. Linda Haygarth's garden was a visual delight and overall the best garden on the tour. It may have lacked the profusion of plants in O'Byrne's and the hominess of Maxine Rowan's, but the design, the pool, the rockwork, and the plants themselves were a delightful and satisfying blend. The main feature of Ray and Catherine Beard's garden was the large pond, complete with koi and waterfalls, excellently designed and executed. The final garden on Sunday was that of Bernard Levine. This was the most unusual garden from the metropolis bed to the four-season pavilion. It is an engineering marvel that protects the large patio area from rain. The overcrowded main garden is jam-packed with many unusual plants, all well-arranged, but overwhelming.

Colorado Gardens

In 1947 and 1948, I was a trail guide at Philmont Scout Ranch in Cimarron, New Mexico. The week after the Eugene meeting of the North American Rock Garden Society, there was a reunion of the

Philmont staff, with about a dozen from those early years planning to attend. What an opportunity to visit gardens in Colorado. Accordingly, on Monday, I flew from Eugene to Denver. Three gardens I knew I wanted to see were those of Gwen and Panayoti Kelaidis, Dick and Ann Bartlett, and Bob and Cindy Nold. The Kelaidis were not coming directly back from the Eugene meeting, but both the Bartletts and Bob Nold extended a warm welcome. Mary Hegedus from Fort Collins was at the meeting, and I arranged to go up there Tuesday morning. Mary has a lovely garden with two beds on either side of her front walk, plus plantings between the sidewalk and the curb. Apparently there was an attempt to require grass lawns and grass strips by the curb. Fortunately it was successfully resisted. Mary's backyard is a shady and restful garden with a handsome dry streambed, using polished black stones. Mary then took me over to Kirk Fiesler's LaPorte Avenue Nursery. Kirk has a large circular rock garden, an alpine house, and a couple of greenhouses. The plants he is growing looked great. From Kirk's, we drove up into the foothills to Pat Baker's garden. Her main garden is shaped like a cirque. Watering is a problem in Colorado, and Pat, being on a well, has a more restricted supply. It was then back to Denver and a visit to the Denver Botanic Garden (DBG). I have not seen many public rock gardens, only that of the Royal Botanic Garden in Edinburgh in the year we built our home and before I started gardening, but the Denver Rock Garden is extensive and must rank as one of the top rock gardens in the world.

Wednesday found me heading down to Littleton. I had called Clark Coe and Sandra Snyder and made arrangements. I was supposed to go to Sandra's in the morning and Clark's in the afternoon. Instead, I showed up at Coe's in the morning, and Clark graciously took time to show me their garden. It was one of the top gardens on my list, beautifully landscaped, beautiful use of rock, and scores of nice alpines, including his collection of Saxifrages. From there, I went to Hudson's, a relatively new garden with Andrew Pierce as director of horticulture and education. It consists of a series of gardens. The rock garden was designed by Panayoti and is only one of sixteen. It is not on the scale of Denver Botanic Garden, but situated to provide a variety of exposures. An impressive feature was a huge circular perennial bed and a large water garden with two volunteers up to their thighs weeding. I went on to see Sandra's garden, but she was not home so I had to be content to just wander and admire it by myself. I encountered a very impressive tall rock garden mound in the front of the house, lovely walls, and garden beds in back. Dick and Ann Bartlett's garden was next on my list. They had just gotten home late Tuesday night, and while Dick showed me around, Ann went off to do errands. Their backyard is one huge rock garden. One leads off the patio while another stretches the entire width of the yard. One side is a shaded area, and on the other, Dick is using flue liners filled with different soil mixes. On one side of the house and up against the house, they have built a large cactus garden. Another mound for a garden has been constructed on the other side of the house. Ann is relegated by choice or design to utilizing the front of the house for her gardens, which are largely shade gardens. It was an extremely interesting garden, and they were most hospitable hosts. Dick then led me over to Bob and Cindy's. We arrived only a few minutes before Bob got home from work. Bob Nold and Loren Russell are two of the more knowledgeable correspondents on Alpine-L while Cindy is a superb photographer, donating a number of slides to the slide collection. It was a pleasure to meet both of them. Bob grows a fantastic number of plants well. He is the gardener; Cindy is the weeder and the woodworker, having built all the garden structures. She is also a water colorist. They invited me to share a Mexican meal, and I gratefully accepted. It rained back in Denver that night. I hoped it had also rained in Lakewood at the Nolds'.

Thursday morning, I headed down to Colorado Springs. Having gotten an early start, I took a mountainous route that took me over a long section of unpaved road. First stop was Stan and Maxine Mesker's. Stan was off working at a golf course, but Maxine was expecting me. She offered me some iced tea, and we sat, toured the garden, and sat some more. The whole back is built up to the alley level with many choice plants. Very impressive was Stan's collection of the troughs he had made and a very unusual red lava rock planted with alpines. A friend from graduate school now lives in the Springs, and I had dinner and stayed the night with them. They have a view of Pike's Peak from their front yard. Friday found me heading south with a stop in Pueblo to see the garden of Karen and Bill Adams. I arrived earlier than expected, but Bill got home just a short time later.

He has a corner lot, and the entire corner out to the curb is where he has located his rock garden. The plants were impressive, but equally impressive was his rock work. He has used a gray stone that blends in beautifully. His crevices are the most natural looking I have seen. Later, he took me down to his nursery and greenhouse. As with Kirk Fieseler's, the plants are well grown. His nursery is Sunscapes Rare Plant Nursery. Either or both nurseries would be well worth ordering from.

Rocky Mountain High I

Fifty years ago, I had two of the best summers of my life. I was a trail guide at Philmont Scout Ranch in northeastern New Mexico. As a guide, I would lead expeditions from one end of the ranch to the other on an eight-day trek. These expeditions consisted of two leaders and twenty to thirty Scouts, who would come from sundry parts of the country. I had groups from Florida. Georgia, Ohio, Illinois, Missouri-Kansas, Kansas, Oklahoma, and other states as well. The Scouts carried their personal belongings, but burros, affectionately known as Rocky Mountain canaries for their melodious braying, carried food, utensils, and bedding. It was my responsibility to work with the leaders, to be in charge of the burros, and to oversee making camp and meals and breaking camp as we hiked from one campsite to the next. A trail guide was the most coveted position at Philmont; one got to be outdoors for three months, sleeping under the stars, communing with nature. A bonus was the opportunity to meet with and get to know many great leaders and wonderful Scouts as we forged bonds of friendship in our short time together.

I have the *Guide Book & Nature Record*[31] in which I checked off the rocks and minerals, trees, shrubs, wildflowers, birds, butterflies, and four-footed animals found on the ranch. An occasional bear was sighted, but I saw only scratches of their presence. Today, I understand they are commonly seen and food has to be stored out of their reach. Whitetail deer, mule deer, and elk were on the ranch, as were bison. Porcupine is a scourge, killing many pines

---

[31] *Guide Book & Nature Record* (Raton, NM: Daily Range, 1947).

in their voracious feeding. The only minerals not checked were limestone and marble. There was gold in them thar hills, and there were abandoned gold mines on the ranch. Ponderosa pine was prevalent in this land of little rainfall. Many other conifers were restricted in their range by altitude, with foxtail pine growing at 11,000 feet elevation. The West has few trees to provide fall color. Quaking aspen is one of the exceptions, and it forms large colonies, which I recently learned is one plant. It grows in a range of 6,000 to over 11,000 feet in elevation, in open and wooded areas and in dry mesas and wet stream banks. At that time, 173 wildflowers were listed as occurring at Philmont. Many of these were familiar to me, but others, such as Spanish bayonet and Indian paintbrush, were not. Others were the same genus but different species. Geraniums, gentians, columbines, and asters come to mind. I don't know whether it is still in print, but my guide to the native plants of the Rockies was *Meet the Natives*.[32] Plants are arranged by zone: alpine, subalpine, mountain, foothills, and plains. Within each zone, there are sections for trees, shrubs, and then herbaceous plants by color. There are also line drawings of some of the flowers. It is a really neat little wildflower guide.

More than one hundred birds have been observed at Philmont, but I had recorded just seventy in the guidebook. One I did not see on Philmont was the roadrunner, but an equally fascinating and unusual bird was the water ouzel. A familiar bird, but with different coloring, was the red-shafted flicker. We have our blue jay, but they had California, stellar, and pinon jays and the Clark nutcracker, as well as the canyon and rock wrens, western and mountain bluebirds, poorwill, canyon and green-tailed towhees, red-backed and gray-headed juncos, and broad-tailed and rufous hummingbirds. I always had a pair of binoculars with me, and I was further aided, as mentioned previously, by the gift of *A Field Guide to Western Birds*.

This summer, I am returning for a reunion. A dozen of us who were on the staff will be renewing friendships and reliving memories of those special years a half century ago. Next issue of *Screeches*, I just might share some of those memories with you.

---

[32] Pesman, *Meet the Natives*.

Rocky Mountain High II

In the last *Screeches*, I related my experiences some fifty years ago at Philmont Scout Ranch in New Mexico. I returned for a reunion in July where a dozen of us old-timers renewed acquaintances and memories of our times at this special place. Returning was a fellow troop member and Eagle Scout, Ed Carty. Ed and I lived on the same hill in north Wilkes-Barre. Both of us were avid birders on this Susquehanna flyway and did a number of Audubon Christmas bird censuses together. I can still remember getting a phone call from an excited Ed to come down and see the 'possum. This was in the early forties as they were extending their range northward. The third troop member, Wayne "Chief" Dietrick, was not able to attend. Two, whom I don't recall, from those early years also ended up working for Corning Glass Works. They were Brad Kinsman and Bill Hudson. With a staff of about one hundred, it was unusual that three from the same troop would be on the staff and that three of us would come to work for the same company.

The Big House, Waite Phillips's home, was the same, and the Tooth of Time had not changed. But the staff has grown from one hundred to more than seven hundred. The number of base and trail camps has quadrupled. The number of Scouts who have the Philmont experience is unbelievable, with groups confirmed two years in advance. Instead of trail guides, who would stay with a group for their trek, they now have rangers who spend only the first few days with a group. And despite this huge increase in programs, Philmont retains that wilderness feel, except around headquarters where there are tent cities for incoming Scouts and for outgoing Scouts. Back in the forties there was only an occasional car at headquarters, and now the parking lot looks like a mall lot.

There is a dark cloud on the horizon. The air force has earmarked several sites for low-level practice bombing runs. One of the sites on the list is Philmont. I cannot imagine being on the trail with my expedition and string of burros and have bombers roar several hundred feet overhead or to be on horseback when the bombers make their practice run.

On Sunday morning, a number of activities were offered. One was a hike up Wheeler Peak, starting from Eagle Nest. I had climbed

Wheeler fifty years ago, starting from Rayado. But climbing from 7,000 feet to 13,151 feet seemed a bit much for this old man. Instead, I opted for a nature walk up and around Uraca Mesa. During my two summers at Philmont, this was one trail I had not taken. The walk was led by a professor of botany at the University of Wyoming, who did his thesis work on the plants of New Mexico. It was great to get on the trail again, albeit for such a short time. There were a variety of habitats as we climbed from 5,000 feet to 6,000 feet and circled the mesa. Some of the plants I recognized; some I did not.

Before getting to Philmont, I was in Eugene, Oregon, at the annual meeting of the North American Rock Garden Society. The day programs were centered on field trips to the Western Cascades and garden visits. I requested moderate field trips, and the two trips assigned to me were listed as "easy to moderate." Each group was divided into a slow and a fast group, with yours truly opting for the fast group. Iron Mountain, at 5,455 feet (rising 850 feet in a mile), and Olallie Ridge on Horsepasture Mountain, at 5,660 feet (a two-mile hike to the summit), were a bit of a challenge for this septuagenarian. But it was well worth the huffing and puffing and the sweat. We were provided with a checklist booklet of Western Cascade plants, which listed the plants reported from all five sites of the field trips.

On our field trip to Iron Mountain, we first stopped at a falls near the headwaters of the McKenzie River—a rainforest with moss everywhere and a nice colony of *Linneae borealis*. On Iron Mountain, particularly impressive was *Gilia aggregata* (skyrocket), *Calchortus subalpinus*, and *Penstemon rupicola*. Along the way, there would be drifts of blue *Delphinium menzeisii*, red *Castilleja miniata*, and mustard-yellow *Mimulus breweri*. The views back through the low-lying clouds and those from the summit were stunning.

The trek up to the summit of Horsepasture Mountain first led through a forest with huge sweeps of vanilla leaf (*Achlys triphylla*) and bunchbery. We left the forest and continued up to the summit where around the old cabin site were German iris. We stayed at the top for some time, just admiring the natural rock garden with myriad clumps of *penstemon rupicola* and, nestled in a crack, a magnificent plant of the fern *Cheilanthes gracillima*. Coming back down, I had to stop and take slides of those stands of vanilla leaf and bunchberry. On both mountains, there were huge clumps of vigorous plants of our familiar false Solomon's seal and on Iron Mountain, its smaller cousin, starry Solomon's seal. We never saw large clumps of beargrass (*Xerophyllum tenax*), but what we saw was impressive. Then it was on to Quaking Aspen Swamp, an area that was denied the previous day's members because of the dense fog. The guide of the fast group took off with none of us looking eight feet above to see the trail sign that this was not the trail to the swamp. But we plunged blindly on until an hour and miles later, our leader finally came to the conclusion that we were not headed for the swamp. Consequently, we did not see shooting stars (*Dodecatheon jeffrey*), the other half of the meeting theme.

In between Eugene and Philmont, I visited gardens in Fort Collins, Denver, Colorado Springs, and Pueblo. Unfortunately, I did not have time to revisit Rocky Mountain National Park or to drive up Pikes Peak.

Best of the West Fern Excursion

British Pteridological Society and Hardy Fern Foundation

This was held two years after the eastern foray. The garden visits are listed first, followed by field trips. This also appeared in the quarterly of the Hardy Fern Foundation.

I grew up in the northeast, went to colleges in the northeast, and have spent my entire professional life in the northeast. I am used to our winters, rejoice in our all-too-brief spring, luxuriate in the summer, and glory in our fall foliage displays. Were I to relocate in the years left to me, it would be to the Pacific Northwest. Oh, the myriad of choices not only in ferns, but also in flowering plants as well (e.g., rhododendrons). Over the last two dozen years, I have had many occasions to travel in the northwest to meetings of both the North American Rock Garden Society and the American Rhododendron Society, and I went on the British Pteridological Society and Hardy Fern Foundation US Pacific Northwest Excursion.

Day 1: Garden Visits

I took an early morning flight from the Elmira-Corning airport to Philadelphia for a connecting flight to Seattle. On arrival, I found my way to Terry Lander Hall at the University of Washington, where we would be rooming. That evening, we were scheduled to visit the Betty Miller Botanical Garden in Shoreline, ten miles north of Seattle. The garden was the home of an Elisabeth Miller and is in an exclusive community on a bluff overlooking Puget Sound. A semicircular sitting area with a view of the lower garden and of Puget Sound adjoins the parking area. We proceeded to the lower garden where food and drink awaited us. Carolyn Miller, director/curator of the garden, and Richie Steffen, coordinator of horticulture, greeted us. Richie was to join us on several days during the week. A large deck provided a place to sit, relax, and enjoy views of the garden and the sound. Both sides of the path in this section were covered with *Epimedium perralchicum*. Many of these would be removed to provide a more diversified planting.

As we were finishing our repast, they offered a brief history of the garden and the life and accomplishments of Betty Miller. The house was built in 1949 on five acres. Betty, a consummate plantswoman, was a cofounder of the Northwest Horticultural Society, the Center for Urban Horticulture at the University of Washington, and the Betty Miller Horticultural Library. Betty died in 1994, but she established an endowment that enables the garden to continue and to evolve. Although there is no admission to the garden, tours are limited to respect the wishes of the neighbors.

From the parking area, we ascended up the steep slope to the modest-looking house. This is a west-facing slope that receives plenty of direct sun and is home to Mediterranean-type plants. A small lawn, bordered by a selection of trees (deciduous and coniferous), shrubs, flowering plants, ferns, and grasses, provides one of the few level areas in the entire garden. We then proceeded to the back of the house where the tall firs provided shade in marked contrast to the slope below the house. At the corner was *Cornus kousa* in full bloom. Here, Richie said, was the collection of hepaticas that were spectacular in the spring when in bloom. Among ferns, such as *Adiatum aleuticum* "Subpumilum" were planted numerous dwarf plants. I was impressed by a large Sargent's weeping hemlock and by a variegated dogwood in this small area. Proceeding up the hill, we entered the woodland garden and viewed a striking specimen of *Polystichum setiferum* "Plumosomultulobum." Of the hundred plus ferns and cultivars in the garden, I recognized only a small percentage. There was one large bed of *Blechnum penna-marina*, a fern that, unfortunately, I am unable to grow. A plant of *Polystichum munitum* was spectacular with the western sun lighting up the tall, erect fronds. There were familiar ferns, such as *Gymnocarpium dryopteris*, albeit growing more lustily, and *Osmunda japonica*, bearing a resemblance to *Osmunda regalis*. While the more ardent fern enthusiasts concentrated on ferns, my gaze was constantly diverted to the flowering plants, such as a huge plant of *Smilacina racemosa* with berries about to ripen. Did I read someplace that this was a tetraploid? I was also taken by a large mass of ground-hugging saxifrage with delicate white flowers. The paths wandered back and forth through this hillside garden. Log rounds, covered with black fish netting and growing with mosses, were used on the path—a most interesting and effective solution. In one area, a late-blooming rhododendron was in flower.

I felt we could have wandered for hours through the woodland garden, the gardens around the house, and the lower garden and still we would not have seen everything. And to see the garden in the spring when the hepaticas were in bloom and in the fall when the maples were ablaze with color made me wish I lived in the northwest. But the dinner bell was ringing and we had to board the cars for the drive past Green Lake to Ivar's Salmon House. There we were ushered to a private dining room overlooking Lake Union. Following a delicious dinner of their salmon barbecued over an alder-wood fire, Bors Vesterby outlined his photographic key for identification of the ferns of the state of Washington. It was now midnight eastern time and my concerns of nodding off did not materialize, the talk being of such absorbing interest. Following the talk, we headed back to Lander Hall and a most welcome sleep.

Day 3: Sylvia Duryee

At 8:00 a.m., Jerry was there with a bus waiting for this motley crew for an 8:30 a.m. departure time to see members' gardens. First up was the garden of Sylvia Duryee. Pulling up to the garden, I saw this nine-foot-high holly hedge with an arched entrance and a swinging gate, great portent of what was inside the gate. The walk leading through the gate to the house was a pebbled concrete lined with brick. The arched entrance reflected the arch in the front entranceway. The courtyard garden was massed with ferns and perennials—including several tall thistles, adding a surprising note. The shrubs and trees (both deciduous and evergreen) practically hid the house. In any other garden, this would be a sign of neglect, but there it was artfully arranged and pruned to present a pleasing composition. This was a person who obviously loved plants in all their variety, although with close to one hundred varieties, ferns played a major role in her landscaping. As if to emphasize this role, a large *Dicksonia fibrosa* tree fern was off to the left of the foundation. The trunk was four feet tall, and the fronds added another six feet to its height. Sylvia had wrapped the trunk to provide winter protection.

In the front border, there was a huge clump of *Adiantum venustum* that seemed to go on and on and then a six-foot-tall *Blechnum chiliense*. To the left was a sweep of lawn with undulating edges that swept around the side of the house to the back beds with trees as background. They were so tall that the neighboring houses were almost invisible. Shrubs were faced off with ferns and flowers. Toward the back border, there was a shady nook with Arisaemas and other shade-loving plants. A tall, irregular boulder with little pockets of moss made a dramatic statement. Off the side porch was a handsome gnarled pine in a raised bed. Other plants that caught my attention were a familiar friend, *Osmunda regalis*, looking very royal indeed at six feet, a *Doodia media* with a several reddish fronds, a five-foot-tall *Dryopteris wallichiana*, a big clump of *Gymnocarpium oyamense*, and a lovely blue gentian planted between two rocks. Walking around the back of the house, I came across Sylvia's workbenches, and in a corner bed, there were some tall Arisaemas.

The courtyard garden was a delightful dense mélange of shrubs, trees, ferns, and low, medium, and tall flowering plants, contrasting with the open lawn area on the east side of the house. The courtyard beds on both sides of the curving path to the front door were filled with an assortment of plants. Carefully placed in these beds were selected rocks and driftwood that accented the plantings. Narrow stone paths comprised of irregular stepping-stones led off the front walk, giving access to these beds. A heuchera with bronze foliage contrasted with a white flowering plant. Low-growing plants, such as *Dryas octopetela*, were cheek to jowl in these beds while thistle plants and tall Arisaemas tower above them. A tree rhododendron provided accent to the front corner of this garden room. It was a delight to see the design and lushness of her garden. It was a perfect beginning to the other private gardens that we were about to see.

Sue Olsen's Garden: Bellevue

From Sylvia's, we headed east to Bellevue to be enchanted by a triad of gardens, beginning with that of Sue Olsen. The house and garden were constructed on a hilly lot. At the bottom of the driveway was the house number backed by a lovely and lacy *Acer palmatum*. On the high side of the driveway, Sue had planted some annuals to fill the spot that in the fall would be ablaze with cyclamen, some with corms three to four inches in diameter. And, of course, there were ferns, notably *Pyrrosia shearii*, sited next to a large rock. Ferns surrounded another rock that had a small basin carved out for water. At the top of the driveway was the carport and a small foundation planting, crowded with fern enthusiasts trying to identify each and every fern. To the right of the front door, there was a raised section with containers of maples and other plants. On the other two sides of the carport were more ferns and plants in the ground and in containers. As we skirted around to the back of the house, to the left was a corner planted with ferns and, yes, more maples. To the right were more ferns and rhododendrons, planted in tubs sunk into the ground—a new concept to me.

At the back of the house, in the corner, we noted the difference between *Athyrium nipponicum* "Ghost" and *A. n. Pictum* Silver Falls. Other ferns that particularly caught my eye were *Athyrium yokoscense*, *Dryopteris crispifolia*, and a magnificent specimen of *Polystichum setiferum Herrenhausen*. To us easterners, Sue pointed out *Pellea glabella* in a round orange ceramic pot, along with *Botrychium virginianum*. The back was terraced off with timbers, creating a lovely concrete pebbled terrace. Above the terrace, there was a large rhododendron ready to bloom shortly after we left. Everywhere we went there were refreshments; the drinks, especially on the hot days, were welcome. At the back of the patio, there was a grated bench holding dozens of plants, mostly maples but also one *Arisaema*. Next to it was a large, eight-foot cut-leaf maple, making a perfect mound of foliage. At the top of the lot, a narrow terrace held a hoop house filled with ferns in all sizes. The bank next to the house was planted with trees, including one maple with gorgeous red leaves. At bottom of the bank, there was a sweep of lawn bordering the house. Sue's attached propagating house is a must for everyone to inspect. Surrounding the small patio were still more plants in tubs and a large tree surrounded by ferns at its base.

Lan Bradner's Garden: Bellevue

The garden was entered via the carport and through a delightfully designed wrought-iron gate. We were immediately confronted with a large stone wall at the base of which were container plants and in the corner a magnificent expanse of *Adiantum venustum* and my favorite hemlock, *Tsuga canadensis* "Cole's Prostrate." On top of the wall were a variety of ferns and grasses, providing a pleasing contrast in form and in color. More rock walls bordered the patio, and in the middle of the patio was a raised bed. With the shade of the tall firs, the flagstone patio, the planting area above the patio, and the small pool, this was a very pleasant and restful garden, and I immediately felt at home in it. But unlike my own garden, it was very neat and well maintained with the dark mulch adding to the restfulness. The waterfall and pool, surrounded by boulders, ferns, a hosta with huge leaves, and *Asarum europaeum* with its dark-green glossy foliage, particularly attracted me. The ibis and the crocodile added a nice touch, as did an unusual wood sculpture. But the nicest touch was the inscribed stone, "How Lovely Is the Silence of Living Things." The planting of *Gymnocarpium dryopteris* in front complemented the setting.

The patio was a very pleasant spot to sit and enjoy the setting while quenching one's thirst and indulging in some delicious biscotti, B. HFF Munitum and B. HFF Adiatum, daughter Kris's original recipes created in honor of the 2003 BPS HFF tour. There was the raised bed to explore and to admire as well as the rhododendrons, ferns, and hostas in the planting bed above the rock wall. Suddenly, I realized that the tree I was sitting under was *Acer japonicum acontifolium*, one of my favorites of the Asian maples. This towered above me and made me wish I could give my two-foot tree growth hormones. Again and again, there were massive clumps of ferns in addition to the *Adiantum venustum, Phyllitis scolopendrium, Dryopteris affinis* "Crispa Gracilis," *Athyrium niponicum*, both green and Pictum, and *Blechnum spicant* to name just a few. The upper level was lawn until last summer when it was torn up, irrigation installed, and a flagstone terrace created. Here the ferns had not had a chance to fill in, but when they did, I hoped they'd invite me for another visit. Here on this terrace, there was a lovely spreading green-leaved Japanese maple in an attractive brown oblong ceramic container. Another tall ellipsoidal container held an erect burgundy-leaved Japanese maple. Oh, and there was an eight-foot-tall *Rhododendron* "Aladdin" in bloom, much too tender for zone 5. Then my eye caught a rock with a bowl hewn out with five stone islands in the tranquil sea.

At that time of year, Lan's garden was essentially a foliage garden with ferns and hostas playing a dominant role. The hostas were in bloom, providing color, as did a large fuchsia, a pink-flowering shrub, and a few other flowering plants. To give us a taste of what the garden was like in other seasons, Lan handed out a small photo album, showing her Matllija poppy, her tree peony with its sixty-five blooms, her *Iris prismatica*, and the seed pods on *Iris foetidisima*. Fall photos included the deep red of *Acer palmatum osakazuki*, the glowing orange of *Acer japonicum acontifolium*, and the golden yellow of her *Ginkgo biloba*. Then at the farewell banquet, she handed out final photos she had taken of our visit to her delightful garden.

I think I might have been the only one in the group who looked at the plantings at the front entrance. There were planting pockets between the steps and the house. On the other side, a tall tree lent accent, and next to it was a low-spreading Japanese maple with dark-green and burgundy leaves. A flowering shrub, several groupings of ferns and hostas, and several boulders completed the planting.

Walking around and up to a landing, I discovered a couple of raised beds with flowers and vegetables. This was Lan's sunny garden, and in addition to the raised beds, there were clumps of ornamental grasses, ferns, and a large trough backed by two large narrow firs.

Pat and Marilyn Kennar's Garden

Our final stop on this four-course feast of gardens was at the garden of the Kennars, Pat and Marilyn. To the left, there was a four-foot-tall hedge and behind it a taller slatted fence and a Japanese-style gate to a small and intimate courtyard garden. One of the first things that caught our eyes as we entered the courtyard was an unusual and attractive tic-tac-toe set of frogs and dragonflies. Immediately, Pat Acock and Robert Sykes had to play a game. There was so much to see in this small space that it was hard to gather it all in. To the left was a small, L-shaped pool, lined by large square stones. There were goldfish in the pool and a fountain providing the sound of running water. Then, of course, there were the ferns, such as *Arachniodes simplicior*, as well as the requisite *Athyrium niponicum* "Pictum" and *Adiantum venustum*, both in large ceramic pots. In another container, there was a nice specimen of *Asplenium trichomanes* and a lovely *Selaginella*. On the far side was a raised bed, containing various ceramic containers planted with a variety of plants. There was a round white bowl with a small Asian maple underplanted with ferns, including *Lygodium japonicum*. To the right was a magnificent specimen of *Adiatum aleuticum*. By the pool was a finely dissected *Acer palmatum*, surrounded by some tall ferns. In another corner dwelled carvings of a hippopotamus and a manatee, with still more ferns in the background. There in the courtyard was a woodland garden in this shady nook. In the corner of the house were ferns but also hosta, as arum, and arisaema, the *Arisaema ringens* looking particularly happy. On the opposite side of the courtyard garden, backed by a fence was another planting crammed with flowering plants and ornamental grasses.

As we went around to the back of the house, we discovered a large deck loaded with planters of every description and benches and chairs to sit in and enjoy the garden. Sitting on one of the benches was Martin Rickard, pouring himself a soft drink. The deck extended outside the railing, providing room for more plants. There were steps off the deck, leading to the garden below. On both sides of the steps were large clumps of *Polystichum munitum*. About the only place where nothing was growing was under the deck and that only for the lack of light. But there were scores of plants in front, a handsome placement of rocks and gravel, and an old leather belt that at first glance appeared to be a snake. There was a good-sized lawn, rimmed with plants of all descriptions. The bed in front of the "potting shed" was ablaze with flowers in white, pink, yellow, blue, and rose. Looking up, there was a sign on the front of the deck announcing that this was the "Palais de Poulet" with demi-douzaine poulets in residence. In addition to the potting shed, there was a greenhouse, and I captured Peter Meegdes as he emerged from an inspection tour. The lawn swept down with more beds on the side, separating the lawn from the shady grove. What a pleasure it must be for Pat and Marilyn to sit out on their deck and survey this wondrous scene.

To the far left, near the back of their lot, there was a path leading into the grove, and to get there, one had to cross a bridge constructed of stone blocks with moss growing in the cracks. This was just one of two such bridges. What a clever way to enter from one part of a garden into another. Inside this garden there were not only plants to enchant one, but a moss-covered Hobbit's home with a stone front, a handsome wood door, and two small windows. The scene even included a mailbox. In another spot was Pat's moss garden, his "MOSS–O–LEUM." Then I came upon a hanging birdbath with four birds perched on the rim. Were these four birds carved out of one stone or two? Another path led beside a carved dump truck carrying a potted plant. I hoped the driver of the truck was not potted. Hanging from one tree in this glade was a hanging fern basket lined with sphagnum moss. And then somewhere in this amazing garden, I came upon a very aptly named *Cardio giganteum* that must have been ten feet, all with large glossy green leaves. And everywhere there were ferns and more ferns, many of them not known to me, but it is always a delight to see these primitive nonflowering plants growing with such abandon.

Day 4: The Ridge Garden

Ilga Janson's and Michael Dryfoos's

I had little clue what was to await us as we walked up the steep driveway and entered the garden through a wooden portal, guarded by two lions. What an incredible site and sight, and to think that it was created in only seven years. The hundreds of fifty-year-old rhododendrons and other mature plantings in the garden belied its age. Oh, to come back in the spring when the rhododendrons were ablaze with color! Their home, blending into the landscape, sat on the ridge overlooking the koi pond. Feeding the pond were a series of waterfalls that tumbled down between huge boulders with mosses, ferns, and hostas softening the edges. The slope from the house to the pond was planted with white and blue hydrangea, ferns, hostas, and ornamental grasses. Large screen structures helped to focus one's view and shield the pump house and other distractions from disturbing the view of the plantings. Bordering the pond was a joglo (or gazebo), a one-hundred-year-old Javanese teak house with carvings on the ceiling and side panels. A pair of curious chairs in the shape of hands provided seating in the joglo. The deck provided access to the koi pond. Ilga demonstrated how one could be kissed by the koi and several members of our group were kissed by the koi as they fed the fish.

Ilga then led us on a tour of the garden. We came upon a sitting area paved with a gray brick and furnished with a stone bench, chairs, planters, and a shrine-like statue. The path leads down past Hotei, the laughing Buddha, behind a collection of round, smooth, river stones and flanked by a rhododendron and ferns. We next came upon the bell tower, containing a massive Japanese gong. Throughout the garden, there were haikus, sculptures, and sitting areas—each one different and all with an Asian flavor. One of these sitting areas was under the rose arbor, a roofed structure providing protection from the noonday sun and the occasional shower. Provided with both a stone and wooden bench, the floor was paved with brick in a circular pattern. Then suddenly there was the tree house, two stories high and adorned with colored banners. There at the top was one of our group gazing down on us. Of course, we all had to go up, restricted to four at a time. On the top deck, there was a bed with red, orange, and purple bedding and an intriguing, brightly colored cylindrical silk sleeve. A small alcove contained an Indian sculpture and Oriental rug. Farther along, we came to another sitting area. Blue-glazed pottery with a large variegated hosta, flanked by ferns, provided color. Behind was a slatted wooden screen. On the screen was a large, intriguing sculpture that might or might not have been a plant. The final resting spot on our outward journey was the "room with a view," a three-sided wooden enclosure open to the sky. A group of windows overlooked a steep drop-off. Rattan chairs and benches provided seating. And always, there were flowers in glazed pottery providing the ambiance. On our return, we came to a large sitting area with a replica of a Lutyens bench, large planters, and a large, bright ceramic fish. This area was paved with red brick and large stones. A small resting area was paved with irregular stone, with creeping plants filling the cracks. On the hillside among ferns and rhododendrons was their moss garden, with large stones covered with a soft green moss. There were about a dozen resting places throughout the garden, each one distinct with different benches and paving amenities. A Vietnamese Buddhist sculpture dominated one attractive alcove. Scattered throughout were sculptures (e.g., a Tachi-gata Japanese lantern and decorative pottery, such as an orange vessel with a lizard emerging). At the top of the driveway was a rock wall, completely covered by low-growing herbs. Leading off to the right was an entry arbor that led to the Garnesha fountain, an upright glass and wooden sculpture flowing with water. Beyond that was Ilga's alpine house with both elevated and platform beds, containing a variety of alpine plants. I kept wandering off, seeing more and more and still not seeing it all. Two things that caught my eye on my final pilgrimage were the walkway panels and a tile flooring sculpture depicting koi in an Escher-like pattern. And then it was time to go, and Robert Sykes was granted the privilege to ring the gong, announcing our imminent departure.

Henry's Plant Farm, Snohomish, Washington

When we arrived, we walked through a large greenhouse with table after table containing ferns, ferns, and more ferns, a prelude to what we were to see over the next several hours. Henry's dated back thirty years when Henry Mollgard moved his greenhouses from south Seattle to the present location in Snohomish. The Nashes purchased the business in 1982, and under their ownership, it expanded to 130,000 square feet (three acres) under glass, poly, and dynaglass and another two acres of outside production. They specialized in producing plants in volume for greenhouse growers. In addition to growing some six-dozen varieties of ferns, they also grew a large variety of herbs, annuals, perennials, groundcovers, begonias, and flowering and foliage houseplants. They also produced their Storytellas African violets, as did propagators in Germany and Canada. Some of their plants were grown for the local market. Most of their plants were contracted for.

After a brief introduction to their operation, we split up into smaller groups and began our respective tours. Our first stop was the greenhouses that contained their stock plants. It was a joy to see such robust and healthy ferns. After the spores were gathered, the plants were given a haircut. The spores were sown into flats, yielding almost three hundred sporophytes. We saw flat after flat of trays with the sporophytes and more flats where they developed their first fronds. We watched as some of the workers plucked out the sporelings and transplanted them, seventy-two to a flat. Occasionally rogue ferns had to be removed. When the ferns had developed sufficiently, they were shipped to the grower. In the case of Canadian growers, they picked them up in their own trucks. Finishing our tour, we were treated to a great repast. After lunch and before departing, we had a chance to wander a bit on our own. I saw row after row of hoop houses and greenhouses, filled with some of the other plants they grew. Outside there was flat after flat of both foliage and flowering plants, the latter making large drifts of white and pink and yellow.

Day 6: Elandan Gardens, Bremerton, Washington

The bus picked us up at our dorm and drove us down to the piers to catch the ferry to Bremerton. Once on the ferry, we piled out of the bus. Some went for coffee; others went up on deck to view the Seattle skyline as we waited for the ferry to cast off. Looking to the west, we could see the islands across the waters and behind them the Olympic Mountains, some marked with snow. After an hour-long ferry ride, we boarded the bus and disembarked. On the drive, we passed the Bremerton Navy Yard and traveled around the end of the inlet. We passed the entrance to Elandan and had to backtrack.

When we arrived, owner/designer Dan Robinson was not there. To the right of the shop was a Japanese maple atop a small rise with a waterfall cascading into a shallow pond, the bottom covered with a large, flat, and rounded stone. As we awaited Dan's arrival, we milled about in the shop. Joy Neal found a fantastic black hat and modeled it for us. There was a collection of bonsai trees for sale on three benches under a shed. What appeared to be a nursery outside made some of us wonder why we had stopped there. There were some interesting plants, but it was disorganized and sections looked junky. At the garden entrance, there was a huge rock resting on three large boulders. Atop the rock was a dead and gnarled tree. Another was an eight- to ten-foot-high narrow stone sculpture. We learned later that these were the work of Dan's son, Will Robinson. There were some handsome, good-sized Japanese maples and then a cypress, the trunk after about eight feet assuming a forty-five-degree angle. Certainly, it was not my style. Scattered about in haphazard fashion were some huge pieces of driftwood. Still awaiting Dan's appearance, I wandered out the rear door and found myself in a veritable paradise. Here was the bonsai garden! This huge garden overlooked the water and was filled with myriad trees of all sizes, trained to perfection. There were huge rocks tastefully placed; an immense trunk and roots of a dead tree; tall, dark, thin weathered trunks; and bleached trunks, all adding up to a dramatic wholeness. One Japanese maple that caught my eye had a large, elongated boulder for a container. In scattered locations throughout the garden were scores of bonsai in brightly colored containers. In a sitting alcove overlooking the water, perched on a table made of stone, was a three-foot-tall bougainvillea with a massive trunk. We learned from Dan that this was bought in Florida as a ten-foot tall tree. It was chopped down to four feet, the resulting sprouts trained, and the upper trunk split. The day we were there, it had scattered blossoms, but it must have been spectacular when covered with bloom. Many of Dan's aged-looking bonsai were created in the same manner. A twenty-foot-tall *Acer palmatum* was cut down to five feet and later reduced to two feet. (This must have been the one planted in the elongated boulder.)

Walking along, I came to a shallow pond with more bonsai, one an ancient-looking tree with a thick, bleached, and gnarled trunk in a round, shallow dish and beyond it a taller but similar tree with a massive trunk, which tapered to a pencil point, planted on a huge two- to three-foot-high boulder. Stretching across the pond were two large logs resting on a boulder in the middle. Growing out of the larger log were two plants. A dramatic accent was a grouping of five upright boulders in the pond, the tallest about five feet. A small patch of water lilies added to the effect. Another solitary boulder sat nearby.

Dan and Martin Rickard had a long discussion on an unusual specimen of *Polypodium glycyrrhiza* that Dan discovered in Oregon. Martin advised Dan to name and publish the name, thus establishing priority.

There were several tables down by the water, and that was where we ate our box lunches. On one side were a half dozen large pieces of driftwood that Dan had found and brought to his garden. On the other side was a grouping of four upright stones with round boulders perched on top. At another spot, there was a triangular carved stone with a blue circle in the center. What it represented I do not know. Before leaving, I wandered around some more and discovered a small, round pond, surrounded by small, round stones and fed by a stream flowing over stones. Then it was time to board our bus for our next stop, the Rhododendron Species Botanical Garden, which housed the Hardy Fern Foundation plantings and propagation facilities.

Rhododendron Species Botanical Garden: Federal Way, Washington

Steve Hootman, codirector of the Rhododendron Species Foundation, greeted us as we arrived. Our first stop was the propagation facilities for the HFF. Two of our group, Michelle Bundy and Becky Reimer, were responsible for the propagation. In addition to seeing the fern facilities, we also got a chance to view the propagation facilities for the Rhododendron Species Foundation. As a member of both, it was great to see where the ferns and rhododendrons I got originated. In one of the hoop houses, there was an array of mature ferns ready to be planted in the garden. There were some beautiful plants of *Dryopteris sieboldii*, but according to John Mickel, it seemed doubtful they would survive in my garden, but *D. tokyoensis*, another handsome fern, would be a welcome addition. In one of the rhododendron houses, there was a flowering vireya with long, tubular red flowers. After we left the propagation area, Steve took us on a tour of the garden. One of the first ferns to catch my eye was *Dryopteris wallichiana* with large, arching fronds five feet tall. Then there was a large clump of *Dryopteris sieboldii* dashing my spirits because I could not duplicate it in my garden. Next, we came upon dozens of pitcher plants, *Sarracenia minor*. We traversed the alpine garden with one area carpeted with a low-growing groundcover with attractive purple blossoms and a clump of a striking primula. Blood grass lent a touch of red to the landscape overtowering a planting of *Antennaria dioica*. No rock garden would be complete without dwarf evergreens, and there were a couple *Tsuga canadensis*. Next we came upon a massive planting of *Adiantum aleuticum subpumilum*, which I would die for, nestled between two boulders. Not to be outdone was an equally large clump of a Washington native, *Penstemon procerus tolmiei*. Another dramatic clumping was a Himalayan gaultheria. Moss-covered paths meandered through this hillside with plantings of rocks, ferns, shrubs, trees, and alpine plants in a harmonious whole. But, back to the ferns. In absolutely every garden, we had seen extensive masses of *Adiatum venustum* and the RSF was no exception. Here was a mat that must be fifty square feet in size. Oh what I would give to see such a mass of the Himalayan maidenhair in my garden! (This fall, I purchased two more plants to try to simulate the effect I have seen in so many gardens.) Equally desirable is saxifrage, making a most attractive groundcover simply covered with tiny white flowers. With the formal tour finished, we were free to explore on our own. In the planting area by the office was a most desirable rhododendron, *R. forrestii forrestii*, but it was much too tender for a zone 5 garden. Two handsome ferns in this planting were *Arachniodes simplicior* var. major and *Cyrtomium macrophyllum*. Could I grow them? Mickel rates them to zone 6. I grow *C. falcatum*. These two were certainly worth a try as was *Blechnum penna-marina* and *B. spicant*, rated to zone 5. I had only managed to have them die on me twice, so would a third try be successful?

Strolling back to our pickup area, I came upon a spectacular clump of the Asian mayapple, *Drysosma pleinthe*, and a little while later an unusual hosta, *H. kikutii* var. *caput-avis*. Then there was a vast expanse of a low-growing rhododendron, *R. calostrotum* var. *keleticum*, unfortunately much too tender for me to even attempt. But then there was a familiar friend, *Mitchella repens* but covering such a large area that it was unbelievable. What a sight that would be when in bloom or when covered with its red berries. Truly, they are red giants in a green sky.

Pacific Rim Bonsai Collection

The Rhododendron Species Botanical Garden is home not only to the Hardy Fern Foundation but also to the Pacific Rim Bonsai Collection. The last time I was there during a Rhododendron annual meeting, our time at RSF was too short to see not only the rhododendrons and ferns but the bonsai collection as well. This day, we had ample time, but as with any garden visit, we could never see everything even by retracing our steps. And in one day, we had seen two superb and excellent bonsai collections, one in a garden setting and the other displayed as in an art museum.

Day 8

Another ferry ride, this time to Bainbridge Island. As we left, we looked back to see Seattle's Space Needle. Our first stop was the local library.

Bainbridge Island Library and Japanese Garden

What a surprise to learn that this attractive low library was surrounded by not only a fern garden but also a perennial garden and a Japanese garden. No formal time was devoted to exploring the perennial garden, but we learned that the Japanese garden was dedicated and maintained by the local Japanese community. What a wonderful community gift. We entered the garden through a gate.

The paving was irregular flagstone carefully fitted together. There were mounds on either side of the stones planted with trees, dwarf evergreens, shrubs, moss, low groundcovers, and an occasional boulder. Numerous haiku verses in Japanese and English were tastefully placed throughout the garden. The path then opened up to a large area. To the right, a large raised area that abutted the library was lined with large boulders. A couple of tall trees dominated the raised bed. At the corner of the building, there was a tall, upright stone flanked by a pine tree and a small, red-leaved Japanese maple. Across the patio, there were two sculpted playful-looking otters, one standing and the other in repose. Across this patio, a path led through a gate and around the building to the fern garden. Large tall windows in the library looked out upon a pool fed by a small waterfall. The gutters led to a chain suspended over the pool. Large boulders and a couple of contorted pines completed the picture.

Fern Garden

Passing through the Japanese garden, we came to a shady area at the back of the library and the fern garden designed and installed by the Hardy Fern Foundation president. A ramp led down to the children's library. What an attractive entrance the children had, with dozens of *Polystichum munitum* on either side of the walk. There was just a mass of greenery under the canopy of the trees. To my mind, the varied shades of green and the difference in growth habit of ferns was not tiring. But still, the use of stone, particularly upright stone, in the garden provided a nice contrast. Also providing contrast were the remains of a partially burned trunk, as well as the trunks of the living trees. A low-spreading gnarled pine at the far end of the garden was striking. But all was not ferns. Several huge gunneras were planted under some willows and lent a nice contrast with their huge leaves and flower-scape.

There were several clumps of hart's-tongue fern, *Phyllitis scolopendrium*, with some of the fronds being crested. A discussion ensued as to whether it was stable. Every other garden we visited had large extents of *Adiantum venustum*, but in this garden, we understood that it had slowly died out. Strange, but maybe not so strange. If plants don't like a particular spot, they decline. Move them a few feet, and they will probably thrive. Some of our eastern ferns, (e.g., *Dryopteris goldiana*) do not take kindly to the Northwest. Why?

There were benches for sitting, reading, relaxing, or just enjoying the serenity of the garden. A newly constructed gazebo had been erected in the garden and would make an ideal place for storytelling.

Jocelyn Horder's Garden

After lunch in Pouslbo, we boarded the bus and headed for our next garden visit at Sylvia Duryee's sister's. Although Jocelyn had difficulty walking, she graciously welcomed us to her lovely home and garden. Both sisters had two passions, gardening and sailing. And what an ideal location for someone who loved both! A single-story brick house with a small alcove at the entrance awaited us as we walked down the driveway from the bus. Both sides of the driveway were filled with trees, shrubs, ferns, grasses, and flowers. What an inviting entrance to a home. The first thing that captured my eye was a small pool, fed by a small waterfall and bordered by large, moss-covered boulders. A small fern was growing in the moss on the boulder, and a large *Polystichum munitum* provided a backdrop to the waterfall. An azalea plus other bushes completed the inviting scene. To the left of this delightful picture was a reddish-leaved Japanese maple, pruned to display its twisted branches.

The water from this pool flowed under the driveway, emerging on the opposite side. The bottom of the stream was covered with flat stones, and water plants floated on the surface. The scene was very restful, in part because of the shade provided by trees and because of the pleasing contrast of foliage and shades of green provided by the grasses, mosses, shrubs, and trees. Boulders of various sizes were tastefully placed, complemented by a tall, thin piece of driftwood. The house side was just a mass of greenery with bushes growing cheek to jowl but retaining their distinctive habit.

The house sits in a small inlet with a view of the Olympic Mountains as a backdrop. As I walk around the house my eye is taken by a tall blanched trunk of a long dead tree with two lower branches bending up and four higher branches bending down. Beyond the tree, closer to the water is a small lighthouse built out of cobblestones. Moored in the water is a sailboat with its mast adding a third dimension to the scene. This is the real front of the house with floor to ceiling windows providing a view of the front garden, the inlet and the mountains. Not a bad life to lead. On one side is a rock garden with masses of color, a half dozen shades of green as well as white and yellow from the foliage and pink, red, orange and shades of purple from the flowering plants with a few boulders for accent. Tucked next to one of these boulders is a sedum covering an area of several square feet. The left side of the front garden is given over to taller plants among them a yellow-foliaged juniper. Other plants provide all shades of green, gray and pink.

Exploring further we come to a large open work area which includes her bonsai collection. Two that caught my attention were two maples in a shallow container and a cascading pine in a tall round container. Lending color to this area was a barrel cactus in a large orange pot just covered with bright orange petals accented by the yellow stamens and pistils. This was not just a work area it was part of the garden

Day 11: Friday, July 25

Lyman Black

Following the superb banquet we were served in Lyman and Liz Black's condominium complex, we were all invited to tour Lyman's newly created garden. It was a small garden on Lake Washington, twenty by forty feet at most. There were lights so that the garden could be enjoyed on summer evenings. A large number of large stones were artfully placed with ferns newly planted in front of and among the stones. A perfect mound of a large, low-spreading *Acer palmatum* formed a nice background for this area. In one corner, Lyman had created a dry streambed, using small, round skipping stones in a variety of colors. I had the pleasure of contributing a few stones I picked up on the beach on the Olympic Peninsula. In one section of the garden was a raised bed with a very distinctive long stone, looking deceptively like an alligator. We spent time enjoying the garden in the twilight.

What Makes a Garden?

Gardens are an expression of an individual's interests, taste, and the hand he or she is dealt. Each of the gardens was in its own way unique, and each appealed to me in a different way; some appealed more than others. Certainly the climate of the Northwest is more conducive to growing a wider variety of plants than here in the southern tier of New York State with our subzero temperatures, but we do share one thing with Seattle. The Ithaca/Corning area has the dubious distinction of coming in second in the nation with the least number of sunny days throughout the year.

I have remarked repeatedly on the large clumps of *Adiantum venustum*, as well as other plants. A single plant is nice, but for drama, one must have a large enough expanse to make a statement. My drift of more than a hundred *Trillium grandiflorum* makes such a statement. Many practices seen in almost all of the gardens are ones that I do not employ—namely the extensive use of containers in which to grow plants, the dramatic use of driftwood and large stones as sculptural accents, and the use of whimsical features. They are just not my style and would not complement the quiet beauty of my garden. But I thoroughly appreciated and enjoyed their use in these Northwest gardens.

But of all the gardens, how do I choose the one that appealed to me most? Certainly, the Miller Botanical Garden has a superb setting with many microclimates, allowing it to grow a wider variety of plants than other gardens in the area. I could spend hours in the woodland garden. Sylvia grows her plants superbly well. Each "room" is a delight in itself. Sue has taken a hilly lot and integrated the house and the lot beautifully. And although she has a nursery, the casual visitor probably would not realize it. And although she specializes in ferns and Japanese maples, they have been combined in a manner that is unobtrusive, unlike many specialized gardens. Lan's garden is the closest to what I have tried to do by making the garden a restful place. She uses her plants and design elements in a restrained way that feels so natural. Pat and Marilyn have four gardens, and I just loved their courtyard garden and their shady grove, being the shade gardener that I am. Ilga and Mike had the wherewithal to create a magnificent and special garden. The library fern garden will only get better and better in the coming years. (I sent a photo of the entrance to the children's library to our local library director.) Again although ferns were the dominant element, other plants were incorporated into the design in a tasteful manner. And what can I say about the Japanese garden except that it was superb? What a gift to the community! The setting for Jocelyn Horder's garden, the inlet, is a beautiful location for a garden, and Jocelyn has done a magnificent job in integrating the house and garden. The use of the waterfall and pool adds a peaceful and restful element to the garden. The use of a variety of low-growing plants in the front garden provides a lovely view of the garden, the inlet, and the Olympic Mountains. Dan Robinson's Elandan Gardens is in a class by itself. Almost everything is done on a grand scale, from his large-scale bonsai to the massive rocks and driftwood he uses so effectively. The Rhododendron Species Botanical Garden is primarily devoted to that species and to a display garden for the Hardy Fern Foundation. But other trees, shrubs, and flowering plants are blended into the overall design of the garden. On our visit, it was not immediately obvious that there were that many rhododendrons in the rock garden. Finally, the small garden of Lyman Black is a new garden with great potential. The backbone of the garden is already there with the rocks and the trees. The ferns are small, but when they fill in, it will make a delightful space not only for Lyman but for the other residents of the condominium.

We saw these gardens for only a fleeting hour on a summer day. To really appreciate gardens, we would have to see them throughout the changing seasons but especially in the spring when the fiddleheads unfurl in all their fantastic beauty.

Out on the Trail

Day 2: Western Cascades: Perry Creek

We were to go to Perry Creek, a federally designated Research Natural Area in the Cascade Mountains. After a breakfast in the dining hall, we boarded the buses at 8:30 and met our driver, Jerry Little, who would be with us for the entire duration of our excursions.

With everyone on board and with Bors Vesterby and Richie Steffen leading the way, we crossed Lake Washington on the floating bridge and got on an interstate heading north. Then it was off on state roads past Lake Stevens and on to Granite Falls. We then took the Mountain Highway and a rest stop at the Verlot Ranger Station before proceeding. Some fifteen miles later, we turned off on the Perry Creek Road and proceeded up to the trailhead. We all piled out of the buses, collected our box lunches, and assembled to await our leaders. To our rear rose a peak with patches of snow visible. Right on the bank at the trailhead was a mat of the delicate *Linnaea borealis*, twinflower. The first part of the trail was dense, dark woods with a lot of deadfall. The trail sign said, "Perry Creek Falls 2 Miles," but it seemed the longest two miles I had ever hiked! *Polystichum munitum*, the western sword fern, was abundant, as it would be in many other sites during the week. Other *Polystichums* I noted were *P. lonchitis*, the mountain holly fern, and *P. andersonii*, identified by the bud on the tip of the frond. We came across a large clump of the western maidenhair, *Adiantum aleuticum*, differing mainly from *Adiantum pedatum* in the shape of the fronds. Two familiar ferns were *Cystopteris fragilis*, fragile fern, and *Gymnocarpium dryopteris*, the northern oak fern. Whereas my oak ferns only grew a few inches tall, those we saw in the northwest were larger in all aspects. After hiking and botanizing in the woods for a period of time, we came to a more open area with large boulders and with the valley quite steep on both sides. Here a few plants of leathery grape fern, *Botrychium multifidum*, were found as well as a number of *Cryptogramma acrostichoides*, American parsley fern. One was nestled quite exposed among a group of large rocks. But the valley ran east to west, and we were on the north-facing slope, so the parsley fern never got a blast of the sun.

A species completely new to me was *Huperzia chinensis*, Pacific fir-moss, in the Lycopodiaceae family. Not content to stay on the trail, the mountain goats among us were botanizing above and below the trail. At one of these sites, Patrick Acock, Bors Vesterby, and Martin Rickard were below looking at something on a big boulder with Robert Sykes perched atop. It was almost noon, and this looked like as good a place as any to open our box of goodies so we did just that. After lunch, it was onward and upward for more botanizing with

Perry Creek Falls as our destination. The entire hillside seemed to be one big rock pile, and the path was rocky and required diligence in planting one's feet. The views were spectacular, and at many places on the opposite wall of the valley, evidence of avalanches could be seen. We crossed a few streams that came down our side and at one stretch traversed through a vast groundcover of lady fern, *Athyrium filix-femina*, with fronds fully five and six feet long. Along the path in one area, there were two plants of *Actaea rubra*, the red baneberry, but one had white seeds. For some distance below the path was Hercules club, with its red fruit. Another red-fruiting bush was the western elderberry, *Sambucus racemosa*. Meanwhile, my old muscles were getting weary, and at one point, I was about to turn back, but the next group of ferners swept me along. The view of the falls was well worth the hike. After a short, welcome respite, I headed back so I would not have to hurry, could enjoy the views, and would be able to place my wobbly legs firmly on solid ground. Besides enjoying the sight of ferns, both familiar and unfamiliar, I also found pleasure in seeing the western columbine, *Aquilegia formosa*, and a lovely blue penstemon. Missed on the way up was a colony of lichen, *Cladonia bellidiflora*, British soldiers, on a moss-covered boulder just off the trail. A tree leaning over the trail had a number of *Polypodium glycyrrhiza* growing on the mossy trunk. Back at the trailhead, I lay down to rest my weary bones. When all were back, we get organized to board the bus and head back to the university and supper. Nobody knew for sure, but the general consensus was the dining room closed at 6:30 p.m. On the road back out of the park, John Scott saw some Equisetums and called to me, sitting in front, to alert Jerry so he could stop the bus and I could retrieve a sample for him. We stopped, and Bors went merrily on, wondering why we had stopped. We got a sample and took off again. A short way down, there was Bors waiting for us. After a quick stop at the ranger station for those in need, we were heading south again. When we got on the interstate, Jerry put the pedal to the metal, as he didn't want to pick up dinner for the lot of us. We made it back in time and learned that the dining room was open until 7:00. End of the second day.

Day 5: Eastern Cascades

North Fork of the Teanaway River

Leaving Leavenworth, we headed south over Blewett Pass at a mere 4071 feet (1205 meters), with a sign that warned that the pass might be closed in winter. We found the turnoff for Teanaway and headed up a macadam road, which after about ten minutes, changed to a dirt road as we headed up the to the north fork of the Teanaway River. After another twenty minutes or so, we crossed a creek and pulled over to await Dr. Art Kruckeberg. Lo and behold, there was a van behind us. Professor Kruckeberg and two of his associates piled out and joined us. On this dry, rocky slope, there were ferns growing in the protection of the rocks. Robert Sykes clambered up the slope to get a better look at *Polystichum lemmonii* while Art pointed out that this fern, found almost exclusively on serpentine soils, was one of the best indicators of serpentine. In addition to the protection of the boulders, the old fronds formed a dense mat, providing still more protection in this dry environment. Also growing on this slope was another indicator of serpentine soils, *Aspidotis densa*, with its very distinctive fronds. We boarded the bus, followed Art's van to a picnic spot, and found a table. Art pulled out a geological map of the area. He pointed out where we were and noted the various soil types along the North Teanaway River and their effects likely to be found on the vegetation. We learned that the toxic serpentine soils were very high in iron and magnesium, high in heavy metals, but low in calcium and potassium. Some plants had evolved and adapted to such soils but might also be found on other soils where there was little or no competition from other plants.

After lunch, we headed across the road to an open wooded area of ponderosa pine, *Pinus ponderosa*, and western white pine. Here we found more *Polystichum lemmonii* and *Aspidotis densa*. There was a small, rapid-flowing stream coming off the hill. One side of the stream was quite dry with sparse vegetation. I spotted an ericaceous-looking low-growing plant and then over by the stream *Rhododendron albiflorum*. Bordering the stream, the vegetation was quite lush with ferns, especially *Pteridium aquilinum*, as well as mosses, grasses, and thistle-like plants. Venturing further on the other side, we came to a swampy area replete with sphagnum mosses and a vast expanse of the serpentine form of *Adiantum aleuticum*. We were also enticed by a host of flowering plants, including an abundance of the white bog orchid, *Habenaria dilatata*. We enthused over the first one we saw, and then there were scores. The brilliant red of *Castilleja miniata*, scarlet paintbrush, and the deep blue of *Gentiana calycosa*, mountain bog gentian, really stood out in the bog. Another blue was *Campanula rotundifolia*, Scottish bluebell, which contrasted with the white *Erigeron peregrinus*, subalpine daisy. *Dodecatheon jeffreyi*, shooting star, was not in flower, but the huge clumps made for an impressive display. Towering over all was *Angelica arguta*, Lyall's angelica.

Then it was up to the trailhead for more botanizing. Dozens of cars were parked on the circle and dozens more on the sides of the road, a horse trailer among them with four tethered horses. We headed up the trail. Looking back, I took in the large craggy mountain on the opposite side of the trailhead. John Scott also took a moment to look back and photograph the scene. On the hillside, we came across a large clump of *Pyrola secunda*, the one-sided evergreen, nestled against a moss-covered boulder. We found two other wintergreens, *Pyrola asarifolia*, common pink wintergreen, and *P. picta*, the white-veined wintergreen. Growing on the slope among mosses was the blue-flowering *Penstemon serrulatus*, the Cascade penstemon, and then the red cliff penstemon, *Penstemon davidsonii*, forming a small mat among the rocks. Many of the group scrambled to the top of the rocky penstemon outcrop to find withered specimens of *Cheilanthes gracillima* and *Selaginella densa*. Others found *Cryptogramma acrostichoides* among the boulders. The gushing mountain stream to our right as we descended was fascinating to watch as it wended its way down among the boulders, forming small pools and then a low waterfall. Back at the bus, we headed down the hill, past our luncheon spot, past our meeting spot by the bridge, finally reaching blacktop and then I-90. Then it was full speed ahead as we headed over Snoqualmie Pass and on to Seattle and Terry Lander Hall.

Day 7: Mount Rainier

We saw Mt. Rainier from the University of Washington campus, from the bridges as we crossed Lake Washington, or whenever we took a ferry over Puget Sound. At 14,411 feet (4,394 meters), it dominated the skyline. We would be encircling it this day as we headed southeast to Mt. Tacoma, the Indian name for this glacier-clad mountain. Two hours later, we entered the park from the north and pulled over to get a glimpse of the mountain over a conifer-clad ridge. The land dropped steeply to a creek far below and then climbed up to a ridge. We caught sight of alpine meadows and rocky protuberances seemingly too steep for plant life. We stopped by a creek, and there was a carpet of the glacial lily, *Erythronium montanum*, sweeping up the hillside. Our first extended stop was at the Grove of the Patriarch Trees. We walked down a wide, well-traveled trail built on the side of the mountain, steep slopes to the left and the right. In one spot, a massive trunk had fallen over the path, partially blocking the trail. Tall dead snags were seen along the trail with *Polystichum munitum* abundant on the hillsides. In one area, there was a beautiful lichen and nearby *Botrychium lanceolatum*. Further on, we crossed the stream on a suspension bridge. The Craddocks had gotten there first, and Linda had her shoes off and was wading in the water—water that must have been ice cold. Then we came to the Patriarchs. A loop boardwalk meandered among these ancient trees. In front of two huge firs, a wide platform had been built, perfect for photo ops, and Alan Ogden posed appropriately. Next, we came to the Patriarch of the Patriarchs, and here the boardwalk completely encircled its mammoth trunk. On the way back, we spotted a *Botrychium multifidum*.

Back on the road, the bus stopped, and Patrick Acock was across the road and halfway up the slope to a *Polystichum* fern growing among the boulders on the hillside. Several miles along, we stopped for another photo op and a beautiful view of Rainier with a quiet pond in the foreground. The opposite bank was lush with vegetation, thanks to the abundant moisture. There were glacial lilies, *Erythronium grandiflorum*, and a large mass of Indian paintbrush, *Castilleja*; a huge clump of lupines; and a colony of shooting stars in a lovely shade of bluish-purple. Not to be outdone was the helleborine orchis with its big wide leaves and tall flower stalk. Unfortunately, we were a week too early to see it in bloom.

Our next stop was Paradise. While the rest of the group went to the scheduled area, the Kohuts and I headed up the mountain. The path was steep, and the sun was hot, causing me to stop frequently. The views along the path and at the top were magnificent, well worth the huffing and puffing. On one side, you were looking down on a peaceful grassy valley with groves of conifers. In the other direction, you looked across another valley to snow-covered peaks and ridges. On the way down, one whole hillside was covered with glacial lilies with a few paintbrushes scattered randomly among them. If we were to make it home for our farewell banquet, we had to leave Paradise and make our good-byes to this jewel among mountains.

Days 9 and 10: The Olympic Peninsula

Leaving Jocelyn Horder's garden, we boarded the bus for the Best Western Inn at Port Angeles. After checking in, some of us visited the information center for the Olympic National Park.

The next day, we headed for the Hoh River Rain Forest in the Olympic National Park. As we started our tour, we had a handout listing some eight ferns for the area. We were to find all of these: *Polystichum munitum*, *Adiantum aleuticum*, *Blechnum spicant*, *Dryopteris expansa*, *Polypodium glycyrrhiza*, *Athyrium filix-femina*, *Pteridium aquilinum*, and *Gymnocarpium dryopteris*. The most impressive feature, however, was the fern ally, *Selaginella oregana*, which festooned the trees like a southern moss.

We learned from our guide that the Hoh Rain Forest received some 160 inches (400 centimeters) of rain a year as the moisture-laden winds from the Pacific encountered the Olympic Mountains. That much rainfall resulted in lush plant life—ferns, flowers, mosses, epiphytes, and immense trees. Dominant trees were Sitka spruce and western hemlock. These trees grew to tremendous heights and girths. When they fell, they left a big hole in the forest and more often than not a tall standing snag. As the snag decayed, it provided life for a host of creatures. The fallen trunk as well was soon covered with mosses, ferns, and tree seedlings. All along the full length of one of these, we saw dozens of young trees growing on the nurse log. Eventually the nurse log rotted, and we saw prime examples of trees with roots beginning several feet above the ground. However, at times, a tree had been weakened, the soil was saturated, and the entire tree was uprooted. The one example of this we saw must have been fifteen to twenty feet across with ferns and other plants growing profusely in the top of the root ball but starting to cultivate the now vertical bottom of the ball. The other distinguishing feature of the temperate rain forests was the plant life that went on above our heads—the mosses hanging from the branches of the big leaf maple and the epiphytes, ferns among them, that grew in the canopy of the maples. The forest floor was a dense green carpet of plants. *Polystichum munitum* was especially prolific, with abundant moisture and the rich soil of the valley.

Ruby Beach

Leaving the Hoh Rain Forest, we continued our counterclockwise circumnavigation of the Olympic Peninsula, our first stop being Ruby Beach. What a fantastic sight as we descended the hundred feet from the parking area to the beach. We encountered a tangled jumble of huge driftwood logs as though some giant was playing pick-up sticks. Navigating over, around, and under this forty-foot-wide obstacle course was treacherous and not to be done lightly. There was a tall, rocky outcrop of an island just offshore and both on and offshore other rocky crags (sea stacks) that had managed to resist the action of wind and water for eons, making for a dramatic scene. On one of these crags, the mountain goats among us, Pat Acock and Peter Meegdes, scrambled up to identify a fern, a *Polypodium*, which had found a foothold on this outcrop. Others of us were marveling at the grotesque forms carved from the rocks by the elements, and still others were off in the woods, searching successfully for *Polypodium scouleri*, a coastal native.

From Ruby Beach, we proceeded to Beach Four, where we teamed up with a park naturalist to learn about life in the tidewater but first paused for a picture of this wild and wooly group. The rocks around us were pitted with myriad round holes an inch or so in diameter, caused by some creature. As we walked along the beach, Robert

Sykes took off his shoes and waded along beside us in the surf. We came to a tidewater pool, and our naturalist looked for animals that lived in these pools. He spotted a starfish, and he and Graham Ackers related its life to us as our bus driver Jerry stared in amazement.

Our destination for the night was Kalaloch Lodge, situated on a bluff overlooking the Pacific. Accommodations were rustic but welcome. After a hearty meal, we relaxed and enjoyed the view of the Pacific, the sun, a glowing ball of fire, coloring the western sky orange as it slowly disappeared. On the morrow, I would go down to the beach and look back as the morning sun brightened the sky. A tall, one-sided conifer provided a dramatic example of the direction of the prevailing wind. Where I descended, there was a palisade of tree trunks protecting the cliff from erosion. Where there was no protection, I found the roots of a tree providing mute evidence of the destructive forces of nature. There were gulls on the beach, and someone had erected a sand pyramid. Climbing back to the top, I found Robert, Joy, and Becky enjoying the sight and sound of the turf. After a breakfast, we were on our way to another beach, Beach One. Here we did not go down to the beach, but on this particular headland, virtually all of the Sitka spruce were sporting boles. We learned that the combination of an insect killing a terminal bud and the salt spray from the Pacific was the likely explanation. These boles provided a nice landing spot for seeds and spores, and many of them were adorned with fronds of *Polypodium scouleri*. Many of the spruce looked bizarre, especially when boles sat virtually on top of one another.

Back on the bus, we headed to the Quinault Valley. Before lunch in the lodge, we had a chance to take a short or long trail to satisfy our appetite for ferns. As we went along a small ravine, we gazed at the other side, which was massed with *Polystichum munitum* and *Adiantum aleuticum*, along with the native vine maple, *Acer circinatum*. Looking down, we could see that our side of the creek was equally adorned. Along our trail, we came upon a tree that got its start on the top of a four-foot high tree trunk with its roots snaking down the sides until they reached the forest floor. Only then could it really begin to grow. Farther on, we came upon the root ball of an uprooted tree that was almost completely covered with our old friend *Polystichum munitum*. The trail was longer than expected—that or the ferns and other plant life too easily distracted us. However, the noon hour was approaching, and we hurried on to Quinault Lodge, where we were seated in the dining room overlooking Lake Quinault. After lunch, we had some time to explore the lodge inside and outside. Out on the porch, my eye was immediately drawn to the totem-inspired rain gauge, which towered seventeen feet. Shortly, it was time to board the bus and leave the Olympic Peninsula, our next stop being Kelso in southern Washington, preparatory to the next day's ascent of Mount St. Helens.

Day 11

Mt. St. Helens

There would be little botanizing this day as we were about to view the aftermath of the eruption that changed Mt. St. Helens from a beautiful cone-shaped dormant volcano to a flat-topped mountain with a glaring hole in its side. Leaving Kelso, we headed up the mountain, our first stop being at the Visitors Center. Outside the center, in a tall spruce, was the nest of a golden eagle. We had time to view a movie of the eruption and to walk the nature trail. As we continued up the mountain, we looked across the valley to the truncated cone of Mt. St. Helens and the valley below us. After climbing up to Johnston Ridge Observatory, we looked down and back where we had come. All looked barren except there was lush growth along the stream in the valley and in every watercourse that came off the mountain. Arriving at the observatory, we piled out of the bus and looked across the intervening valley at the gaping hole in the side of the volcano. There was a short trail on the ridge, which afforded a close-up view of both the destruction and the recovery but also a panoramic view of the entire area. There were the remains of stumps from the blast and a yellow-flowering plant on the slope, perhaps *Hypericum*, and a lovely violet-blue penstemon. From the *Mt. St. Helens Plant List*, I learned that there were two ferns found growing within the crater. We would expect to find *Pteridium aquilinum*, bracken fern, but perhaps not *Asplenium viride*, green spleenwort.

On the way off the mountain, we stopped at Coldwater Ridge Visitor Center to view a lake created by the eruption. It was now a lovely blue lake, but on the opposite side, the hill was strewn with trees that had received the hot blast from the eruption. Other sections of the hill were forested with trees that were protected from the blast. After a final stop at the Forest Learning Center, we headed back to Seattle and our farewell dinner. There I met up with my wife, who had been visiting her sister in Walla Walla while I was trekking and touring gardens.

CHAPTER 12
GARDEN QUOTES

My favorite:

> *If you have a Garden and a Library, you have everything you need.*
>
> Marcus Tullius Cicero

And one recently received from Cousin Jack:

> *All through the long winter I dream of my garden. On the first warm day of spring I dig my fingers deep into the soft earth. I can feel its energy, and my spirits soar.*
>
> Helen Hayes, 1900–1993

> *Trees have entwined the heart of man ever since he became a sentient being they hold a prominent place in the legends and sacred writings of all people.*
>
> E. H. Wilson

> *How cunningly nature hides every wrinkle of her unconceivable antiquity under roses and violets and morning dew.*
>
> Ralph Waldo Emerson

Flowers always make people better, happier, and more helpful; they are sunshine, food and medicine to the soul.

Luther Burbank

Bury your face in the hanging snow, or breathe it far off, the scent is softly hypnotic; you are compelled to stillness, to let the cloud enclose you.

H.V.P. Wilson

Let no one be discouraged by the thought of how much there is to learn ..."

Gertrude Jekyll

A garden is like those pernicious machineries which catch a man's coat-skirt or his hand and draws in his arm, his leg, and his whole body to irresistible destruction

Ralph Waldo Emerson

Every garden is a chore sometimes, but no real garden is nothing but a chore.

Nancy Grasby

No two gardens are the same. No two days are the same in one garden.

Hugh Johnson

If a man be weary with over much-study, there is no better place in the world to recreate himself than in a garden.

William Coles

To create a little flower is the labour of ages.

William Blake

At any one season one sees only part of the symphony, just one movement. Flower gardening is an ephemeral art, like music and dance.

J. Van Sweden

Perhaps no word of six letters concentrates so much human satisfaction as the word 'garden'

Richard LeGallienne

Gardening is such a mixture of mistakes and successes. And I often think the mistakes are the most important.

Barbara Dodge Borland

Heaven is under our feet as well as over our heads.

H. D.Thoreau

I will no longer permit the avid and eager eye to steal away my whole attention. I will learn to enjoy more completely all the varied wonders of the earth.

David Grayson

Each within his inclosure is a creator, and no two shall reach the same conclusion.

Louise Beeber Wilder

Give fools their gold, and knaves their power Let fortune's bubbles rise and fall; Who sows a field, or trains a flower Or plants a tree, is more than all

John Greenleaf Whittier

If I could do what I wanted, I would build a house under those trees, sit down, read books, and eat ice cream for the rest of my life.

E. I. DuPont

Gardening gives me fun and health and knowledge. It gives me laugher and colour. It gives me pictures of almost incredible beauty.

John F. Kenyon

The kinds of gardens are as varied as the gardeners who make them. They each serve a need by simply giving pleasure.

Anonymous

Keep a green tree in your heart, and perhaps a bird will come.

Chinese proverb

Gardening has compensation out of all proportion to its goals. It is creation in the purest sense.

Phyllis McGinley

The bountitude of nature is both infinite and infectious...contact with garden beauty sets free the better impulses of human nature.

E. H.Wilson

Though an old man, I am but a young gardener.

Thomas Jefferson

A garden is a grand teacher. It teaches patience and careful watchfulness; it teaches industry and thrift; above all it teaches entire trust.

Gertrude Jekyll

Nature has something to say, and the gardener has something to say, and their voices should harmonize.

Ruth Levitan

The purpose of a garden is to give happiness and repose of mind.

Hugh Johnson

Life begins the day you start a garden

Chinese proverb

All gardeners live in beautiful places, because they make them so.

Joseph Joubert

When at last I took the time to look into the heart of a flower, it opened up a whole new world ... as if a window had been opened to let in the sun.

Princess Grace

Gardeners. I think, dream bigger dreams than emperors.

Mary Cantwell

Gardening is a matter of your enthusiasm holding up until your back gets used to it.

Anonymous

In his way a gardener is an artist, but his art is unique. Paint a picture and it may be finished within weeks ... but a gardener's work is never complete.

To dig one's spade into one's own earth! Has life anything better to offer than this?

Beverly Nichols

Oh, Adam was a gardener,
And God who made him sees
That half a proper gardener's
work, is done upon his knees

Rudyard Kipling

One of the worst mistakes you can make as a gardener is to think you're in charge. You aren't.

James Gillespie

What a man needs in gardening is a cast-iron back,
with a hinge in it.

Charles Dudley Warner

I hope I will never get too old or too self-important to
listen to a bird singing ... For if I do I will be of as little
use to the world as I will to myself.

W. A. Birdwell

Flowers preach to us if we will hear.

C. G. Rossetti

Of all human activities, apart from the procreation of
children, gardening is the most optimistic and hopeful.
The gardener is by definition one who plans for and
believes and trusts in future, whether in the short or
the longer term.

Susan Hill

Talke of perfect happinesse or pleasure, and what place
was so fit for that, as the garden place.

John Gerard

"..paradise is an ancient Persian word ...
still found in our dictionaries ... meaning garden or
park.

'Pokin' round mid ferns and mosses
Like a hop-toad or a snail
Somehow seems to lighten crosses
Where my heart would elsewhere fail

Woolson

The more one gardens the more one learns;
And the more one learns, the more one realizes
how little one knows. I suppose the whole of life
Is like that.

Vita Sackville-West

The best gardeners are three-hundred-and-sixty-five-day-a-year gardeners, For long experience has taught them that some of the darkest days may also be among the brightest.

B. Nichols

If you would know strength and patience, welcome the company of trees.

Hal Borland

REFERENCES

Bruce, Hal. *How to Grow Wildflowers and Wild Shrubs and Trees in Your Garden*. New York: Alfred A. Knopf, 1976.

Bull, John. *Birds of New York State*. Garden City, New York: Doubleday / Natural History Press, 1974.

Case, Frederick W., Jr., and Roberta B. Case. *Trilliums*. Timber Press, 1997.

Davison, Verne E. *Attracting Birds from the Prairies to the Atlantic*. New York: Thomas Y. Crowell Company, 1967.

Dietz, Marjorie. *The Concise Encyclopedia of Favorite Wild Flowers* Garden City, NY: Doubleday & Company, Inc., 1965.

Fernald, Merritt Lyndon, and Alfred Charles Kinsey. *Edible Wild Plants of Eastern North America*. New York: Idlewild Press, 1943.

Foster, Gordon. *The Gardener's Fern Book*. Princeton, NJ: D. Van Nostrand Company, Inc., 1964.

Foster, H. Lincoln. *Rock Gardening: A Guide to Growing Alpines and Other Wildflowers in the American Garden*. Boston: Houghton Mifflin Company, 1968.

Gracie, Carol. *Spring Wildflowers of the Northeast*. Princeton, NJ: Princeton University Press, 2012.

Greer, Harold E. *Greer's Guide to Available Rhododendrons*. Eugene, OR: Offset Publications, 1982.

Montgomery, James D., and David Fairbrother. *New Jersey Ferns and Fern Allies*. New Brunswick, NJ: Rutgers University Press, 1992.

Morse, Harriet K. *Gardening in the Shade*. New York: Charles Scribner's Sons, 1967.

Newcomb, Lawrence. *Newcomb's Wildflower Guide*. Boston: Little Brown & Company, 1977. *National Register of Big Trees*. 1994 Edition.

Pesman, M. Walter. *Meet the Natives: An Easy Way to Recognize Mountain Wild Flowers, Trees and Shrubs*. Denver: The Smith Brooks Printing Company, 1946.

Peterson, Roger Tory. *A Field Guide to Western Birds*. MA: The Riverside Press, 1941.

Wiley, Leonard. *Rare Wild Flowers of North America*. Published by the author, 1969.

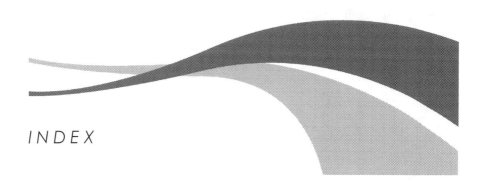

INDEX

bulbs, 16, 24, 40, 48, 124, 128. *See also specific bulbs*

bunchberry (*Cornus canadensis*), 52, 76, 86, 99

Bundy, Michelle, 181

Burbank, Luther, 200

Burtch, V., 12

butter-and-eggs, 68

buttercup anemone (*Anemone ranunculoides*), 64, 65

C

Calycanthus floridus (Carolina allspice), 14

Camptosorus rhizophyllus (walking fern), 29, 33, 36

Canada anemone, 64

Canada mayflower (wild lily of the valley), 50–51

Canadian fleabane, 75

Canadian hemlock, 24

candling, 149

candytuft, 115

cannibis, 73

Cantwell, Mary, 203

Carbo, Tony and Carol, 159

cardinal flower, 5, 67, 74, 78–79

Carolina allspice (*Calycanthus floridus*), 14

Carolina silverbell, 72

Carty, Ed, 166

Caulophyllum thalictroides (blue cohosh), 16, 62, 63, 76, 119, 126

cedar waxwings, 4

cedars, 4, 103, 111

celandine poppy (*Stylophorum diphyllum*), 83

Cercis canadensis alba (white-flowering redbud), 18, 117

chestnut oak (*Quercus prinus*), 1, 10, 107–108, 111

chickadees, 5

chicory, 5, 68

Chinese celadine poppy (*Stylophorum lasiocarpum*), 83

Chinese dogwood *(Cornus kousa chinensis*), 18, 84, 97, 98, 102, 116

chiondoxa, 16, 24, 115, 128, 131

Christmas fern (*Polystichum acrostichoides*), 14, 27, 28, 30, 31–32, 34, 118, 138, 139

Chrysogonum virginianum (goldenstar) (green-and-gold) (gold star), 17, 63, 140

Cicero, Marcus Tullius, vi, 199

Cimicifuga, 61, 74

Cimicifuga americana, 62

Cimicifuga dahurica, 62

Cimicifuga elata, 62

Cimicifuga foetida, 62

Cimicifuga japonica, 62

Cimicifuga laciniata, 62

Cimicifuga rubifolia, 62

Cimicifuga simplex, 62

cinnamon fern, 28, 29

Clayton, John, 43

Claytonia, 43

Claytonia caroliniana, 45

Claytonia virginica, 45

cliff brakes, 36

climbing fern, 36

clintonia (bluebead), 76

Cloud 9 (dogwood), 100

coast redwood, 111

cobra lily, 54

coccinea (Indian paintbrush), 73

cockspur hawthorn, 105

Coe, Clark, 162

E

eastern hemlock, 4, 103
eastern larch, 103
ebony spleenwort, 29, 31, 32, 33, 70
Eddie's White Wonder, 98
edellebere, 41
Edible Wild Plants of Eastern North America (Fernald and Kinsey), 44
elaisome, 42, 45, 47
Elandan Gardens, 179–180, 188
Emerson, Ralph Waldo, 199, 200
English cowslip, 71
enkianthus, 126, 139
Enkianthus campanulata (red-veined Enkianthus), 18
ephemerals of spring, 41–46, 66, 71
Epigea repens (trailing arbutus), 15, 39–40, 60, 61, 131
Epimedium rubrum, 20, 81, 82
epimediums, 20, 81, 116
Erica, 141
Ericaceous family, 18
Erigeron, 75
Eriocaulon, 70
eupatorium, 69
European anemones, 64
European beech, 101
European ginger, 56, 79, 81, 115
European milkwort, 69
evergreen ferns, 30, 32
evergreen shield fern, 32
evergreen trees, 3, 6, 27, 92, 103, 125, 126, 127, 129, 134, 135, 148, 149. *See also specific trees*
exposure, 124–125

F

Fairbrother, David, 158
fairy bells (*Digitalis purpurea*), 72, 126
fairy candles, 61
fairy spuds, 44
Fais, Jennifer, 105
false anemone (*Anemonopsis japonica*), 25
false hellebore (Indian poke) (white hellebore), 73
false miterwort, 48
false Solomon's seal (*Smilacina racemosa*), 14, 49, 55, 76, 126
Fawn's breath, 73
Federated Garden Clubs of New York, 21
Felco pruners, 151
Fernald, Merritt L., 44
ferns
    appearance of in author's garden, 115, 118
    as asexual, 33
    author's interest in, 27–28
    in fourth tier of trees, 138
    identification of, 28
    impact of lack of moisture on, 132
    indoor ferns, 36
    introduction of into author's garden, 15
    reproduction of, 33, 35
    varieties of, 26–38. *See also specific ferns*
fertilizing, 89, 101, 136, 144
fescue, 132
fever root (feverwort) (horse gentian), 69
fiddlehead, 25, 30, 41
Fiddlehead Forum, 26
field garlic, 66

ginger, 115. *See also* European
    ginger; wild ginger (*Asarum
    canadensis*)
ginseng (*Panax quinquefolia*), 57,
    76, 126
glade fern (narrow-leaved
    spleenwort), 31, 35
global warming, 133
glories-of-the-snow, 115
goatsbeard (*Aruncus dioicus*),
    56–57
golden locust, 126
golden poppies, 82–83
golden ragwort, 70
goldenrod, 14, 25, 52, 76–78, 79,
    119, 139
golden-shafted flicker, 9–10
goldenstar (*Chrysogonum
    virginianum*), 17, 140
Goldie's fern, 27, 35, 118
good morning spring, 44
Gordon Foster Fern Collection,
    156–157
Gottesman, Eve and Len, 161
Gouchaultii, 85
Graham, Paul and Grace, 35, 77
grape ferns, 30, 36
grape hyacinth, 24, 115
Grasby, Nancy, 200
gray birch, 112
gray dogwood (*Cornus racemosa*),
    76, 85
Grayson, David, 201
great blue lobelia, 78
great Indian plantain, 73
great laurel, 90
great-leaved aster, 78
green ash, 112
Green Luster, 92
green thumb, use of term, 146

green-and-gold (gold star)
    (*Chrysogonum virginianum*),
    63, 140
greenhouse effect, 132
Greenwood Forest Wildlife
    Management Area, 157
groundnut, 44
Guide Book & Nature Record, 164
Guiles, Catharine, 155, 160
gypsy moths, 110, 127

H

hackmatack, 103–104
hairy lip fern, 36
harbingers of spring, 39–41
hardening-off process, 134
hardiness zones, 133–134, 137
Hardy Fern Foundation, 37, 155,
    168, 181, 183, 188
harebell, 72
hart's tongue fern (*Asplenium
    scolopendrium*), 27, 36
Harvey, Paul, 31
hawthorns, 4, 14, 75–76, 105–106, 111
Hayes, Helen, 199
Haygarth, Linda, 161
hay-scented fern, 27
heath, 24, 131, 135, 141
heather, 135
Heck, Otto, 155
hederophyllum, 117
hedge garlic, 68
hedge nettle, 71
Hegedus, Mary, 162
hellebore, 24, 73, 115
helleborine orchid, 68
hemlock, 4, 14, 23, 24, 92, 103, 112,
    121, 146, 149
hemp, 73, 75
Henry IV (Shakespeare), 28
Henry's Plant Farm, 178–179

Mid-Atlantic Fern Foray, 155–160
milkwort, 69
Miller, Carolyn, 168
Miller, Elisabeth, 168
Miller Botanical Garden, 186
miniature lady fern
     (*minutissima*), 38
minilopper, 151
minutissima (miniature lady
     fern), 38
Mitchell, John, 60
Mitchella repens (partridgeberry),
     14, 51, 75, 138, 139
miterwort (bishop's cap), 14, 48–49,
     80, 117, 138
Mollgard, Henry, 178–179
monkshood (wolfbane), 75
Monotropa uniflora (Indian pipe),
     51, 59–60, 73
Montgomery, Jim, 155, 158, 159
moosewood, 102, 106–107,
     127, 138
Moran, Robbin, 156
Morris Arboretum, 159
mountain andromeda, 115
mountain dogwood (*Cornus
     nutallii*), 98
mountain laurel (*Kalmia latifolia*),
     14, 88–90, 112, 118–119, 127,
     132, 138, 139
mountain sweetbell, 72
Mt. St. Helens, 197–198
mulching, 89, 95, 114, 125, 128,
     133, 134, 136, 137
musclewood, 101–102, 106
mustard root, 68
myrtle, 24, 95

N

naive pinxterbloom azalea
     (*Rhododendron
     periclymenoides*), 20
narcissi, 65, 128
narrow-leaved spleenwort
     (*Athyrium pycnocarpum*),
     31, 35
narrow-leaved spleenwort
     (*Diplazium pycnocarpum*), 35
National Park Service, 111
native wildflowers, 15, 16, 45
Nearing, Guy, 19
netted chain fern, 31, 36
New England aster (*Aster novae-
     angliae*), xv, 79
*New Jersey Ferns and Fern
     Allies* (Montgomery and
     Fairbrother), 158
New York aster, 78
New York fern, 31
Nichols, Beverly, 203, 205
nipplewort (dockcress), 69
noble liverwort, 41
nodding trillium, 48, 117
Nold, Bob and Cindy, 162, 163
nonnative ferns, 28, 37
nonnative shrubs, as poor
     choices, 24
North American Rock Garden
     Society, 160, 167, 168
northern beech fern, 35
northern blue violet, 52
northern exposure, 124–125
northern maidenhair (*Adiatum
     pedatum*), 26, 29, 34
northwest maidenhair (*Adiantum
     aleuticum*), 34
Norway maple, 4, 102, 111,
     125, 138

wild onion (*Allium stellatum*), 66
wild potato, 44
wild sarsparilla (*Aralia nudicaulis*),
    14, 51, 55
wild strawberry, 24, 79, 140
wild sweet William, 70
Wilder, Louise Beeber, 201
wildflowers, 15, 16, 27, 40. *See also*
    native wildflowers; *specific*
    wildflowers
Wilen, Ellen, 157
Wiley, Leonard, 59–60
Wilhelm, Donna, 157, 159
Williams, Gray, 157
Wilson, E. H., 199, 202
Wilson, H. V. P., 200
Wilt-Pruf, 135
Windbeam (rhododendron), 20, 93,
    94, 117–118, 137, 151
windchill factor, 134
winter aconite, 16, 80, 115, 131
winterberry, 4, 14
wintergreen (*Gaultheria*
    procumbens), 51, 59, 75
Winterthur (*viburnum nudum*), 87
witch hazel, 5, 14, 112, 115, 126,
    131, 138
wolfbane (monkshood), 75
wood anemone, 64, 65, 115–116
wood boneset, 69
wood ferns, 14, 27, 28, 30, 32, 37,
    38, 138
wood poppy, 82, 83
woodland aster, 14
woodland phlox (*Phlox*
    divaricata), 57
woodland plants, 17, 125
Woodsia plummerae (Plummer's
    woodsia), 37
woodsias, 36, 37
Woolson, 204

worts, 68–71
woundwort, 71
Wye Oak, 108, 111
Wyman, Donald, 17, 18, 133

X

xeriscaping, 132

Y

yak, 94
yellow birch, 101, 112, 126, 138
yellow epimedium, 81
yellow lady's slipper (*Cypripedium*
    parviflorum), 56
yellow mandarin, 72
yellow trillium (*Trillium luteum*),
    16, 117
yellow warbler, 9
yellow wax bells (*Kirengeshoma*
    palmata), xv, 79
yellow-bellied sapsucker, 11
yellow-flowering epimedium,
    20, 81
yews, 92–93, 135, 149

Z

zineb, 101

Printed in the United States
By Bookmasters